THIS ISLAND
WAS TAKEN POSSESSION OF
DECEMBER 24th 1846
IN THE NAME OF HER MAJESTY
VICTORIA
QUEEN OF GREAT BRITAIN AND IRELAND
UNDER THE DIRECTION OF
HIS EXCELLENCY REAR ADMIRAL
SIR THOMAS COCHRANE C.B
COMMANDER IN CHIEF
BY
CAPTAIN G.R. MUNDY
COMMANDING
H.M.S. IRIS

THE CORONA LIBRARY

NORTH BORNEO

NORTH BORNEO

BY

K. G. TREGONNING

LONDON
HER MAJESTY'S STATIONERY OFFICE
1960

Frontispiece
The Gomanton Caves, source of edible birds'-nests

THE CORONA LIBRARY

A series of illustrated volumes under the
sponsorship of the Colonial Office dealing
with the United Kingdom's dependent
territories, the way their peoples live, and
how they are governed. The series has
been designed to fill the place between
official Blue Books on the one hand and
the writings of occasional visitors on the
other, to be authoritative and readable,
and to give a vivid yet accurate picture.
The books are being written by established authors whose qualifications include, where possible, experience of
colonial administration and first-hand
knowledge of the territory concerned.
Neither Her Majesty's Government in the
United Kingdom nor the Governments
of the territories necessarily associate
themselves with the personal views expressed by the authors. Each volume will
contain maps and be fully illustrated.

FOREWORD

By the Rt. Hon. Sir Winston S. Churchill
K.G., O.M., C.H., M.P.

NOT since the days of the Roman Empire has a single nation carried so great a responsibility for the lives of men and women born outside her shores as Great Britain does today. Within her forty or so dependent territories dwell eighty million people for whose welfare and enlightenment Britain is, to a greater or lesser degree, answerable.

There has been no lack of critics, at home and abroad, to belittle Britain's colonial achievement and to impugn her motives. But the record confounds them. Look where you will, you will find that the British have ended wars, put a stop to savage customs, opened churches, schools and hospitals, built railways, roads and harbours, and developed the natural resources of the countries so as to mitigate the almost universal, desperate poverty. They have given freely in money and materials and in the services of a devoted band of Civil Servants; yet no tax is imposed upon any of the colonial peoples that is not spent by their own governments on projects for their own good.

I write 'their own governments' advisedly, for however much diverse conditions may necessitate different approaches, the British have for long had one goal in view for their overseas territories: their ultimate development into nations freely associated with the Commonwealth framework. The present state of the Commonwealth is the proof of the sincerity of this policy.

It is because I believe that Britain's colonial record is too little known and her policies too little understood that I welcome the books of the Corona Library. The aim of these books is to present a contemporary portrait, at once reliable and attractive, of each territory. I warmly commend the series to the attention of the public at home and abroad, for if these publications do even a little to clear away the clouds of misunderstanding and prejudice that have gathered round the very idea of colonial government, they will have been well worth while.

Winston S. Churchill

CONTENTS

Drawings and Jacket by Geraldine Horton

Folding map at the end of volume by Directorate of Overseas Surveys

ILLUSTRATIONS

PLATES

DRAWINGS

ENDPAPERS

Front: A Voyage to Borneo by Captain Daniel Beekman was published in 1718. *Below* these pages from it is a picture of the Dyaks attacking the boats of the *Iris* and *Phlegethon*, from Capt. Rodney Mundy's *Narrative of Events in Borneo and Celebes* (1848). *Above, right,* shows the attack on the Dido's boats by Capt. the Hon. Henry Keppel's *Expedition to Borneo* (2nd edn. 1846). The memorial stone (*below*) commemorates the cession of Labuan to the British Crown. *Bottom, right,* also from Mundy's book is the drawing of Pangeran Mumin, Prime Minister to the Sultan of Borneo (1843).

Back: (*Left, above*) This group is of the Court of Directors of the British North Borneo Company with the Dyak police contingent which took part in Queen Victoria's Diamond Jubilee celebrations. Seated are (*left to right*) Harrington G. Forbes, Sir Charles J. Jessell, Bt., Richard B. Martin (chairman), William C. Cowie and Edward Dent. Behind Martin stands Capt. W. Raffles Flint. (*Below*) signing the treaty for the cession of Labuan, 1846. (*Right, above*) Ilanun pirate *prahu* 'off the Kinabalu mountain, Borneo', also from Mundy's *Narrative*. (*Below*) The stamps illustrate (*top row*) a Malay stag, buffalo sledge, tapir. (*Middle row*) Blowpipe, the arms of the colony, Bajau chief. (*Bottom row*) buffalo sledge with Japanese Occupation overprinting, historic group, *prahu.*

ACKNOWLEDGEMENTS

We are very grateful to the Fellows of the Royal Commonwealth Society, and in particular to the Librarian, Mr. D. H. Simpson, for allowing us to reproduce plates from the Society's valuable collection in the endpapers, to Messrs. H. E. Wingfield & Co. for providing the postage stamps for the back endpaper, and to Messrs. Constable and Co. Ltd. for permission to reproduce the extract from Owen Rutter's *British North Borneo.*

PREFACE

THIS is a travel book, the outcome of a two-month tour in 1957 of North Borneo. At the beginning of it I met a planter in Jesselton who said some very rude things about young men who wrote books on the superficial impressions of a brief visit, so I should explain perhaps that this is my second book on North Borneo, that previously I had spent three years, at Oxford and in London, studying from a mass of material the history of the country, and that already, in 1953 and 1954, I had toured the territory from my home in Singapore and had worked among the archives in Jesselton. This book may still be superficial, but it embodies far more than the snap observations of a two-month visit.

Although this tour, from Singapore to Jesselton, the capital on the west coast, up and down that coast and then into the interior, round to the east coast, and finally back to Brunei and the oil fields, was sponsored by the Colonial Office and arranged by the Department of Broadcasting and Information, whose Director, R. J. Brookes, I thank, and although in most places my host was a government officer, the views expressed in this book cannot be taken as official. No restriction, no control whatever was placed on me, and I write merely as an informed, favoured, but unofficial traveller.

Information of all kinds was readily supplied me by the government officers and the many others whom I met on my journey, and I am grateful to them all. For particular kindnesses, however, I would like to record my thanks to the late Philip Lee Tau Sang, C.B.E.; I would also like to thank, in Jesselton, Donald Stephens, and Mr. and Mrs. R. J. Brookes, G. L. Gray, C.M.G., O.B.E., A. N. Goode, O.B.E., and P. Gillett; on the west coast and interior, Mr. and Mrs. J. H. Alman, R. H. W. de la Poer Beresford-Peirse, M. Pike and I. Peck, and Messrs. P. Hewitt, J. F. G. Dingle and Father Smit; in Kudat, Messrs. J. Nicholson and Lo Cham En; on the east coast, Mr. and Mrs. P. Edge, K. Summers, C. J. Bridge and D. Ireton, and Messrs. G. F. Douglas and G. L. Carson; and on Labuan and in Brunei, R. Robbins, R. W. Rule, T. Carter, G. Hedley and P. Pierce.

1. THE JUNGLE

THE plane roared steadily over the South China Sea. Ahead lay the coast of Borneo. We had left Singapore at dawn, the sun shining heavily through the haze and sending long shafts of heat through the coconut trees that surround this most modern of airports. In its Chinese air-hostesses, neat in slim cheongsams, in its languorous Indian passengers, waiting in classical saris, in its Europeans and its dozing Malay policemen it now reflects all the cosmopolitanism tradition-ally associated with its harbour, over which we flew a few minutes later.

Here Borneo begins. Here, between the offshore mole and the car-packed Collyer Quay, anchor the little ships, squatting like brooding hens surrounded by chickens, as tongkangs and sampans receive over the side or deliver for storage the im-ports and exports of Borneo and the islands beyond; here, up Singapore's river, bustling with barges, are the warehouses that sort, select, grade and pack the primary products brought from the jungles of Sandakan and Sibu; and here, in cool air-conditioned offices, sit many of the men whose firms and businesses stretch their tentacles to the remotest kampongs in the territory towards which we were flying.

As we climbed after take-off a few incurious *Orang Sungei* (river-folk) glanced up from their *prahus* by the mangrove-lined Seletar river, pagan people who have lived a nomadic watery life unchanged since they were first described in the sixteenth century, unchanged in essentials since neolithic times, unchanged now although living alongside a great ocean highway, and within a minute of the twentieth century.

The workmanlike Dakota droned on, its stereotyped routine—'Magazine, sir? Coffee, sir?'—reducing to normalcy this eastward venture. Next to me sat a Chinese businessman, in Dacron pants and transparent nylon shirt. With his casual shoes slipped off, gregarious and cheerful, on his way home to Kuching, in Sarawak, he discussed business prospects in

1

South-East Asia. A student of history, he felt that the European in the East had become too respectable.

'A hundred years ago,' he said, 'you weren't respectable, you were booming. Whenever a million was made, you made it, and we scratched for the crumbs. Even thirty years ago, when China was like a rich melon, it was the European who secured the biggest bites. You weren't frightened then. But take the position today, for example in Indonesia. There is a state of affairs very similar to China thirty years ago—war lords, or army commanders, corruption and much wealth. But it is we who are profiting now, we who are the Merchant Adventurers, and you have become too timid to take advantage of this new anarchy. Your respectability has become a vice, yet you call yourselves the new Elizabethans!'

I heard these same sentiments expressed several months later when I was in Tawau, the east coast port of North Borneo, that faces the ill-governed Celebes and Sulu Archipelago, and where, by the maintenance of law and order, by the establishment of an honest currency and by the provision of ample goods, all is a bustle as the Chinese businessmen buy and sell to those less fortunate than they, who sail their small craft on hazardous journeys to this British beacon. But I witnessed also the continuing British penetration of this same market, and one does not need to live long in Singapore to meet many Europeans well able to adapt themselves to the changing conditions. Both in Borneo, where we were now heading, and in the other, less well-administered countries of South-East Asia, my Chinese friend would face stiff opposition.

So too would the Indian textile man, sitting across from me, impeccably dressed with an immaculate white shirt, cuff-linked and tied, hanging outside a *dhoti*. He was the heir of two millennia of merchants, Indians who had traded through these waters since before the time of Christ, merchants who had sold their peppers in China and their cottons in South-East Asia before the Romans first came to Britain. He was young, barely out of his teens, and he epitomized the younger sons all down the ages, who had been sent forth from the family base to bargain, sell and perhaps stay, in some remote river where possibilities seemed encouraging. In such a way

2

had Indian influence spread through this area; through such a man had the seeds of culture first been sown; and by the union of such a man with an indigenous beauty had states such as Cambodia and Champa, Majapahit and Sri Vijaya first begun.

In whose hands lay the future of Borneo I wondered? I sat in the nose, and watched for the first sign of land, as a raw-

North Borneo woman and child

boned Australian pilot pointed to half-remembered dials and knobs. Behind me in the aircraft were four other Australians, two engineers for the Brunei oil fields, a teacher for the Sarawak government, a district officer for North Borneo. 'What do you think of Australia's new imperialism?' I was asked. 'What do you think of the Colombo Plan?' The Australian impact in British Borneo is unmistakable, but as yet it is minor, and the future still rests, the foreseeable future, with the one type not evident in that aircraft: the Englishman.

Borneo crept under our wing, and I renewed my acquaintance with a landscape already familiar to me, hills and valleys of jungle, thick forest trees, creepers and ferns fighting for life, killing or being killed in a desperate striving for sun and water. Packed tumultuously together, this was the jungle that had burst asunder the massive temples of Angkor and had covered the once great city of Ayuthia. This was the jungle that was covering a hundred discarded South Pacific air strips, and which, if left unchecked, would claim again all man-made clearings in this tropic land. Man existed here, one felt, only on sufferance, and only by continual effort, only by a successful defiance of his great enemy, the jungle, did he remain. Let him relax for a moment and the battle was lost.

From the air, as one flies up Sarawak towards North Borneo, the jungle looks innocuous, a charming pattern in variegated greens, A stronger impression of the vigour and hostility of the terrain is given to the traveller who reaches Borneo by ship, which in this and in many other ways provides a better introduction to the island. The Straits Steamship Company, a subsidiary of Holt's of Liverpool, sends every Friday from Singapore one of its diminutive vessels, and as it chugs across to North Borneo, which it reaches every Sunday, one absorbs, well before arrival, some of the characteristics and a little of the tempo and attitude of mind of this still remote territory.

These ships vary from the *Kimanis*, the pride of the fleet, which boasts of several decks of cabins and a real dining saloon, to the *Kajang*, an ancient vessel of great charm, merely several holds, an old engine and a few cabins opening on to a minute square of deck near the stern. An immense Chinese jar furnishes water for showering in the traditional style.

Infinitely preferable to the impersonal aircraft that fly over her, the *Kajang* has been sailing from Singapore across to Labuan Island, on to Jesselton, the capital on the west coast, up to Kudat in the north, and on round to Sandakan, Lahad Datu and Tawau at the south-eastern end of the territory, where she turns round and the voyage back to Singapore begins again, since before World War I. To travel on her, to sit in a comfortable rattan chair near the rail while Chinese junks head for a sunset, to call down the ventilator for more

4

drinks and to listen to the tales of the old Borneo hands returning to their lovely land is a lesson in peaceful tranquillity.

The jungle of Borneo, when first seen from the deck of one of these ships, stretches smooth and unbroken along the distant shore, for all the world like a green ice cap. It is as dangerous as an ice cap, and as empty, and as vast. It rises from the coast in tier after tier, climbing the precipitous slopes of the Crocker Range which runs down the west coast some twenty miles inland, and then spreading scarcely without interruption over the tangled mass of hills, mountains and valleys that stretch across to the distant Sulu and Celebes Sea. North Borneo is as big as Ireland; it is virtually all jungle.

Inhospitable, unfriendly though it is, it yet produces for a few a precarious livelihood, and when the European at last came to settle, late in the last century, he was forced to rely almost exclusively on the jungle for a revenue. The superstructure of British administration that was erected was paid for, in the first instance, by a small export tax on the *rattans*, the thick twisting creeper that is used for 'cane' furniture throughout the tropics, on *damar*, a gum extracted from the base of various trees, used in the production of varnishes and lacquers, and on such minor items as *gutta percha*, another type of gum extracted from trees (and useful for its property of becoming soft and plastic on immersion in hot water, and retaining any shape then given it on cooling, when it again becomes hard), crocodile skins, elephants' tusks and beeswax.

The natives who collected this jungle produce were joined, during the Depression, by an adventuresome but impoverished Englishman named Hardwick. R. K. Hardwick, who has just retired from South-East Asia, has lived an incredible life of adventure, and his exploits as a fully-blooded Dyak, wandering the jungle, dressed and living as one of them, are no more astounding than his career in wild western Queensland in the nineteen-hundreds, or his cloak and dagger excursions in the islands during the war. He is known and remembered all over North Borneo today, his bee-collecting experience being typical of the life he led as a jungle collector.

The wild bees in the Borneo jungle make their nests usually in the *mengaris* tree, which rises to a great height before sending out a branch. The ascent is hazardous and as Hardwick relates, unpleasant.

'It is most advisable to go up stark naked, because if you wear clothes the bees in thousands work their way in and may sting so seriously as to cause you to lose your hold in trying to beat them off, and a drop means certain death. You make your ladder as you go up by hammering in a sharpened wooden peg a foot over your head, connecting this with the one on which you are standing with a rattan, mount again, drive a new peg in and so on; thus you gradually mount your way up step by step.

'Having arrived at the top, about 120 feet from the ground, I straddled the first branch in which was a large nest and sent down the rattan which had been attached to my waist. The idea is for the men below to send up in a basket torches made of resin, matches, etc., so that on arrival at the bees' nest you brush its huge sides with flaming torches in each hand, thereby causing the sleepy bees inside to come outside and drop.

'This is the only practical way adopted by natives, and if any collect and sting one must bear them with utmost fortitude and never attempt to brush them off because this would probably result in falling. In my case I suppose thousands of bees followed out this theory by falling in a sleepy state to the ground, but from the innumerable stings I received on my naked body I should gather that most of the swarm found and settled on me.

'Frantically I worked, yelling loudly with the pain and receiving shouts of consternation and warnings from my men not to care but to hold on. The number of stings eventually produced a sort of anaesthesia and I became indifferent to them. Breaking off huge lumps of the nest I filled the basket, lowered it and filled it several times again until the whole comb was finished. Having had more than enough by now and being dreadfully swollen and nearly fainting I returned; the descent was deadlier than the ascent. Never have I felt such relief as I did when my feet touched terra firma. . . . We eventually returned to our camp with about 60 pounds of honey-comb, but I had to lie in my jungle hut for three days, being quite unable to move owing to my swollen condition.'

Outstanding among the scanty produce of the jungle are the edible birds' nests, a Chinese delicacy, sought by them for centuries in various caves not merely in North Borneo but in Sarawak and other parts of South-East Asia as well. The greatest single source for these birds' nests has remained the

Gomanton caves on the east coast of Borneo, near to the Kinabatangan River, and without doubt it has been the constant coming and going of the Chinese merchants in their junks that has given this broad, massive river, the longest and loneliest in North Borneo, its Chinese name. (Kina = China.)

During the Pacific War the small side stream that led the traveller conveniently close to the caves became clogged with weed, and the path to the Gomanton hill now ignores the Kinabatangan and begins, in essence, by the foreshore market of Sandakan. Here, several weeks after my arrival in North Borneo and thanks to the kindness of the Conservator of Forests, Mr. G. L. Carson, who controls the birds' nests, I was loaded early one morning on to a small decrepit launch, along with *Pengiran* Digadong, the native in charge of the caves, three Dusun porters, and Michael Wong, my young Forestry guide.

We headed out from the market, passing a half-dozen freighters anchored in Sandakan Harbour, busy loading timber from large rafts that floated against their sides. We chugged across the immensity of the bay, which stretches into North Borneo's flank for thirty miles or more. Broader than Sydney Harbour, it surpasses in magnificence any land-locked stretch of water I have seen in Great Britain. Perhaps Rio and San Francisco alone can claim pre-eminence. It lay before me, silent, still, a vast stretch of calm blue water vanishing to a shore where for mile after mile stood stacks of towering timber, virgin jungle down to the water's edge, and then mangrove beyond. It took us two hours of steady progress to cross, passing perhaps once or twice an anchored fishing junk, seeing scarcely a sign of native life in all that immensity, until finally the shores closed in, our wash rippled over muddy banks and the dense packed jungle was all around.

We wound up a narrowing river, that split and resplit its course, to become a stream, shallow and turgid, until three hours after leaving Sandakan we reached almost our first small village. The launch could go no farther, and we gently edged our way in among a collection of dug-outs, to tie up at a crude jetty. And immediately the heat of the tropics, which we had escaped on the bay, rose up and hit us again. Here the *pengiran* entertained me to the hospitality that the Muslim religion appears to have made traditional to the different races of island South-East Asia. In Sumatra, Kedah, North Borneo, the Celebes, the coastal people are quite distinct, although speaking variations of the same tongue, Malay, and practising the same religion, Islam. Amongst them all, the hospitality to a passing guest is very similar. One cannot hurry past; foolishly I had forgotten, and only remembered when I said to Michael Wong as we landed, 'Well, let's start walking,' and saw the look of astonishment on his face.

The *pengiran* showed us to the verandah of his house, built like nearly all houses in North Borneo, be they native, Chinese or European, on stilts. We took off our shoes, shook gentle hands with a number of elders (the firm grip of the west must quickly be forgotten), and sat down to a meal of pink sweet cakes, biscuits and orange pop. One is a long way from Mecca in Borneo, and it is an accepted custom that there is nothing sinful in a glass of beer, so soon warm bottles of Carlsberg and Anchor were added to the table, and reminiscences of the days of Tuan Keith, the pre-war Conservator, waxed apace. His photograph hung between some six or seven of the Queen, and innumerable group photographs of the *pengiran*, on the verandah wall that led to the inner rooms. Throughout my wanderings in North Borneo, even in the far interior with the primitive Muruts, I found these two characteristics; photographs of the young Queen and her children, as well as many of the Duchess of Kent, whose visit in 1953 was such a success, and clear vivid memories of the pre-war Europeans whose lives had touched upon theirs.

Finally we left our *pengiran* and his friends, and set off down the foot-track to the caves, some four or five hours away. I had had no breakfast except some useless black coffee, and now for lunch only pink cake and warm beer. Thus fortified, I sauntered off. Each of my three porters, who became my friends long before I returned, was loaded with an immense *bongon*, a large container fitted on the back and rising to head height, which can carry a tremendous weight of equipment. With army recollections in my mind I felt rather ridiculous setting off into the jungle carrying nothing but a light stick; but that is the way you walk in the jungle today, and I soon thanked heaven for it.

The track to the caves is filthy. Within five minutes I was perspiring, within fifteen minutes I was saturated, with sweat rolling down my face, dripping from my chin, pouring down my back and front, and blurring my eyes, as I stumbled, gasping for breath and coolness. The track, narrow and indistinct, wound for an hour or more through flat slushy mangrove and thin, closely packed trees. Constantly our feet sank in the mud, constantly we slithered precariously over small streams on flimsy branches laid as inadequate bridges. '*Pelahan pelahan*,' Wong kept saying. 'Slowly, slowly.' But however slowly I crossed, a muddy foot would slip, and splash! into the stream I'd go.

On leaving the mud and mangrove we entered thick jungle, and our track rose and fell over numerous slopes, slippery from rain. Here the biggest curse was not the occasional toss, but the numerous leeches. Sometimes you could see them on the leaves or track ahead of you, thin waving tentacles, as small as a gesticulating match, that would swing and cling with incredible rapidity, with amazing speed, as you brushed by. But most times you were unaware of the loathsome creatures until you felt a pricking in your leg, or thigh, and discovered, through your sweat and mud, a fat slug, as thick as your finger, busily sucking your blood. The experts in Sandakan had advised me to rub tobacco on them, or to put a lighted match to them, and they would drop off. I found the procedure too deliberate, too slow for me, and my reaction was to curse and grab. It worked just as well.

In the late afternoon we reached the small kampong, a cluster of seven ramshackle huts which house the nest-collectors, and washed our filth away in a clear pebbly stream flowing nearby. The Forestry Department maintain a storage hut here, and amid the piles of nests our beds were made. It is a unique kampong, in that the inhabitants are all men; they come for the season (March or June), while their wives wait at the other end of the track. They work hard and dangerously, and the kampong was black and silent not long after sunset, while outside our hut the minute baby, featherless swifts, ejected from their nests now neatly stacked, fought and flapped a pathetic, hopeless fight for life. By dawn, all were dead, covered with ants.

9

Hard by this minute clearing in the jungle rises the Gomanton hill, a limestone outcrop some seven hundred feet high, resembling many of the sheer limestone hills one finds in Malaya. Down through this limestone, for countless ages, water has percolated, eroding and carving vast chambers, corridors and shafts that provide for the small darting swifts ideal nesting places. They share the miles of caverns with innumerable bats; and as I was up at dawn, I saw the latter pouring into the mountain, and the swifts pouring out, in what seemed an unbreakable column for more than an hour. At sunset the process is reversed, as the swifts (*collocalia* is their scientific name) return, and the bats depart. I have never seen an official figure, but I do not think that one can doubt that daily a million swifts and bats move in and out.

There are two immense caves in Gomanton, one at the base, and another a few hundred feet up. The lower cave is tremendous, its floor of guano soft, squashy, oily, foul, stinking and alive with hungry spiders and beetles, its walls rising eighty to a hundred feet high into darkness, a mighty cathedral of a place, with long rattan ropes rising from the guano to bamboo or rattan platforms, on which the collectors cling, leaning and reaching out long poles to hook or disconnect the nests from crevices and ledges.

The higher cave, set off to one side, is longitudinal in character rather than vertical, entrance to it being down a steep slope rather like the open mouth of a tremendous stone shark, with a choice of several chambers that vanish, as broad avenues, deep into the hill. One can walk into these caverns for over an hour, and their intricacies and tortuous branches are known to few; it is an eerie business, even with a strong torch, to pad along, bats banking and brushing over you, impenetrable darkness at your back and before you, and the musty smell, reminiscent of mustard gas, growing stronger all the time. No wonder the Chinese never disputed the collecting, and contented themselves with the purchasing.

We climbed at last to the top of the hill, a strenuous climb for us all, as the path rises vertically in places. Bamboo ladders are fixed in the rock, and even where ladders are not used one is constantly down on hands and knees, clawing at creeper

.or boulder for support. Our porters, whom I had thought utterly exhausted the previous day, and whose tubercular coughing close to my stretcher had continued through most of the night, came on this little venture purely for fun, and when I reached the flat top, and could do little but flop to the ground, they busied themselves with the making of coffee.

A small hut on the top watches a vertical shaft which extends down for five hundred feet or more. It is one of the main routes of exit and entrance; William Pryer, the founder of Sandakan, who wrote the earliest account of the caves, in 1885 (although accounts of the export of the edible nests date back to the Ming Annals), had descended this shaft for some distance. From the time when in London I had studied Pryer's activities, until long past the time when I wrote his brief biography, I had admired him, and so I too determined to descend the shaft.

The rattan step ladder was thick, and fastened to large stubs, firmly anchored, but I had forgotten my exhausting climb, and I had lowered myself scarcely ten rungs of the ladder when I slipped and lost my footing. Clinging desperately with my hands, I swung back against the wall of the shaft, hung on for a moment, and shamefacedly climbed out. More exhausted than by the seven-hundred-feet climb, I decided that Pryer was a better man than I was, and descended again to the peaceful kampong below.

These nests, so prized by Chinese gourmets, are formed from a glutinous substance produced from an abnormally developed gland in the birds; there are white nests and black nests, made by the different types of swift. The former are much rarer, and much more expensive. I have eaten them both, and as I find they taste so alike as to be indistinguishable, I feel that the Chinese must have the same outlook as shown by many a westerner, who judges the quality of his wine by its price.

The walk back was just as muddy and exasperating as before, but it was filled with slightly more incident. In the tramp to the caves, I had passed, so it seemed to me, millions of trees but nothing else. My small circle of vision that moved with me down the path had seen nothing; nothing but greenery and tree trunks. And this is usually what happens, for the noise of your progress moves out of sight the birds and animals that live in the jungle, and it is possible to travel on and on, day after day for weeks and never see a single thing.

However, on one of our pauses, when we rested quietly in a small clearing and waited for our porters to come into view, Wong suddenly pointed to an indistinct blob on a tree; '*Maias*,' he said excitedly. It moved out of sight as soon as he spoke, but I had seen what to most in North Borneo is merely an ancient legend, the orang-utan, the wild man of the forest.

With a few herds of skinny elephants the *maias* lives on the east coast of North Borneo, and at several points in Indonesian Borneo (Kalimantan) and Sarawak. The subject of highly fanciful literature for three hundred years, and often confused in popular imagination with the African gorilla, the orang-utan is a very harmless creature as a rule, loving and affectionate if captured as a child, but its colossal strength makes it dangerous when fully grown, and then it must go back to the jungle to hunt again, usually in family groups, for the fruits it loves. It is protected under ordinance but it is a rarity today, and I was fortunate to see one.

Native legend, in both Sarawak and North Borneo, is full of tales about women being carried off by orang-utans. The favourite, retold in English by Rutter in *British North Borneo*, and elsewhere, tells of how a native woman, kept prisoner by an orang-utan, bore him a son, but contriving one day to escape, fled with the infant to a stream. Here she stumbled on a *prahu*, a native canoe, and the paddlers in it, seeing the orang-utan in close pursuit, called, 'Quickly, throw him the child.' She turned and tossed the baby to him; this momentarily delayed him and they managed to gain the safety of mid-stream. Seeing her escape, the orang-utan tore the child in half, tossing one part into the jungle, the other to the humans, a symbolic division that reflects the attitude of the natives to this man of the jungle.

The orang-utan has never been a menace to crops as has the wild pig, nor has it threatened humans as much as the crocodile has. This too I saw as we chugged downstream in our small launch, an arm-chair this time provided on the forward deck, the mangrove slipping past the side as the tide rapidly ebbed. And there he lay, a prehistoric monster, sole survivor through aeons of time, basking in the warm mud.

Again a rarity in the jungle streams today, he was mentioned in all accounts of Borneo a hundred years ago; no stream was safe, he had been known to carry off grown men and women, and bear them screaming downstream. Innumerable cattle and children had vanished, and hunting crocodiles was a recognized livelihood. All that has changed, and although there are crocodiles in the streams, orang-utans and pythons, elephants and cobras in the jungle, I have met men who have lived there a decade or more and never seen any of them. The green enveloping blanket that spreads over North Borneo is a dangerous cover, but your greatest danger lies in getting lost. To wander off the path, and suddenly to discover you are alone, is indeed a most terrifying experience.

The jungle alone has killed few men. It needed the alliance of man to perform one of the great tragedies of our time, the Sandakan Death March, when the Japanese drove 2,400 prisoners to their death. More Australian prisoners of war died in the Borneo jungle than on the Siamese railway. Out of 1,800 Australians who entered the jungle, only six survived; of the 600 British, none survived. The jungle, or the Japanese, killed them all.

A few years after the war the Australian and British Governments sent a small mission, led by Major H. W. S. Jackson of the Australian Imperial Forces, to repay and reward the people of North Borneo who had aided and succoured our prisoners of war. The script of a radio documentary by Colin Simpson, a veteran Australian journalist who accompanied the mission and who retraced, as far as possible, the track of the terrible Death Marches, is as yet the only account in existence of this unforgettable episode in the jungle of Borneo. It deserves a more lasting memorial than that.

Most of the prisoners brought to Sandakan, on the east coast of North Borneo, had been captured in Singapore, but some of the British units had been previously interned in Java. Set to work eight miles outside the town to build a military airstrip, for the first year they had passable food and treatment; the death rate had been kept down to an average rate of three a month, largely through the work of an underground network led by the Australian, Dr. J. P. Taylor, who escaped internment as the doctor in charge of the Sandakan Hospital. He slipped in medicines, milk and money, and also morale-building test tubes, from which radio valves were made.

In July 1943, however, Taylor, Captain L. C. Mathews, who built and operated the secret set, and sixty-three other officers and members of the Asian underground were arrested and moved to Kuching, in Sarawak, where most of the civilian internees were already imprisoned. Here Mathews was executed with eight of his supporters, and the pressure of work and the reduction in diet began in Sandakan. By December 1944 the food ration was down to three ounces of rice per day, with a little *ubi kayu* (tapioca root). For those caught stealing food a regular punishment was confinement in a wooden cage twelve feet by seven, and five feet high, out in the tropic sun. Here Botterill, one of the six Australian survivors, spent forty days and nights with seventeen others, the first three days without water, the first week without food.

By the end of 1944 the American and Australian forces were returning, and one of the most pathetic aspects of this tragedy is that by January 1945, when the first evacuation of Sandakan began, a landing near the prison camp would have been perfectly feasible. Sandakan was lightly guarded, and well within allied striking range; but it did not figure in the strategic plan of MacArthur the American or Blamey the Australian, and while the forces of the South-West Pacific moved steadily closer to Japan, the east coast of North Borneo was by-passed.

To the planners, however, the oil in what was then Dutch Borneo, at Tarakan, was a prize of inestimable value, and Australian forces landed there on May 15th, 1945. As a side-show, to divert the attention of the reeling Japanese from the major assault, a feint attack was made on Sandakan, several hundreds of miles to its north. Bombers sailed in and completely devastated the town; not one single building was left standing, while small P.T. boats shelled the coastal area and then steamed brazenly into the harbour.

That sealed the fate of the remaining prisoners. The first walk-out in January had taken four hundred and seventy men in nine parties; each party consisted of fifty-odd men, guarded by thirty Japanese. Weak as they were after three years of internment, and heavily guarded, there was little chance of escape, but of those who made the attempt two survived; in Sandakan between January and May the death rate climbed to over a hundred a month, and neat stacks of boxes labelled 'International Red Cross—Packed in U.S.A.' were paraded for the living to envy. Then, after the mock attack on the 15th, the Japanese pulled out completely. All the remaining prisoners who could walk were moved to Ranau, high in the interior, a hundred and fifty miles away.

These men, some hobbling on sticks, some with ulcers through to the bone, the 'walking wounded' of a three-year war with malnutrition, maltreatment, malaria, dysentery and beri-beri, men with distended stomachs and swollen limbs, men whose heads wobbled from side to side, left Sandakan in the belief that the war was over. It was only when they reached the main road, and turned not left to the town but right to the road's end and the wall of jungle that they knew that this was a march not to freedom but to death.

Over the camp they left hung the smell of death too. Sick men left in the open between the ash piles of the burned-down huts were pitiful characters in a story we shall never fully know, but a story of horror as bad as anything east of Belsen. There was a third Death March, of seventy-five men; but their bodies have never been found. Those left died terribly of starvation, diseases and exposure, without one single thread of hope or comfort. Chinese have told me of tortured death, of skeletons found clutching weeds for un-availing nutriment, of at least one crucifixion. A massacre of twenty-three occurred on the aerodrome, and finally, an Australian private, the last survivor, was executed a few weeks before the war was over.

The route to Ranau, 1,500 feet high, which took the marchers four weeks, led through treacherous dragging mud for days at a time, swamps that sucked at tired limbs, and then went, for over a hundred miles, up and down the green razor-backs of Borneo. Men died, or were killed, all along that track. At Muanad Crossing seventy-three were massacred. Daily the agonized crawl of the living was punctuated by the rifle shots that ended the trek for those too weak to move. Finally, after indescribable brutalities and neglect, 183 men out of the 537 who had begun the second Death March staggered into the little green cup that is Ranau.

Of the first marchers in January, although 313 prisoners had survived the trek, only six walking skeletons, five Australians and one Englishman, greeted the new arrivals on June 25th. Disease, starvation and the death task imposed on them, a twenty-six-mile portage over long hills of fifty-pound rice sacks, had killed the rest. The fate in store for the newcomers was obvious and inevitable.

It is incredible, but four managed to escape from Ranau, sick, filthy, unmistakably dying, yet determined to live. Four Australians, one a survivor from the first march, staggered into the jungle, climbed to nearly 4,000 feet and were befriended by Dusun natives; here they were discovered by a Services Reconnaissance Department detachment operating secretly in the vicinity. When contacted their weight ranged from six to four and a half stone, and only a flicker of life remained. The six-foot commando who discovered these four pathetic ghosts, dying in a cave, sat down beside them and unashamedly wept. Only their indomitable courage had pulled them through.

In Ranau itself the beatings, the savagery, the executions by the Japanese quickly emptied the crowded camp. When the Australians landed on the west coast, at Brunei, Labuan and Weston, only a few remained, and the last of these men, still alive after Japan had surrendered, and after leaflets announcing the surrender had been dropped to the Japanese at Ranau, were carried, or marched if they could walk, to the cemetery nearby, and there massacred.

But six had survived; Campbell and Braithwaite, who had escaped on the track, and Short, Botterill, Moxham and Sticepewich, who had escaped after reaching Ranau. Their evidence, presented to a War Crimes Court held on Labuan Island shortly after the war, presided over by Maxwell Hall, a former chief justice of North Borneo and then serving in the Australian forces, brought swift retribution to some of those who had killed their captives in what Australians regard, perhaps even more than the British, as the greatest tragedy in the Pacific War. Certainly the jungle of North Borneo had never witnessed such mass murder as the Death Marches to Ranau.

Ranau today, twelve years after, shows no signs of war whatever. The wooded hills that surround this green cup once more lie peaceful under a tropic sun. To climb the track behind Ranau village near sunset, to watch a thin column of wood smoke rise in the valley, and to hear the Dusun urge his tired buffalo home across the *padi* field, is to witness a charming rustic scene. In the little village itself, where a tumbling mountain stream nearby passes under Borneo's only covered bridge, the Chinese cigar-maker is the only sign of effort; busily making cigars from the tobacco leaf grown by the Dusuns on the surrounding slopes, and flying them out by the small aircraft which daily bring him his beer and provisions, even he, induced by his Dusun wife, has succumbed somewhat to the leisurely tempo, and pauses to talk and rest.

In the centre of the small valley the narrow fields are replaced by what appears from the plane to be a flat green board, an airstrip, with a building which combines the functions of airport and post office alongside. It must be one of the few airports in the world that does not show a car or two alongside as you fly over. There is no road, as yet, to the outside world; you are in a Shangri-la, and once you leave the plane you must of necessity walk.

The Rest House, primitive, charming, full of character, looks down from its knoll on to the grounds of representatives of the Borneo Evangelical Mission. In the centre of these grounds is a concrete plinth bearing a reference to a rebel of the late nineteenth century, Mat Salleh, who was eventually killed by the government. There is no sign whatever that it is also the site of the mass grave of the British and Australians who trekked to Ranau, for here, hard by the strip they built, was their camp site and graveyard. No monument in Borneo honours their memory, nor those who died befriending them. Yet it cannot be said that Borneo has forgotten them.

There were some who thought that it would be fitting if

there was some memorial, not a narrow national one merely to the Australian prisoners, or to the executed Chinese, but something by which the living of all races in North Borneo could honour the valour of their dead. A movement, headed by G. S. Carter, of Brunei, who parachuted into Sarawak in 1945, was anxious to make it international as well as inter-racial, a monument that would claim the support and merge the emotions of all the peoples of British Borneo. From the remembrance of the cause to which all paid service in the past, a nation of the future might be born.

Rising high over Ranau, dominating the jungle of North Borneo, visible from almost the entire territory, is the magnificent mountain of Kinabalu, a jagged monolith that stands as the highest peak (13,455 feet) in all South-East Asia. It thrusts its sheer stone slopes high above the jungle, too steep and cold for trees, aloof and mysterious, the object of veneration to all the neighbouring peoples, who regard it as the place whence all spirits depart. Here will be this most fitting memorial.

In all North Borneo there is only one small bird sanctuary; there are no National Parks, there are no sanatoria or hill stations. Just ten miles from Ranau lies the little plateau of Kundassan at an altitude of 4,000 feet, and commanding a magnificent view of nearby Kinabalu. It was in this glorious setting that the last four survivors of the death march were found. Here a permanent and fitting tribute to their memory will be raised; a constructive tribute of potential value to all three territories of Borneo.

The challenge and grandeur of Kinabalu are attracting more and more attention from climbers and tourists anxious to see something of this most beautiful part of a lovely land. The mountain, sweeping up from its western side almost from sea level in a towering mass of granite, contains a wealth of almost untapped interest and research for the botanist, the ornithologist and the social anthropologist. Here grow unique orchids, while near the craggy top flies Borneo's rarest bird, the 'mountain black eye' (*chlorocharis*), along with many other imperfectly studied specimens.

Although subject at times to heavy rain, the climate at Kundassan is invigorating. All the humidity of the coast has

Mount Kinabalu

*'Here grow unique orchids, while near the craggy top flies Borneo's
rarest bird, the "mountain black eye"'*

gone; one can move without perspiring, and the days, pleasantly sunny, are followed by cold nights, which call for blankets and fires. All this is within a day's drive from Jesselton on the coast, for a road link of great scenic beauty is on the point of completion, and by air within less than a day from any other point in steaming, humid, enervating Borneo.

Here on this plateau could be built a convalescent home for the sick, a research centre for the agriculturist, a rest house or hotel for the traveller. It would be ideal for the establishment of Boy Scout and Girl Guide camps, whereby the youth of all races would be brought together, and it would be hard to find a more appropriate site for an Outward Bound School, if that enterprising institution for training young men in the practical principles of citizenship and self-reliance could be introduced into Borneo as it has already into Malaya.

All this needs money—£25,000 is an estimate, and £5,000 has already been raised—but a stroke of the pen is all that is needed at least to save this plateau and the neighbouring peak as a bird sanctuary and National Park, and once half the estimated cost has been raised the organizers are willing to make a start in getting the park declared, leaving its further development until later. Some central commemorative symbol, as dramatic as the Cross on the Andes, is needed to catch the imagination; around this there could arise, in the jungle of Borneo, a project of direct and indirect benefit to the loyal-hearted peoples of Borneo, and a focal point of interest and appeal to people throughout the Commonwealth who wish this country well. The colonies of Britain are not prone to imaginative gestures; here could be the exception.

2. CAPITAL CITY

MEANWHILE, as my plane carried me from Singapore towards Jesselton, the *padi* fields and the jungles of the west coast of North Borneo were covered with thick cloud. We had left Kuching, capital of Sarawak, to the south, far behind; Sibu, Sarawak's second city (merely a strip in stumpy jungle, and the blazing heat of a hut at midday), and Labuan Island, the other stop, where news of the unserviceability of the Jesselton strip for heavy aircraft had necessitated a long pause and a change of plane, had become already a moment in time. Jesselton, the capital of North Borneo, was somewhere ahead, and the small De Havilland Rapide biplane, a wooden relic of twenty years ago, shook and shuddered in a tropic storm as it searched for its journey's end.

A few miles off its track loomed Kinabalu, nearly fourteen thousand feet of malevolence; the rain lashed the tiny plane, the clouds enveloped it, and the five hundred boxed chickens, with whom I shared the back seat, squeaked and twittered in terror. Opposite me a mother with three small children— mothers who travel always seem to have three small children —peered in vain through the perspex windows. 'Is that Kuala Penyu?' she wondered hopefully, at a brief glimpse of the China Sea. 'Was that the Kimanis?'

The Kimanis River was where it all began. Today it is again a small west coast river, with a rubber estate a little upstream, and a kampong of sorts nearby, with nothing to show (except for one granite headstone), that it was here that the first European settlement on the mainland of North Borneo was made, and there are not many who know that it was a colony of Americans in 1865 which set in motion a chain of events that led to the acquisition of the territory by a British Chartered Company in 1881, and eventually to its incorporation as a British Colony in 1946.

Before 1865, and for many years after, North Borneo was a wilderness. The only power on the west coast had been Brunei. At one time it had been powerful, active, and perhaps all the rivers of Borneo had paid tribute to it, and observed a tolerable peace. But that had been centuries before. Political competency has been vouchsafed to few Malay States in the past, and the system of delegating rivers and responsibilities to relatives merely encouraged the latent anarchism in their mentality. The old supposition, that all the evils of piracy and dissolution of seventeenth- and eighteenth-century South-East Asia were the fault of the Dutch, who monopolized the trade of the islands to the great detriment of all others, can scarcely be defended. In Borneo waters, east, north and west, the Dutch never came, and trade was never controlled; yet here the states collapsed just the same, and by the middle of the nineteenth century, apart from the small area of law and order in the south, at Kuching, where the eccentric James Brooke was ruling, and at Labuan, the island off Brunei acquired by the British in 1847, Brunei was in a state of decay.

The man who first thought there might be money in this was an American named Moses. He arrived in Labuan from Singapore, and had to borrow money to pay his fare, so he could not have been a very successful businessman there; he then secured a ten-year lease of the northern part of Borneo from the aged Sultan, and immediately sailed, not back to Singapore, but to Hong Kong, which also suggests a certain lack of credit. Before he arrived at Labuan, claiming to be the United States Consul, we know absolutely nothing about him except that he had been in the United States Navy; he may have been with Captain Balastier U.S.N. in 1850, when he concluded a most-favoured-nation treaty with the Sultan; perhaps Moses conceived the idea of developing North Borneo then; but where he came from and what he was, is still obscure. Yet he was the vital first actor in a play that ended with North Borneo as part of the Commonwealth.

Somewhere about the Baram, the river boundary of Brunei and Sarawak, the arc of overseas contacts shifts from Singapore to Hong Kong. North Borneo looks to Hong Kong, Sarawak to Singapore. It was fitting then that while James Brooke came from Singapore, Moses should go to Hong Kong. Here he met some minor businessmen, Americans like himself, and on to them he quickly unloaded his title deeds. He painted a

22

most optimistic picture of a virgin territory waiting to be exploited, gold, diamonds, timber, the birds' nests that sold in Hong Kong for fabulous prices, spices and peppers, all were commodities that Hong Kong and the hinterland of China desired, all could be secured in North Borneo. Naïve, trusting, these most untypical New Englanders fell for the bait and bought. Led by Joseph Torrey, from Massachusetts, they quickly formed a company, interested Chinese associates and decided on a settlement at Kimanis, where a track wound inland over the coastal mountain range. By December 1865 some sixty Chinese labourers and half a dozen Americans were established there, and the stars and stripes was waving over Borneo.

It did not wave for long. Torrey and his colleagues had enterprise, but they had little money, and the settlement began to fail very quickly. Torrey was forced to lead a most active life, dodging between Hong Kong, Labuan and Kimanis in a frantic effort both to raise more capital and to avoid those from whom he had borrowed already. He completely failed to raise any more money, but he managed to withhold any payments to Moses until he contacted a disreputable gang in Hong Kong, and persuaded them to embark on a general filibustering raid on Borneo.

These pirates were a mixed bag of Germans, gold miners largely drifting from Alaska to the new fields in Australia. One, their leader, Rhode, had fought in the Tai'ping revolt. Moses gave them the American flag, they acquired an old schooner, and in her in August 1866 they sailed for Brunei, to cause consternation among the British officials on Labuan, and panic among the ruling circles in Brunei. They need not have worried. The little settlement on the Kimanis was almost exhausted; there were no easy pickings to be secured there, or in Brunei, and in disgust and without incident the bedraggled adventurers returned to Hong Kong.

The Kimanis settlement was abandoned soon after. The area chosen for the project had been most unsuitable—thick jungle beside a small river, with none of the necessities of life provided—and the Americans had no experience and little capital. Towards the end of 1866 the few Americans remaining brought their Chinese labourers to Labuan, where they secured employment for them in the coal-mine, while they themselves returned to Hong Kong. In a few months the jungle had claimed its own again, and the terraced slopes and the solitary grave of Mr. Thomas B. Harris, of Walton, New York, vanished for over forty years.

The cessions granted to Moses, who left Brunei in disgust in 1867 to disappear from our story, had been for a period of ten years, and although Torrey had failed to form a settlement on the ceded territory he had not lost hope of exploiting them in some way; for nearly a decade in Hong Kong he persistently pressed them upon anyone likely to buy them from him. Slowly he was successful. In 1875, shortly before they were to expire, he persuaded Von Overbeck, an Austrian who had retired from North Pacific whaling to enter business in Hong Kong, that something might be made out of them. Overbeck had recently acquired a barony, in recognition of his efforts in collecting oriental pieces for the great Vienna Exhibition of 1873, and he had wider horizons than the men with whom we have previously dealt. The great expansion of European powers, the scramble for Africa, the annexation or partition of large parts of Asia, were beginning. Here, reasoned Overbeck, was a unique opportunity to acquire territory that later could be resold to Austria. In Vienna and London he convinced some financiers, who advanced him capital, and he then sailed to Borneo. Although he and Torrey failed to secure another cession deed from the Sultan, who had never received a penny for his troubles, the heir to the throne was more approachable, and with him an agreement was concluded.

Only now did Britain enter the scene. Overbeck's finances, strained by the visit to Borneo, steadily deteriorated. Austria remained indifferent to such a dubious offer, and refused to consider any occupation. Overbeck, after several other contacts had failed, approached Alfred Dent, the son of a former employer of his, of the great eastern house of Dent Brothers. Dent had capital, enthusiasm, drive and vision. On condition that the chief direction of the affair passed to him, he advanced Overbeck £10,000 and sent him back to conclude agreements with the Sultan.

Here he encountered two difficulties. One was W. H.

Treacher, the governor of Labuan Island, who viewed with disfavour any undertaking that might result in North Borneo passing to alien hands; another was the fact that the east coast of North Borneo, which the Sultan had blithely included in earlier cessions, was the property of the Sultan of Sulu, and had been since at least the eighteenth century.

Overbeck was able to surmount both these problems. Treacher he pacified by promising that if North Borneo was granted to Dent and himself (as it was by a new agreement of December 1877), they would develop it by a Chartered Company, and they would not endeavour to sell it to a foreign power; and by a quick visit to the Sultan of Sulu, who was fighting the Spaniards from Manila throughout his archipelago, he secured a cession deed from him ceding all his North Borneo territory for an annual payment of $5,000.

These cession moneys are still being paid, for after the Sultanate was abolished by Americano-Filipino democracy early in this century, the recognition of the rightful heirs to the Sultan proved difficult and took some time. It was not until 1939 that North Borneo listed those eligible, and it was not until some years after the war that most of the heirs felt able to accept payment. Moneys due to deceased heirs are paid into deposit accounts, and the Estimates each year included $5,300 to which their successors can lay claim.

With 28,000 square miles of North Borneo firmly and legally ceded to him, Overbeck followed Dent to London. For a brief period, despite his promises to Treacher, he endeavoured to interest Austria and then Bismarck into buying these title deeds from him. He failed here, and he failed to withstand Dent, who gradually deprived him of all power in the matter, so that slowly he too dropped from the scene. Dent alone remained, doggedly driving the British Government into some form of official recognition of his cessions.

Finally he won through. He had been helped considerably by various assets denied his predecessors. In London he had the friendship of the Permanent Under-Secretary at the Foreign Office, a Civil Servant of great power, Sir Julian Pauncefote, who was as convinced as Dent was that Britain should acquire this territory. In Borneo he had the success of the solitary Residents whom Overbeck had planted there, particularly Pryer in Sandakan Bay, who demonstrated clearly that the concern was active and useful. And in the actual position of North Borneo, lying unattended on the flank of the immense British trade with China and Japan, he had perhaps his most important asset of all.

In 1882 Gladstone invaded Egypt to protect this trade route to the Orient, and the year previously, for the same reason, he had quietly acquiesced in the granting of a Royal Charter to the company that Dent had formed. Politically reluctant to allow any expansion of the Empire, which would thus make North Borneo (Sabah as it was called then) a direct burden on the Crown, fearful of the consequences if it lapsed to foreign hands, Gladstone welcomed the Chartered Company, a Civil Service compromise, as the cheap way out.

This company, the British North Borneo Chartered Company, drew its strength from the City of London. Despite great hopes, little other outside capital, Chinese, Malayan or otherwise, ever flowed into North Borneo, and the country's development depended almost entirely on unofficial British investment. It became British, acquiring the status of a Protectorate in 1888; but it never cost the taxpayer a penny, as the Chartered Company administered it from 1881 to 1941 from its own scanty sources. Such an admirable state of affairs ended only in 1946, when following the ravages of war (North Borneo was the most devastated part of the Commonwealth), the Colonial Office assumed administrative and financial responsibility, and the territory became the youngest Colony of the Crown, with Jesselton, where we were on the point of landing, the youngest capital.

Jesselton's airstrip, built by the Japanese with forced labour during the war, is only six feet above, and a few hundred yards from, the sea. Built for light 'Zero' aircraft, and subjected to some hundred inches of rain per year, it did not long survive the first few years of peace, and the saying spread, as the strip became unserviceable for days, then for weeks at a time, 'If you have time to spare, travel by air.'

It was purely a coincidence, but my arrival with the chickens, the harassed mother and the tropical storm marked the end of all this, and in a way typified the stage reached by the Colony as a whole. Since 1946, when the territory was

26

flat on its back, with scarcely a house standing, having been occupied and run-down for three and a half years, the talk was all on reconstruction; improvisation was makeshift, repairs were temporary, war equipment was salvaged and adapted. When I visited the Colony in 1953, and again in 1954, this pre-occupation with the dismal past, this lack of new spirit, was depressingly obvious, in Jesselton most of all. Now this has ended; reconstruction is a word never used; 'development' has taken its place, and what was a dispirited town is bursting with vigour. Jesselton is taking on the appearance of a capital city more and more, while North Borneo is growing increasingly confident and beginning to boom. It is in a most interesting stage of development, with numerous exciting projects at last beginning to show fruit. A new era is beginning, and a bad one is ending. I was there to see the change.

For example, by the time I left North Borneo, two months after my slithering approach in the Rapide, a new, higher strip had been made by the Public Works Department, with equipment unheard of before. Metalled and surfaced, this can take all the landings possibly demanded of it, while an even larger and stronger one is planned nearby. Air communications these days are long past the period when only V.I.P.'s flew, and North Borneo is determined to ensure that if business enterprise is on the wing, it will be able to fly in here.

In most cases in the East the European wisely has retained the native name of the locality he chose for his abode, and cities such as Singapore, Kuala Lumpur and others have borne indigenous titles; where he has endeavoured to Europeanize his settlement, with some such title as Prince of Wales Island or Batavia, they have not lasted; Prince of Wales Island became Penang again long before European control was removed, Batavia reverted to the ancient Djakarta soon after. North Borneo has three localities named after Europeans, Jesselton, Beaufort and Weston; they were all nonentities, and their names still seem out of character. But before the European came in each case the area of the town site was uninhabited, and as the concept of a settlement was European, there seems no reason why a European name should

27

not be given to it. Nevertheless, it seems a pity that Jesselton at least was not given some adaption of the old-Malay name for the area, '*Singga Mata*' (where the eye loves to dwell), for it is indeed a lovely spot.

Jesselton lies on a broad bay, facing a green hilly island, Gaya Island. In the eighteen-eighties this island had been one of the earliest posts of the Chartered Company. The land where Jesselton now stands had not been part of one of the rivers included in the cessions of the Sultan of Brunei, as it and a few others had become the personal property of some of his relatives. The Company, with a recollection of late eighteenth- and early nineteenth-century Colonial practice, which had established posts on a variety of uninhabited off-shore islands—Balembangan (1773), Penang (1786), Singapore (1819), Hong Kong (1848) and Labuan (1847)—had placed its west coast administrator here, on Gaya Island.

Here grew a small settlement. It was severely handicapped by the lack of water, but it was a small circle of peace and justice. Chinese traders settled, and people from the surrounding rivers sailed across to buy and sell their wares. In 1897, however, the post was attacked, looted and burnt to the ground by the famous rebel Mat (Mahommed) Salleh. Much of his support had come from the little streams nearby, and as they were under the suzerainty of the Sultan of Brunei, however nominal, he was presented with a tremendous bill for damage. These streams, wedged into the side of Chartered Company territory, had become a nuisance long before this devastating Gaya raid, as Brunei slave dealers were permitted access to the interior tribes, particularly to the Muruts, who readily exchanged their unwanted children for arms. In addition, escaping convicts could take refuge there, and in this and in other ways administration was hampered. So using this raid on Gaya as a convenient excuse, the Company began negotiations with Brunei and acquired the rivers, putting all of Gaya Bay under Chartered Company rule, and making the west coast a compact unit.

Sixty miles south of Gaya Bay a railway was being built inland from the coast. The piece of mangrove there which later became the port was named Weston, after West, the man who built the railway. It was useless as a port, being far too shallow, and following the acquisition of Gaya Bay it was decided to build a deep water port there. The first choice was Gantisan, near the entrance to the bay, but when that was proved unsatisfactory, as being too exposed, the site was moved in 1899 to what was called Jesselton, after Sir Charles Jessel, a Director of the Company.

It is a narrow stretch of level ground, much wider now than fifty years ago, but still extremely thin, lying at the foot of a steep razor-back, a green slope of jungle that affords for those fortunate few who can afford it, a home site unexcelled in all Borneo. Down below lies the town; beyond it the blue waters of Gaya Bay. Glimpsed through magnificent timber, heavy with vine and fern, the coral underneath the bay patterns the scene with translucent colour. Sailing between the reefs come the Bajaus, truly *orang-laut*, men of the sea, their *prahus* distinguished by a most characteristic broad stripe in their one big sail. They anchor by the sea wall, or beach on the shallow bank nearby, unship and secure their sail and mast, and come ashore to sell their fish, caught among the islands, Gaya and the others, that lie off shore.

From the sprawling green mass of Gaya comes at dusk another visitor to Jesselton, the flying fox, heading for the *mangosteens, rambutans* and other fruit trees of the mainland. His outstretched wings provide the motif for the burgee of the local yacht club, one of those cheerful, multi-racial affairs that provides a quicker and clearer insight into the essential atmosphere of Jesselton and North Borneo than many a textbook or Annual Report.

The most outstanding characteristic of North Borneo, placing it apart from the remainder of South-East Asia, is its racial tolerance and goodwill. Whereas in Malaya, Indonesia, Burma and Indo-China racial antagonisms are sharp, and violence and disorder are controlled only imperfectly, North Borneo is a peaceful and happy land.

This peace, this goodwill, is all the more remarkable when one realizes that for long after the first permanent occupation of the territory by the British North Borneo Chartered Company, North Borneo was a poverty-stricken, fragmented, anarchical wilderness, and that even today, although its population numbers merely 400,000, it is as polyglot as the Tower

Murut

Malay

N. Borneo
woman
a child

Bajau chief

Tamil

of Babel. On the coast there are the Brunei Malays and Kedazans, stretching from Brunei to Jesselton, then Bajaus and Illanuns, Suluks and Obians, all embracing the tenets of Islam. Behind them are the Dusuns, agriculturalists on the coastal and interior plains; they are pagan or Christian. In the interior roam the Muruts, primitive pagans. In the towns are the Chinese, small pieces of the mosaic that is South China, with a unique colony of Northern Chinese as well. There are Europeans, Anglo-Indians and Burmese, Sikhs and Ceylonese. People from different homelands, professing different faiths, living different lives; yet between them all there flows a broad generous stream of tolerance and racial goodwill.

The greater part of this population lives on the narrow coastal plain that runs down to the west coast, and I was able to see people from most of these different ethnic groups as I wandered about Jesselton's dusty streets. As I walked past piledrivers and nearly-completed shops, as I sauntered along the new sea wall, smelled the hot dry coral that is being used as a filler, and watched the new reclamations, as I coughed with the dust of cement bags being unloaded, and watched the Chinese women labourers at work, with their distinctive broad-brimmed hats with black cotton face-curtains hanging from them, I was constantly rubbing shoulders with this amazing assortment of peoples, going their own way, living at peace with their neighbours.

Jesselton itself, like all the other towns, is a Chinese town, full of Hokkiens and Cantonese. These are the shopkeepers, the businessmen, while the third great subdivision, the Hakka, are the smallholders in the countryside behind the towns, the vegetable growers and pig rearers. At the same time, they are often Government clerks or junior officers, because it is they who are the converted Christians and have learned English at school, whereas the others are still Confucians, Buddhists or Taoists, and have studied at Chinese schools.

In Malaya it is the Hakka who is often the communist. With the Hailamese, the islanders regarded by the others as uncouth, they crowd forlornly the foot of the ladder leading to success. No relative or connection reaches down to help

31

them, and despised and scorned, secretive and resentful, they become fit targets for communist persuasion. Not so in North Borneo. There is no communist party, there are no secret societies. The Hakka is a cheerful peasant, with all the land he wants. Again different from his counterpart in Malaya, he is friendly with, and often married to the indigenous people amongst whom he works. In many cases both pray to the same Christian God, for both were pagans until recently converted. The Hailamese, just as contentedly, runs the coffee-shops of Jesselton, Sandakan and Tawau, and prepares, for a highly satisfied clientele, the best food this side of Heaven.

The coffee-shop is a feature of the whole of South-East Asia. It appears to have missed the attention of sociologists, anthropologists and even historians, for there are no texts on 'Coffee in South-East Asia', nothing to compare to the flood of material on Tea in England, and while the significance, both economical and political, of the tea-shop has been analysed thoroughly, I have seen no estimate of the power of the coffee-shop. But it has an important role in the countries of South-East Asia, for it is there that the Chinese have gathered. Until recently nearly all of their business deals would be arranged there; even now some aspect of them, their initiation or conclusion, is performed there, and now not merely economics are talked there, but politics as well, North Borneo not excluded.

The coffee-shop probably has a history as old as the Chinese in South-East Asia, and I would suggest that in the first place it was a tea-shop. Tea has been drunk in China since Han times, since before the time of Christ, and the little handle-less cups are far more a piece of traditional China than the thick heavy cup and saucer of the present day coffee-shop. Perhaps the change to coffee came with the Dutch period in South-East Asia, in the seventeenth century above all, but really I do not know, and where is my social historian to tell me?

There is an amazing sameness about these establishments, which fill the roles of club, secret society rendezvous, employment agency, committee and board room, as well as restaurant, and throughout South-East Asia they all contain certain essentials. There are rarely doors or windows, one merely walks in from the sidewalk, and sits at the very traditional circular marble table, usually in a fairly old rickety wooden chair.

In Jesselton one of the young Europeans I met had been trying for weeks to sell a new line that his firm was promoting. It was a coffee-shop table, circular, identical in all respects to those already in use, but made of a plastic that looked identical to marble and sold at a third of the price. He could not give them away. You will never find, anywhere in South-East Asia, a coffee-shop table that is not of marble.

On the marble table you usually find an ashtray, heavy, half full of water, in which float the disintegrating remains of your predecessor's cigarettes. This is unfortunate for the squeamish, but as over your head a fan will be whirling, it is better that the butt be drowned than the ash lodged in your eye. Alongside it there will be placed as you sit down, if it is not already waiting, possibly a plate of small stale cakes, possibly a packet of warm soft chocolate. Often to one side at the front there is a glass case, and the same wares will be displayed for the passer-by, with in addition, always, the inevitable packets of cigarettes.

At the back of the shop, or to one side, is the refrigerator, rather black now round the edges and handle, for the humidity is always high, and sweaty moist hands take little time to remove the enamel and shine; but even if there is no electricity the refrigerator is usually the *pièce de résistance*, providing for those who want it the light North German type of ales and the beer brewed in Singapore that have spread through the Oriental tropics.

Even in Singapore or British Borneo the light British beers find few customers among the Chinese, who constitute the greater proportion of the alcohol-consuming public, and it is Carlsberg, Becks, Anchor and Tiger that jostle for position and coldness in the coffee-shop refrigerators. But beer emerges usually only in the evening; it is coffee that holds sway most of the time, brought to you by one of the waiters, clad in shorts and singlet, shuffling on red wooden clogs, and although I suppose I drank a hundred cups of that coffee on my tour of North Borneo, and I have drunk a thousand other cups before and since, I have never yet had it in a cup from

33

which it had not already slopped over. From the research and cross-questioning I have done on this subject, I fear that this is an inevitable occupational hazard, and is as typical of the coffee-shop as the circular table.

Over this establishment there hangs a certain undefinable air, a raffish quality more in keeping with earlier days than this twentieth century. In South-East Asia today the characters of Conrad and Maugham are difficult to come by; much of the East has become too ordinary, and occasionally too sophisticated. It is not without character, but it is a character far removed from the East of twenty or fifty years ago. Yet in the coffee-shops of Borneo you are back again, back in the romantic raffish past, and a European with a stubble and a pair of chewed-up, dirty whites, even if he is only the Dutchman in charge of the dredger, is not out of place at all; nor are the group of Bajaus, their thick uncombed hair burnt brown, nor the Chinese in old-fashioned laced-across jacket and voluminous black shiny trousers. These are of the East as it was, when to the European it was exciting and mysterious, before the layers of its character began to burn and shrivel under western heat, and a protective artificial coating of superficial culture took its place. Here in the coffee-shop is one of the residual layers of the East.

The refrigerator and the German beer, even the coffee cups, may be seen as something extraneous. Not so the food. Here no attempt is made to provide anything but that which is of China, food prepared by Hailamese, the best cooks of the South. There is sharks'-fin soup for example, a glutinous soup that is an excellent beginning to any banquet, which can be followed by delicious sweet-and-sour pork, delivered, as would be the soup, in a big bowl in the centre of the table, from which you may transfer what you want to your own small bowl. Other fish, rice and meat dishes will follow, some with hot chillies that will burn your throat, some with long flat beans that will cool it. An excellent way of ending is with lychees, small fruits that rest in juice among blocks of ice. Such a meal with every course increases your *bonhomie* with the world, and adds to your appreciation of your hosts, the Chinese. The next best thing to learning their language, if you wish to understand the Chinese, is to love their food.

While both should be attempted, the latter is much easier and much more enjoyable; and a Jesselton coffee-shop is not such a bad place to begin.

Far removed from the coffee-shop in the social context, united with it as a legacy of the past, and as something equally as valuable in performing a service of many different kinds, is Government House. In Jesselton it stands on the ridge behind the town, its Union Jack visible to all who live in peace under and because of it. Agnes Keith, in her delightful book on Borneo, *Land Below the Wind*, has captured the essence, the charm, of official British hospitality far better than I can hope to do. She went to a Garden Party at Government House, and a Dinner, when His Excellency lived in Sandakan. He now lives in Jesselton, but the picture is much the same.

'If one paints the picture in more detail, one sees inside rooms which are large and dignified and always made gay with flowers, tables with *Tatler*, *Punch*, the London *Times*, the *Manchester Guardian* and the photographs of the children who are at home in their English nurseries. Chinese servants . . . will be bustling in with gin and bitters and whiskey and soda, and native servants in sarongs and wound head cloths will be smiling brilliantly and moving languidly, and women in flowered evening dresses will be talking about the weather, and men in mess jackets . . . will be standing erect and presenting a more handsome than comfortable appearance. And if one listens at the open door of such a gracious room there will be heard the soft tones of pleasant voices.'

The coffee-shop is largely the rendezvous of the Chinese, while Government House is partly, though not nearly as exclusively, the rendezvous of the European. Where the two races mingle most, and associate with the other races of North Borneo, is on the *padang*, the playing field, which is to North Borneo what the village green is to England.

The Jesselton *padang*, the shadiest in the territory, is tucked into a fold of the steep slope that crowds the town into the sea. Here is turf almost as sacrosanct as that of Lords, and cricket equally as solemn; here the ceremonial parade on the Queen's Birthday, the Boys Scouts' Annual Display, the Police Sports, the Inter-Territorial Athletic Competitions. Here above all is soccer, for soccer is the most widespread and most popular of sports in Borneo, with teams representing every possible combination, where European, Chinese, Dusun, Bajau and Murut all meet together, accept the same rules, respect each other's skill, and enjoy one another's company. It may well be Britain's most lasting legacy to the East.

The *padang* competes with the new sea wall as a place of relaxation, and while the young extroverts practise their soccer, their basket-ball or their athletic techniques, the middle-aged stroll in the cool of the late afternoon by the water's edge, past the newly planned and recently opened market, past the new three-storied hotel, the new shop-houses and clean new banks, to where the new wharf ends the narrow stretch of level land, and the sailing yachts ride gently at anchor. At the other end of town the temporary makeshift rows of shops, erected hurriedly over the chaos that was Jesselton in 1945, still stand, their flimsy walls and highly combustible roofs a nightmare to the Insurance Agents, their presence a challenge to the town planner to finish the job and to present Jesselton as the first completed new town in the territory.

Jesselton is the capital, the seat of government; the new wharf, already in danger of being considered inadequate, as the imports and exports continue to rise in quantity and value each year, is tucked away discreetly at one end of the town. One has the feeling that if commerce must rear its ugly head in Jesselton it should do so as much as possible out of sight. Is it only a coincidence, or does it reflect subconsciously the attitude of the peoples of Jesselton, that whereas the favourite walk of the Chinese is along the sea wall to the end of town, to the wharf, where the lighted hatches and the whirring derricks of some Straits Steamship provide noise and interest, the favourite drive of the European, usually a Civil Servant, is out of town the other way, where a golf club hides among *casuarina* pines by the sea, and no sign of commerce or industry mars the view?

The difference in their modes of behaviour reflects merely a different attitude to relaxation, and although the rivalry between commerce and government in North Borneo is traditional, nevertheless the work they do is aimed at a common goal, the development of the territory. In this they have achieved considerable success. In 1947 the combined figure for imports and exports was a little under $40 million. Ten years later it was a little over $240 million. Similarly, shipping figures rose from under one to over five million gross tons, and there is no sign of a slackening in that rise.

On to the wharves of the territory, Jesselton's included, rumble constantly the Land Rovers and decrepit trucks of the hard working Chinese, to disgorge an ever-increasing quantity of rubber, timber and copra, manila hemp and tobacco, cattle and *cutch*, and to load not only the food, the cigarettes, the textiles and the equipment that a growing population with a rising standard of living is demanding, but also the bags of cement, the steel girders and the heavy machinery for a government's increasing capital expenditure.

Great Britain plays the dominant role in this trade. Despite comments that her deliveries are too slow and her prices too high, she sells far more to the country than any other, averaging some 25 per cent of all imports. And she alone buys an equal amount from North Borneo. Other Commonwealth countries participate, particularly Hong Kong, second to Great Britain in the value of imports which she supplies to North Borneo, Malaya, Australia and New Zealand.

The economy of North Borneo is a simple one, and the revenue of the state is secured very largely by export duties, usually 10 per cent on its primary products and a similar import duty on the manufactured goods that come in. The export duties, on an export trade valued in 1956 at over $120 million, were over $6 million. Double that amount came from the import duties on a $117 million export trade. The item yielding the largest single contribution to the revenue, just on $4 million, was the duty on cigarettes.

Smaller amounts of revenue are raised by licences, posts and telegraphs, port and harbour dues, and other minor charges. The dues from entertainment and petroleum storage licences steadily increase as films and cars, those western necessities, are embraced by more and more. All in all, over $30 million was raised by the Government in revenue in 1956, and a little under $30 million was spent.

A new imposition, at first fiercely denounced as endangering the stability of the state, but now accepted grudgingly as inevitable, was the introduction in 1955 of income tax. It is a very low tax, standing at $3\frac{1}{2}$ per cent until an income of over £1,500 is reached, and rising no higher than 5 per cent until more than £3,000 is earned. It is administered with an efficiency and a lack of red tape that compares favourably with United Kingdom procedure, and with countries closer to the territory, such as Singapore and Malaya.

I witnessed one taxation scene that reflected this efficiency, and which also epitomized the friendly informality of the country, in which the bureaucrats of Jesselton participate almostly as freely as anyone else.

We were sitting late one afternoon on the verandah of the Jesselton golf club. It is a simple wooden building, in the shape of an L, raised slightly from the ground. It is separated from Tanjong Aru, one of Borneo's loveliest stretches of beach, five or six miles of golden sand lined with tall cool *casuarina* pines, by a few yards of lawn. Here play the children, on the grass, or the sands through the pines, or in the calm safe waters of the China Sea, while their parents play golf.

On the other side of the club house is the golf course. The links at present unfortunately lack one hole, as the seventh, a difficult one, used to pass close to the house of the manager of Cable and Wireless, the firm owning the land. His predecessor had not minded, and his servants had made a small fortune from the recovery of lost balls and their subsequent sale to the next ham-handed golfer who plunged past. But with a change in 'number one's' (as the manager of an Eastern firm is always referred to), objections were raised; the hole was abandoned, and the loss had not been made good when I left. Doubtless, as a vital issue, the position has by now been rectified.

We were discussing which airline would be the first to accept golf clubs as personal luggage, and so ensure a waiting list of travelling directors for years ahead, when a rather rough-and-ready gentleman approached us, and said to one of my companions, 'Excuse me, are you the income tax bloke?' My friend intimated that such was indeed the case, and when the other replied, 'Well, look, I've been here on contract, I'm off back to Australia on Tuesday, and I thought I'd better get things straight with your mob first.' My friend invited him to sit down, asked him a few questions, jotted down the answers on the back of a gin chit, and then said, 'You owe me such and such.' The visitor wrote him a cheque on Singapore, and the 'income tax bloke' wrote across the old chit 'Paid,' signed it and handed it over to him. A drink all round and the business was concluded.

Excellent, I thought, excellent; I could detect no flaw, for as my income tax friend had earlier commented, and as the history of the territory bears out, North Borneo is incredibly honest. The European in many cases is forced to live up to a higher standard of morality than that which he left. I heard amazing tales of honesty—a wallet left lying in the seat of an open car, houses never locked, possessions never guarded. All were safe—safer than if guarded by a dozen policemen. Similarly, people told the truth; perhaps in each case the answer is that there are so few people in North Borneo that should you steal something, or should you tell a lie, someone will soon recognize the stolen object, or detect the falsehood. Even the Chinese, whose incomes are notoriously difficult to assess, present little difficulty, for too many know them already. But I like to think that is only partly the answer, for Chartered Company records, before the turn of the century, tell of all the Company's coin being carried to the Interior district offices in open bags, and never being tampered with, of goods dropped and discovered by someone else, who would place them in a prominent position. Even today it is the custom for Interior natives, Muruts, to come with jungle produce to the road, dump their goods there and depart, trusting the Chinese trader to collect it and leave payment there for their subsequent return.

Even the few criminals in North Borneo have the saving grace of a sense of humour. I heard of one rogue who crept out of Jesselton gaol one night (it was easy enough, for in those days it consisted of a loose wire fence and little else), and it being Christmas Eve, entered the residence of the Commissioner of Police, and stole his Christmas brandy and cake. When his escape from gaol was discovered, he took refuge in the safest place of all, under the Commissioner's house, where he quietly consumed his Christmas dinner.

North Borneo, peaceful, happy, is an extremely honest land, and one of the ironies of officialdom is that the Comptroller of Income Tax, one of those who should not worry, has been the only Civil Servant in a decade to have a suspected ulcer. But he secured that on leave; a few weeks at his post and he was a relaxed man again.

Officialdom rather dominates Jesselton. Formerly the Government offices were on the ridge behind the town, near the graveyard; this led to much conjecture about the relative speed of the occupants, and even about which was which. The difference is easy to tell; whereas in one the very young and old are buried, the other houses a multitude of men in the prime of life. They reside now in the largest building in North Borneo, an octopus in stone, distant from the planned street and shop-houses of the town proper, but standing on the flat a mile or so closer than the growing suburb of Tanjong Aru.

Tanjong Aru has supplanted the ridge as the most popular place of residence, for although it has not the glorious views of sea and island, nor the shady walks by towering tree and creeper, it is alongside a most magnificent beach; there is ample flat land for building (though not, it would seem, for a garden, for no home possesses one), and always there is the distant view of Borneo's tangle of mountains, with Kinabalu over all.

Another suburb, Likas, is now springing up behind the Jesselton ridge, out of sight of sea and beach, but convenient for building purposes. Here live many of the junior Civil Service, the clerks, the educated Dusuns, and the young Chinese anxious to quit the crowded shop-houses of their fathers, or the ramshackle conglomeration of huts over the water, reached by long wooden paths, that is tacked on to the town, and which houses the poorer Chinese and natives.

Between Likas and Tanjong Aru, between government and commerce as it were, lives Philip Lee Tau Sang, C.B.E., the best known Chinese in North Borneo today. He may not be the richest, although he is a merchant of repute, with big rubber, timber and import interests, is the general manager of the Tuaran Transport Co., and is concerned in the cinemas of North Borneo as well, but he is the most public-spirited. His importance is on the political stage, not the economic, and it lies in his innate adaptability to all political situations.

He is the senior unofficial Adviser to the Governor; he serves on half a dozen crucial Legislative Council committees and has done extremely valuable work for the Government, but he has never forgotten that he is not of that Government, but that he is an unofficial, one of the governed, a Hakka Chinese. By them he is regarded as their leader, the champion of their causes, and in various disputes and grievances it has been his ability to see both points of view, and to translate this vision into a compromise formula acceptable to all, that has earned him not merely the thanks of the Governor but the gratitude of the Chinese community as well.

Like most other leaders of North Borneo whom it was my privilege to meet, he is a young man, barely forty. I was most surprised to meet him for I had read of Philip Lee for years, as representing the colony at the Coronation and at various Colombo Plan conferences, as being the founder and President of the Junior Civil Service Union of North Borneo, the state's one and only union, and as being on the Legislative Council since its inception in 1950. I had pictured someone rather like the rubber towkeys of Singapore, big, tough, hard Chinese. Philip Lee is a small rubber ball, cheerful, bouncing with good humour, his twinkling eyes reflecting nothing but *bonhomie*. But he must be as tough as my Singapore friends.

He was the only student in pre-war North Borneo to secure a Cambridge School Certificate. He became a dresser in a Government hospital. During the war, 'I lived,' he said, as if that was accomplishment enough. But the British Government in 1946 gave him the King's Medal, and the Australians awarded him the Certificate of Merit for aiding internees and P.O.Ws. I doubt whether this was merely for staying alive. After the war he went into business, starting from scratch, and built himself up to his present powerful position. You do not do all that with twinkling eyes and cheerful stories; Lee Tau Sang is a brave and very clever man.

The present Legislative Council (if I am not already out of date), is a nominated body, consisting of thirteen officials including the Governor as President and ten unofficials, the latter being chosen by the Governor from names put forward by various representative bodies. Among the unofficials the Governor has had to include several chiefs already in the service as Assistant District Officers, since so few chiefs are able to represent their peoples; thus in the twenty-three-man chamber the unofficial voice, divided as it is by race and interests, is rather weak. It would be much weaker, far less effective than it now is, but for Lee Tau Sang.

His ability to interpret his countrymen to the Legislative Council was most to the fore several years ago when a new east coast timber regulation, passed without much notice by the Legislative Council, suddenly aroused a storm among the annual licensees, small timber concessionaires in Sandakan. There was an intense dispute; it has left lingering flames, and I was quite unable to secure a moderate, reasoned account of it. For a moment Government and governed, separated even more than by the mere physical division of the jungle, were quite unable to meet on common ground. News of the quarrel, in the usual garbled form, reached London. Philip Lee, with no interests involved, was almost solely responsible for effecting a compromise, and for drawing together two hostile points of view.

At the age of forty Philip Lee is a young man, and politically conscious as he is, he looks forward to a gradual strengthening of his influence. The history of British colonies is a broad path, leading at last to responsible power being in the hands of the elected representatives of the people. He intends to be that representative. He is fully aware of the pitfall that has attended the career of other politicians, prominent unofficials in other Legislative Councils, and he has learned from their mistakes not to neglect the potential electorate. He is now President of the Chinese Chamber of Commerce, Vice-President of the Boy Scouts, the St. John Ambulance, the British Borneo Amateur Athletics, President of the Hakka Association, and Committee Member of the Jesselton Chinese Middle School and the Sacred Heart Secondary School, where he was educated. At a meeting of the Jesselton Town Board, or the arrival of a Visiting Justice of the Prisons, whatever the occasion, Philip Lee is there, his smile as ready as his pocket-book. An important man now, and a very likeable one, he is a man of the future.[1]

He has an outlook somewhat to the right of Lim Yew Hock, his friend, the Singapore People's Alliance Leader. He is a fervent supporter of free enterprise; he is opposed to communism. He is a leading light in all educational discussions, and feels that the present composition of the senior Civil Service, which is virtually 100 per cent European, is due to a lack of education in North Borneo. He is a great friend of Donald Stephens, the leader of the Dusuns, and there may well be, one day, a political alliance between this small engaging Hakka and his big lumbering friend, his colleague on the Legislative Council. Should it be so, North Borneo will be in good hands; even better if there remains a British representative of the calibre of the present Governor, Sir Roland Turnbull, to watch, advise and encourage.

Prominent among Philip Lee's interests is the development of Jesselton. Among the new concrete buildings going up, which are brushing away the post-war temporary wooden structures that have stayed too long, is a Community Centre, a modest building in comparison to the new Secretariat (respective costs are $180,000 and $1,800,000), but one in which Philip Lee and many others have great hopes. Jesselton is showing signs of forgetting its racial tolerance, and the appearance of clubs closed to other races is a disquieting pointer to the future. The Community Centre is meant, in part, to combat this insidious racial cleavage, and to help preserve this wonderful legacy from the past that North Borneo possesses, this mutual friendship and goodwill.

The Town Board of Jesselton, of which he is an unofficial member, and which still is presided over by the District Officer, deals with an annual budget of over $500,000. Buildings now being completed within its field of responsibility include the new secretariat and the new market ($400,000); the new jetty cost $1,700,000, the Americans helping in this. This is big money. It has been well spent, thanks not least to Philip Lee and the other canny Chinese on the Town Board.

[1] Alas, he is a man of the past, for he died while this book was in the press, in 1959.

All in all Jesselton has a population of 12,000 people, second only to Sandakan (15,000), its great east coast rival. Sandakan has its bay, but Jesselton has its sunsets, and of the two I would choose the latter. From the blue horizon every evening there advances across to the coast of Borneo towering mountains and masses of cloud, now the cleanest white, then shot with colour, from the strongest red to the gentlest of pink, a tremendous sky charged with irresistible movement and majesty, huge clouds suggesting the crescendo of Beethoven; yet under it the calmest of peaceful waters, perhaps a solitary white sail, and while overhead these battlements of blazing colour cry out for passion and noise, beneath it there is yet an incredible silence. The sun sets, and the night in a whisper rushes over the land.

3. BAJAU COUNTRY

THE Coat of Arms of the Colony of North Borneo is with
one addition that of the pre-war territory, which was devised
by the Chartered Company in 1882. On the customary
heraldic shield the lower panel has a nineteenth-century
trading schooner (taken from the Labuan arms) sailing in
front of Kinabalu. On the panel above is a lion, placed there
by directors anxious to suggest to reluctant shareholders that
the territory was in some way officially British. (This also
made them insist on calling their cession 'British' North
Borneo when its correct title was North Borneo.) Above that
are two arms, European and native, clutching in united effort
a flagstaff on which flies another lion. Beneath it all is the
motto *Pergo et perago* (I persevere and I achieve).

To this old Coat of Arms a post-war country, grateful
beyond measure for its liberation from the Japanese by the
Australian 9th Division, has added to the mainsail of the
schooner the letter 'T', this being the Australians' shoulder
flash, granted to them after their dogged defence of Tobruk
three long years before.

The time has come to change this, it seems to me, or at
least to add to it, if the symbolism in the Arms is to remain
clear. Wherever you go in North Borneo today the development of the country that you perceive on every hand is linked
inseparably not to a nineteenth-century schooner but to the
twentieth-century Land Rover. It is everywhere, and room
should be found for this ubiquitous vehicle which now assists
man in nearly all his undertakings. The motto as it stands is
an apt description of its efforts.

One place where the Land Rovers crowd close upon you
is before the new market of Jesselton. Here stand, line upon
line, the bus and taxi ranks of the town. Some suburban bus
routes are now so busy and so profitable that real buses,
brightly painted, are in use; but there still remains the jack-
of-all-work, the Land Rover, which runs for many *entre-
preneurs*, usually Chinese shopowners, spasmodic services to

45

remote kampongs along the tracks that converge on Jesselton. Vegetables, *padi* and people come in, provisions and people go out, in many cases still by a person-to-person arrangement. On such a basis, and in such a Land Rover, I secured a passage to Kota Belud, the centre of the Bajau country forty miles to the north of Jesselton.

Travel by bus in many parts of the East has about it a certain fluster, a refreshing suggestion of adventure that disappeared in the west with the exit of the stage coach, and it is sensible not to panic at the confusion and noise that usually precedes departure. In this respect Siamese buses perhaps excel; but North Borneo is close behind. The Land Rover of Tan Fong Bee would leave the market at 8.30, the hotel receptionist told me. No, it would call at the hotel for me at nine. No, I should go to the market at eight. These varying directives, preceded and accompanied by a considerable amount of telephonic shouting, in Malay, Hokkien and English, helped me a little in remembering where I was, and in forewarning me of the chaos likely to be discovered at the market.

In fact, although there was gesticulation and argument, there was also action. The Land Rover, with a trailer attached, was carrying commodities to Mr. Tan's shop in Kota Belud. It was not the only Land Rover heading up that road, and a certain competition was obvious. But Tan's rates must have been acceptable, for gradually the trailer was filled with flour, beer and crates of tinned food, the seats in the Land Rover were occupied with the usual variety of humans one meets in North Borneo, and off we moved at the early hour of ten a.m.

The East has had its movement restricted for so long, over so many uncertain millennia, that now it loves to travel, and at times it seems as if the whole of Asia is on the move. The unchanging, unmoving East is a thing of the past. It is quite amazing to discover what distances have been covered, what countries seen, by old greybeards you would think had never moved from their remote village, or by youngsters still attending school. Among the most restless are the Anglo-Indians, unfortunate Eurasians searching for a home and a nationality. There was one who travelled with me to Kota Belud, a young man scarcely out of his teens. He spoke ten languages, had travelled in twenty countries, including the whole of Australia and all the countries of South-East Asia. Now he hoped there was a firm future for him in North Borneo; I think there is.

For the first twenty miles the road ran north, skirting the mangrove of the coast, and passing placid little settlements of *padi* and rubber. The road was bitumen, the surface flat, and we sped along. It was not uninteresting, for there was constant change; now we were crossing flooded fields in which a buffalo was pulling a simple wooden plough, with a Dusun plodding through the mire behind him; next we drove through rubber trees, planted so closely together that they obviously belonged to a smallholder; we skirted the mangrove at one stage, and had a quick glimpse of stacked firewood and a long shallow inlet leading to the coast; and several times we drove through small villages, consisting of a row or so of identical shop-houses, where we tooted frantically in the hope of further custom. But the inhabitants of Inanam, Menggatal and Telipok remained oblivious of our charms, and our overcrowded Land Rover suffered no further imposition.

It was a pleasant run, but it gave no warning of the magnificence ahead, when we turned north-east, headed in from the coast, and left the plains behind. For one thing the people began to change. Previously there had been a steady stream of them on the road, a sure indication of its worth, and its superiority over any railway line. Dusuns in black, Chinese women with their broad-brimmed black-veiled Hakka hats, Malays; many on bikes, sturdy British makes that have a monopoly through their quality, many more in decrepit cars and Land Rovers; not many on foot. But now as we climbed into the hills, and as Kinabalu loomed before us, we passed small groups coming into the road down side tracks, carrying the immense *bongons* I have mentioned already, and young men on horseback; the Chinese disappeared and only the wound cloth headgear of the Bajau remained.

And as the people changed, so too did the character of the land. The *padi* fields now were small pockets between steep green slopes, the shop-houses vanished and poor little kam-

47

pongs of *attap* huts on stilts took their place. Pigs, rooting underneath a few, indicated a Dusun or pagan village; where there were no pigs it was safe to infer it was inhabited by Muslims, probably Bajaus. The kampongs became fewer, as we climbed, twisting and gyrating, plunging and climbing again, across several sharp spurs of the Crocker Range that ran diagonally across our track almost to the coast.

The jungle view was breathtaking, panoramas of mountains packed with thick foliage, tremendous trees themselves embraced passionately by fern and creeper. At times you were turning high on some ridge, above a pulsating valley, and at others sweeping down to some minute clearing of smoothly planted *padi*, and again climbing, pushing through the jungle that hung over the road, and apart from the road the jungle seemed untouched, as if it had stood there ever inviolate; truly a virgin jungle.

Ever and anon the Land Rover would wheeze to a halt and rocks would be placed under the wheels. A message would be bellowed to some distant razor-back where a solitary hut was precariously perched, until a faraway figure would emerge, wave an arm, and plunge down the hill. We would deposit a package or two beside the track and start off again. Everyone participated in these operations. It was with a feeling of joint accomplishment and in an aura of mutual goodwill that we would drive on, and it was almost as a united team that we stopped at one little place and had a cup of coffee together. I have travelled on some country buses in Australia where the driver pulls up, strides to some daughter or wife by the fence, and casually has his afternoon tea, while we've sat waiting thirstily in the bus. This was far better, and most enjoyable.

This route to Kota Belud crosses many streams. At times they are gently flowing, the playground of children; sometimes after a storm (and over a hundred inches of rain a year falls in these mountains) a stream rises thirty feet or more, staying up for several days. When the Chartered Company began pushing a pony path through to Kota Belud, and then followed it up by converting it to a track and then a road, it was faced with the problem of bridging these rivers, and it solved it in a very sensible way. A high bridge would have been extremely expensive, and money was very hard to come by. So it built strong cement bridges close above the usual flow of the stream. It gave them no parapets, narrowed the edges in the manner of the wing of a plane, and then when it flooded, well it was just too bad; if you could not get across in a car, you could try a *prahu*; and if you could not do that, you went back to the nearest village and drank *tapai* (rice alcohol) until the flood subsided. I do not think a single one of these irresistible bridges has ever been washed away, and they are still doing excellent service, at a tenth of the price of the elaborate over-the-flood type being built elsewhere today.

Kota Belud (the 'Hill Fort') is situated beside the Tempasuk River, in the centre of a large plain and rolling hills, bounded by the sea, a belt of foothills and inland a mountain country that culminates in Kinabalu. It stands in contrast to most of Borneo, in that instead of dense restricting jungle the plains and rolling hills are bare, growing a coarse grass, with timber and lush vegetation, only along the river courses. The open view given to you in this area is most refreshing, and for fifty years it has been accepted as possibly the most pleasant district in North Borneo.

The Bajaus who live here were formerly sea pirates, as they still are on the east coast, where they remain primitive *orang laut*, men of the sea, living in their boats throughout the year, identical to the *orang laut* of Johore and Singapore, from whence their legends say they originated. A hundred years ago, even less, they roamed far and wide; bold, independent, lawless, they were classed as pirates equalling the dreaded Balignini and Illanun in savagery and ferocity. Much of this has vanished, particularly in the Tempasuk district, and it is hard to believe that this area contributed much to the nautical prowess of the race, for they are firmly settled on this land, they grow *padi* and tend cattle, have only one fast asleep little village of four or five huts on the coast, no traditions of sailing, and while independent, lawless rogues in Kota Belud, are nothing but sea-sick amateurs in a boat.

The Tempasuk attracted one of the three men whom Overbeck put ashore in 1878 as living 'keep off' signs after his acquisition of the territory for Dent. W. Pryer, one of his entourage, was deposited in Sandakan Bay on his way back from the Sulu Islands, H. Leicester, another young Englishman, was deposited among the Dusuns on the Papar River, near the ill-fated Kimanis settlement, and W. Pretyman was dropped over the bar at the mouth of the Tempasuk.

Pretyman had the devil of a time. Then as now Abai, the little coastal village, was hindered by the bar across the river, and he could not induce the occasional coasting steamers to call, except very infrequently. He had the minimum of power; for a time another European and the dubious support of a servant or two. The area which he began to explore was, as it is now, full of Bajaus and Dusuns, with a pocket or two of Illanuns to the north. Buffaloes were run, and fought over, *padi* was planted and fought over. No paramount chief kept

Taking soundings at first light in Darvel Ba

Getting about North Borneo. *Above:* Mt. Kinabalu from the air. *Below:* A jeep and a ubiquitous Land-Rover on a jeep track between Tamporuli and Ranau. *Right:* Bales of rubber being transferred to a motor vessel for shipment to Singapore

The gorge of the Padas River where it passes through t

r Range is the site of the proposed Hydro-Electric dam

Above: The wastage of war. A pony grazes at Kudat where the pre-war street stood. *Right:* Labuan War Cemetery. *Below:* A Chinese village on the water front at Sandakan

Above: The new Karamunting road, shown under construction, was planned to open up new land for agriculture and for transporting timber.
Below: Villagers crossing a wire bridge at Kota Belud

Sunset over Darvel Bay

the peace, no one was particularly respectful to the Europeans, no one was very much inclined to accept their decisions. He stuck it for two years, then the post, Fort Alfred he had called it, was pulled out from near Abai and moved to Gaya Island, and the Bajaus were left to their own devices.

For the first twenty years of its existence the Chartered Company clung to the territory largely through the economic success of the east coast, not the west, through the timber, rattans and birds' nests of Sandakan, and the thirty or so tobacco estates that sprang up on the long east coast rivers. It was not until near the turn of the century that the west coast became important, with the railway line and the advent of rubber. Then it became more than ever necessary for a controlling hand to be placed over these independent 'Jack's-as-good-as-his-master' people, the 'Asian Australians' as I have heard them called; in 1902 a European was posted to Kota Belud, where a Native Chief (Dato Rambangan) and a few police had been since 1899.

From this post vigorous young district officers, under the benevolent but distant eye of the West Coast Resident in Jesselton (it was a four-day journey by boat and track before the road was made in the nineteen-thirties), gradually laid down layers of peaceful existence, and today a native woman can wander here without fear and a European without worry.

The Tempasuk district, however, is one of the few in North Borneo where the Chinese still steps warily, and he is largely confined to the township. This, like so many other activities and enterprises in North Borneo, had emerged from its long cocoon of post-war planning and was near completion when I arrived in 1957. American airmen had obliterated it in 1945, as they had all the other towns, in a most unnecessary surge of devastation. When I visited it in 1953 it was still a cluster of temporary buildings, but now the P.W.D. has finalized plans and a new town is rising.

The shop-houses in these new towns are 'according to an approved model' say the P.W.D. This means they are identical. Every shop-house, in every town in Borneo, will look the same. If you were suddenly placed between two rows of them, for the plans always call for rows, it would be impossible to tell where you were. In Kota Belud, however, there is one saving grace; the shop-houses form an open U, opening on to the village *padang*, an imaginative stroke that might well be copied.

One drops into this Chinese outpost from the spurs of jungle that divide it from Jesselton, and the new atmosphere is apparent at once. The Bajaus are everywhere, brown lean men with big hats, broad-brimmed in the manner of the Australian slouch hats. Long thin pants cling tightly to their ankles, and show an incredible slimness of waist. Almost invariably they carry a light cane switch, and somewhere near at hand is their pony or their lumbering buffalo. There is no social distinction between the two, but one of them they always have. They never walk; they always ride. They are great cattlemen now too, and a new word has entered their language, 'cowboy', or 'coboy', as they write it.

Above the new shop-houses of Kota Belud is the spur or hill that gave it its name. On this ridge lives the district officer; a track runs along the crest to office, courthouse and police barracks. It was this prominent ridge, with the Tempasuk River running noisily and shallowly over pebbles and boulders below, that led to its selection as a police post. And once the European had come the Chinese followed, to shelter close under his Residence, with its magnificent view. 'There you are', my host, Beresford-Peirse, exclaimed, sweeping his arms to the horizon, 'cinemascope on the broad screen.' From the Mantanani Islands, far out to sea, over all his domain to Mt. Kinabalu, virtually his entire district was visible, east to west, north to south.

Kota Belud used to boast of one of the most charming of Rest Houses, but is now the possessor of a stone and tin monstrosity that bears a faint resemblance to modern suburban architecture, and is most out of place in Borneo. Its rooms are stuffy and airless and it is impossible to see Kinabalu from the lounge. Shortly after the war the then district officer was told that the governor was coming up, and expected to stay at the Rest House. There was no Rest House, so one was hurriedly built. It was still standing in 1953, a large sprawling wooden building on sturdy stilts, with a high attap roof, and wide covered verandahs. The rooms were large and uncluttered, while the walls rose only six feet or so, with a gap left to the roof, so that air constantly circulated. A pleasant lounge with plenty of rattan easy chairs gave an incomparable view of the mountain in all her moods, sometimes with water cascading down her sheer slopes, sometimes pink in the sunset or steel grey in the late afternoon. In this cool comfortable building one could relax, and assimilate the atmosphere of North Borneo; but not in its modern successor.

Fortunately at present the new Rest House of Kota Belud is the exception rather than the rule. Throughout the remainder of the territory the Government Rest Houses are full of character, reflecting something distinctively North Borneo-ish in them. The idea, of course, came from the Malay States, which in turn had accepted the idea of Government Rest Houses from its administrators who came from India in the East India Company days. Nearly everything and everybody of worth introduced into North Borneo by the Chartered Company came from Malaya, and it was this firm link with all that was best in British colonial administration in the Far East that distinguished it from the less successful Chartered Companies, in East, South and West Africa, which copied its Charter and little else. One of the best ideas that was borrowed was this building of small Rest Houses, and it is a great pity that the Kota Belud structure is now so untypical. Despite this, as it is now reached easily from Jesselton by a bitumen road, and the old isolation has gone, as it surveys one of the most attractive scenes in North Borneo, as it is cooler, fresher than the coast, and as it has a weekly *tamu*, it has become the most popular Rest House in the territory.

The *tamu*, or native market, of Kota Belud is now an institution of some antiquity, as time runs in North Borneo. It has functioned for fifty years or more. As soon as the young British officer and his detachment of police made their base on the ridge of land beside the Tempasuk, the various villagers began exchanging their wares on the shady strip of bank below. The quiet presence of a few police, the unobtrusive saunter and gossip of the D.O., the imposition of some necessary regulations (no one could attend armed, all ponies and buffaloes must be tethered outside, a small rental must be paid, people wishing to sell must display their goods in the same area, etc.), and firm dealing with any nonsense, ensured that the villagers from this populous area could have trade in peace.

The *tamu* is now administered by the native chiefs themselves. The D.O. does not interfere in any way. Among themselves order is kept, new regulations enforced, improvements made. For example the profit made from the renting of space on the *tamu* ground, particularly under the broad spreading trees, has permitted the erection of semi-permanent stalls, with a roof to keep off the glare for many more, and the erection of a barbed wire fence, which keeps loose buffaloes at bay.

It is situated beside the Tempasuk River, which here runs shallowly over stones. From early in the morning solid Dusuns are plodding across on their lurching buffaloes, and the more colourful Bajau is cantering through the splashing water on his pony, spear or rifle in hand, fully conscious of his gay apparel. Amongst numerous tall trees that throw a welcome shade there is a wired-off area. Inside there are five long rows of squatting women, their wares spread out before them. I do not think men participate in the selling to any extent, although in a few sections some were so engaged; but not many. Those unable to rent a stall or to find shade usually have a Japanese stiff paper umbrella stuck in a stick of bamboo, open above their heads. Encircling the rows of sellers are the food stalls, where the tired can sit and the hungry eat.

The fascination of the *tamu* is twofold; in the diversity of the wares and of the people. Spread on the ground before you, scarcely visible by the crush of people, one discovers, for example, a large section given over to the sale of tobacco. This is not Virginia tobacco, for in fact there is scarcely any western object here at all, but native or Dusun tobacco, strong and cheap, grown near Ranau and the foothills of Kinabalu, four days' walk away. Those whose *bongons* are stacked beside the tree, and those weary late-comers splashing across the river have walked for four or five days to sell their tobacco, for here they are assured of a good price.

From the coast a day's walk away, or an hour in a Chinese Land Rover from Usakan or Abai, come the supplies for an-

54

other big section, that given over to fishes, prawns, crabs and oysters. One had to be careful in the crush here, for when a crab for example was sold it was handed over with its body encircled once in a thin shred of rattan; often its nippers swung lazily backwards and forwards, ready to make one last defiant gesture.

Another popular section sold pineapples, pomelos, bananas, coconuts, durians, rambutans, limes and other tropical fruit. The European seldom eats the durian, because of its strong odour. I have been told that it conceals an exquisite taste, but I, along with the majority of my countrymen, have failed to conquer my loathing for the smell. The diminutive limes are often used as substitutes in the East for the lemon. These, and all the other tropical fruits, were spread out cleanly on large banana leaves, and were selling well.

There was a small section, the only one handled by men, that displayed bundles of local ropes; quite a few single-furrow wooden ploughs were for sale, there were some brightly-designed rattan food covers, a little matting—that brought from the Mantanani Islands being the most attractive—and a group of women were selling distinctive Bajau material, thick cloth of broad red and black design with a silver thread, of quite some artistry. It seemed to me odd, that with Kinabalu dominating the landscape, the basis of the Dusun religion, and the site, even to the Muslim Bajaus, of portents and gods, it did not figure in any way in their matting designs, and that in their artistry they ignored it.

Another large section, densely crowded, was selling meats of incredible colours and parentage, skewered, bits of bright red chicken on a stick, pieces of buffalo, black old slabs that seemed in great demand, alongside sweetmeats and jellies, bright yellow and green, and betel-nut, that were selling all the time, for nearly everyone, in a crowd of four or five thousand, seemed to be eating.

In this crowd the 'coboys' stood out, sauntering with unaffected grace, with bright shirts and tight pants, broad hat and switch, looking strangely wild western but not out of place at all in this Eastern setting. Old Bajau chiefs, with wrapped-around headgear, each slightly different in colour or arrangement, signifying a different village, mingled with attractive Dusun women, clad unfortunately in black, but with magnificent belts of Hong Kong silver dollars, the virgins intimating their status by several rings of red beads round their chests. Old Dusuns, in shorts and grimy head cloths, Malays in sarongs, Islanders with skin peeling from ankle and throat through salt and heat were there in hundreds. The loveliest creatures present were the Bajau girls, squatting by their wares, in beautiful sarongs and *kebaya*, and with nonchalant pieces of flowered material arranged over their smooth black hair, their deep, dark eyes surveying you saucily, enticingly, mischievously, as you groped for words which were really unnecessary.

Benignly presiding over this peaceful, slow-moving crowd was a group of elders, surveying the scene from a structure resembling somewhat a bandstand in a park. A month before they had lost their most outstanding leader, Chief Hasbullah bin Hadji Mohammed Arshad, who had died after a long life, and they had placed the *tamu* in mourning. So cockfighting, which they all love, and which brings in much revenue to the *tamu*, was abandoned and the section devoted to that was empty; and there was no gong beating, which is another great attraction to these cheerful people. Their mourning was deep and sincere, and I could not regret the absence of these sideshows in my recognition of an honest emotion.

O.K.K. Hasbullah (O.K.K. = *Orang Kaya Kaya*, a Chief, First Class), was the son of a man equally as renowned, Hadji Mohammed Arshad, a Banjerese, who left his home in the South Celebes in 1899 and sailed with his father to Java, intending to open a business in gold. It did not flourish, and within a few months they had moved to Sarsan Island, off what was then Dutch Borneo, and thence on to Labuan. From here they crossed to Brunei. Brunei in 1899 was in the last stages of anarchy and tyranny, and the two moved on quickly.

His uncle, Dato Amat, living in Brunei, introduced them to Dato Temenggong, who was of the Bajau people on Labuan. He told them of the trade between Labuan and North Borneo in tobacco, and it was arranged that the two voyagers would work with him. In his *prahu* they sailed to

Menggatal, on the coast near the Tempasuk region, a typical Malay coastal village built on stilts over the water, hidden discreetly inside a bay. Here they stayed for several months, acting as learner-agents for the Dato, and discovering the idiosyncrasies of the Dusuns who carried in the tobacco. Then, leaving his father behind, Arshad sailed for the Tempasuk, crossed its dangerous bar, and went upstream to Kota Belud.

It had not then been established as a Government post, and existed as a small kampong. Arshad, in a manner typical of the Bajau, particularly before the war, made friends with some Dusuns, strictly in the big brother counsellor and defender manner, and journeyed with them to Bundu Tuhan, near Kinabalu, the centre of the tobacco area. Arrangements agreeable to all were made, and, assured of a regular supply of tobacco, Arshad made Kota Belud his headquarters.

He was perhaps the only person in the area who could read and write (in Jawi), and could manage simple mathematics, and this secured his selection as Government clerk when Kota Belud was selected as a station and Dato Rambangan installed as a Government officer. It would seem that his arrival in 1899 virtually coincided with this. Owing to his official position his influence over the Dusuns increased, and he made many trips between Menggatal and Bundu Tuhan. He married a Bajau girl, of great beauty and high parentage, and by force of character gradually came to the fore.

The immediate incentive for the founding of Kota Belud was the disturbance created by the rebel Mat Salleh, who after several killings and much confusion on the east coast, had raided and sacked Gaya on the west coast, had retreated into the Interior, gathering many Bajaus with him, had been pardoned stupidly by the Chairman of the Company, had become more and more lawless, and by the end of 1899 was being attacked again in the Interior. The Tempasuk area was a good recruiting ground and sally port; this it was hoped would be denied him by the establishment of the police post.

Arshad was called on to guide one of the columns converging on Salleh in the Interior, and he led them round the flank of Kinabalu via Bundu Tuhan. The expedition was allowed to climb the valleys and drop over in Ranau without challenge, but in the attack on Mat Salleh in Ranau a European and several others were killed. Mat Salleh escaped and fled over the hills to Tambunan, where he built another fort. Arshad returned to Kota Belud; Tambunan was too distant, too remote, for him, and he played no part in Salleh's final defeat and death in 1900.

It was Arshad's urgent warning, however, sent overland to the District Officer in Kudat, that first acquainted him of the impending raid on the town by the survivors of the Mat Salleh gang, led by his most ferocious lieutenants, and it possibly saved Kudat from disaster. In hunting down the wanted criminals, and in constant service to the officer at Kota Belud, Arshad proved his worth. For thirty-one years, until his death in 1933, he was the invaluable right hand man of this District Officer.

Native society in North Borneo is largely amorphous. There is no such thing as a paramount leader; there have rarely been more than a few outstanding leaders over the whole territory, and only a few score before the war had the prestige to warrant the title *Orang Kaya Kaya*. Arshad and his son Hasbullah were two of these, while Nuar, a younger son, is an O.K.K. today.

The Government had come to place even greater reliance on the energy and ability of Hasbullah than on his father, for Kota Belud was selected as an area suitable for the establishment of a Local Authority. The post-war policy of the Government has been to associate the people of the territory ever more closely with the management of their affairs, and a most important advance in this direction was made in 1952. Taking advantage of the great strength of native institutions in Kota Belud, and the virile attitude apparent there, and leaning heavily on Hasbullah, the Government established a Local Authority in the area.

The Tempasuk region was given control of its own finances, and enabled to raise and to spend them without reference to Jesselton. Forty-five chiefs and selected Village Headmen were brought together, under the Presidency of the District Officer and the Vice-Presidency of his native assistant, who was Hasbullah. As the President would only attend when invited, Hasbullah generally presided, and until the middle of 1957 it was his grasp of the issues concerned that advanced the Local Authority from strength to strength, and which encouraged the Government to institute Local Authorities elsewhere.

At the time of his death Hasbullah, as the elected Vice-President of the Kota Belud Local Authority, was controlling 21,000 people, Bajaus, Dusuns and Illanuns, divided into over ninety villages and the town of Kota Belud. The problem of fair representation had been solved in the early stages of the scheme, as fortunately the villages sort themselves clearly into distinct groups, linked by close racial and social ties. From each group the most acceptable chief was chosen, usually after somewhat informal, if serious, discussion and selection. The time is not ripe for elections, nor are they necessary or useful. There is a time-honoured method of selecting chiefs, and the system of chiefs and headmen has functioned for the stability of the people for a longer period than democratic voting methods have worked for the west.

These chiefs, numbering forty-six by 1957, meet at Kota Belud, under their own locally-designed flag, once every three months. To deal with the everyday work of the area there are seven committees which meet far more often, and which act on matters affecting Livestock Management, Education, Health, Irrigation and Agriculture, Municipality, Finance, and the *tamu*.

The Kota Belud Local Authority is a separate financial body, preparing its own estimates of revenue and expenditure. It has shown great courage, unfortunately not emulated elsewhere, in imposing its own taxes to raise money to pay for services or works which it desired but the Government would not initiate. Unfortunately to the very primitive and uneducated, with a narrow circumscribed outlook, the idea of Local Authority tends to fasten on this aspect of it, that it will lead to more taxes, and an effort by the central Government to introduce a Local Authority in the Interior met with such opposition from people perfectly happy with their district officer, that it had to be shelved. Nevertheless the Local Authority, as a means of teaching self-reliance, and of bringing the local people into a closer appreciation of the problems and opportunities of government, cannot be bettered. It is firmly established in Kota Belud, and all the signs are that it will survive the death of O.K.K. Hasbullah.

The Kota Belud Local Authority secures the revenue it needs for financing its activities in three ways. When it was formed, in January 1952, the Government made over to it certain taxes, which were placed completely at its disposal. These included the Poll Tax within the Tempasuk area, the Hawker's Licence, the fines imposed in the Native Court, and a half share of all Rents on land held under Native Title. In addition to these taxes the Authority was given the right to impose other taxes, and this it has done. There is a Ferry Cess, for crossing the Tempasuk and other rivers, there is an export tax on cattle and poultry leaving the district, there is a *tamu* fee, and there is an Educational Cess. These two types of tax are not sufficient to pay for the administration and development of the area; in 1957 it was estimated that they would raise some $58,000, of which the Cattle Cess was the largest, bringing in $22,000, the Educational Cess securing $6,500, the Poll Tax $7,450, the *tamu* fees $6,500 and the Ferry Cess $2,000. But the estimated expenditure was over $167,000, and reliance for the remainder had to be placed as in previous years on aid from the Government.

This Government grant, which is made also to other Local Authorities, is earmarked as a capital grant for development purposes. The local taxes and the surrendered taxes of government are expected to be sufficient to pay for all recurrent expenditure on salaries, administration, health, education and agriculture. Thus a large measure of responsibility is thrust on these local chiefs, and mistakes necessarily occur. But as the District Officer observed to me after greeting an elderly chief, who, clad only in a dirty sarong, had stepped from a most primitive piece of wood that he called optimistically a *prahu*, 'He is on the Education Committee of the Local Authority. Of course it's often completely over his head. But whoever learned to swim by standing in the shallows?'

There is evident in Kota Belud a certain feeling of pride at the achievements of the Local Authority, and an *esprit de corps* has grown up since 1952. The Local Authority flag, which waves beside the Union Jack, epitomizes this, and it augurs well for the future. But without doubt, if the area is to continue to develop largely by means of local participation in local affairs, the chiefs will have to acquire considerable experience in matters now outside their field of view, and they will have to be assisted by a populace far better educated than at present.

The lack of education is a nettle that has been grasped firmly by the Local Authority, which realizes only too well the necessity of schooling in this modern age, and which has taken over the responsibility for all the Vernacular Schools—that is the Malay Government Schools—in the Tempasuk area. Each school has a Board of Management which regularly inspects the school and reports to the Education Committee of the Local Authority. It pays the salaries and ensures the upkeep of the schools, and is encouraging the building of others by communal effort. By 1957 three of these had been opened, and to pay for their maintenance, and the salary of the teachers, the Local Authority decided to impose an Educational Cess, of 25 cents per acre of land, or 50 cents added to the Poll Tax for those not owning land.

In addition the Local Authority decided to establish a Central School in Kota Belud itself, to act as the centre of its growing school network. A beginning has been made, a double class school has been built, and all children reaching a certain level (Standard V and VI) in the village schools now finish at Kota Belud.

The Local Authority lists several other achievements apart from its initiative in education. There is in Jesselton a rather impressive section of the P.W.D. named Drainage and Irrigation. This once inspected the broad flat plain that constitutes the seaward end of the Tempasuk area, and attempted unsuccessfully to drain and irrigate it. The failures of Government departments are fit objects for humour; what added to the joy of the Dusuns and Bajaus was the subsequent success of their own Local Authority, which concreted two irrigation dams, dams of local manufacture that had catered for local needs with commendable efficiency for many years. The concrete and the modern sluice-gates cost money, but the labour for the erection and installation and the widening and straightening of the channel was all voluntary. It resulted in two major *padi* areas being completely free of crop failure through lack of rain. Another result, all those at Kota Belud hope, is that Jesselton has learned not to ignore local experience.

Another venture of the Local Authority that has caused great goodwill was its acquisition of an old Government *padi* store near the *padang* in Kota Belud and the transformation of it into a Sports and Pony Club. The Bajau loves a game of polo, and is equally as enthusiastic over a race-meeting. The Local Authority has organized these on a regular basis, thus saving it, if any rescue was needed, from becoming a stuffy administrator. The younger set, Dusun or Bajau, has taken to athletics, and from Kota Belud, with the blessing of the Local Authority, both Sium bin Diau and B. Gabuh journeyed to Melbourne to participate in the hop, step and jump event in the Olympic Games. The latter was placed in the same event in the Commonwealth Games at Cardiff in 1958.

He and others like him reflect the youth of today. Another who has effected the change, who is adapting himself to a world where civilization has come close to Kinabalu, and which he must face, is Ashkar, son of Hasbullah, grandson of the almost legendary Arshad. Ashkar is the Learner Manager of the Local Authority's greatest pride, one of the most interesting developmental projects in North Borneo, the Sorob Cattle Farm.

This farm, of over 6,000 acres of rough grazing land, hilly or rolling countryside for the most place, with a thick rough grass growing to five feet or more, and with some flat lush land, of Borneo jungle, on the banks of the waterways, was established in 1953. Its main advocate had been J. S. Chisholm, an ex-Chartered Company officer who had returned to North Borneo after internment, and had continued his service with the Colonial Government. A tall, lanky New Zealander, his insistence over the years that the Bajau cattle farmers could be led by example greatly to improve their stock bore fruit with the initiation of this project.

On the grass-covered hills within a five-mile radius of Kota Belud there wander, in a manner as wild as their masters, some 20,000 head of cattle. Owing to poor management and grazing their quality is low and their losses high. So Sorob was founded, with the objects of improving their livestock by supervision of health, by professional breeding and by managed feeding, and of improving by fencing the grazing grounds, the cultivation of grasses, and the rotation of cattle on them. With these objects went also the intention of making a profit. All this has been done.

In the five years that the Sorob farm has been functioning it has known two managers, the first paid for by a Colonial Development and Welfare grant. This man, W. Reece, was a tall, rangy New Zealander of the same physical and mental construction as the father of the scheme, J. S. Chisholm. He was a cattle man, and he began the collection of a herd, the building of a perimeter fence, thirteen miles in length, and of some paddock fencing, the establishment of a farm site and the erection of the farm buildings, the forming of a rough track from Kota Belud to the farm and the constant supervision of a largely hostile collection of animals.

By 1956, when he handed over his charge to W. E. Gore, a Kentish farmer with considerable grass experience, much had been done, and by 1957 it was possible to look forward to the day when the Local Authority, as well as owning the cattle, the farm and the lands, would have their own man experienced enough to take over the running of a very efficient and unique experiment in South-East Asian animal husbandry.

All the capital projects that were initiated as a result of the decision to establish Sorob have now been completed, and the farm is a going concern. There is an earth road from Kota Belud through to the farm house, linking up there with tracks over the farm itself. It is completely fenced, and metalled posts largely replace the earlier soft-wood type. (One of the early difficulties had been teaching Bajaus how to erect a wire fence, the art being completely unknown to them.) Twenty-six paddocks have been formed inside the farm, and the last of the wild cattle originally fed into Sorob have been caught and largely tamed.

A permanent labour force of Bajaus, no mean achievement, has been held together for several years, and their proud title

'Sorob coboy' is well known. Their accustomed presence, together with routine salting and feeding of molasses, has had a great influence towards producing a quieter stock. Most of this stock is of the Indian *Zebu* type, progeny of Zebus brought to North Borneo well before the war, and which subsequently ran wild and bred unrestrainedly. It is eminently suited to the heat of the tropics, and the Sorob aim is to select and segregate a small herd from its three hundred head, and through this establish a type of animal that may evolve eventually into a definite Sorob strain of cattle with all the benefits associated with pure breeding.

There are still many difficulties ahead, for this venture has little precedent to guide it. It was only in 1957 that it was realized, for instance, that the local strain of Zebu cattle, possibly owing to nutritional and environmental causes, had an erratic breeding cycle of perhaps eighteen months or longer. But gradually the strain is being improved and as the Local Authority declared a second 3 per cent dividend on the 36,000 one-dollar shares, issued to the owners of the cattle which had entered Sorob, its activity began to be copied by individual Bajaus outside.

O.K.K. Nuar bin Hadji Mohd Arshad, brother of the late Hasbullah and uncle to young Ashkar, was the first to apply to his cattle the methods of fencing and control at nearby Sorob. He has his fifty head now moving from paddock to paddock on his three-hundred-acre ranch. Two other small ranches in the Sorob manner have been established, one by another chief, the other by a group of Bajaus. The largest cattle-owner in the Tempasuk, who runs eight hundred head on 4,000 acres, so far stands aloof. But as the wire fences spring up, and the coarse feed inside is squashed and munched to form a green sward, as a Zebu strain is evolved and prices rise for it in Jesselton, the Brunei oil fields, Singapore and Manila, no doubt he too will be forced to acknowledge the example of Sorob, and do likewise. Whenever he does he will find a sympathetic hearing from the Credit Corporation, a Government loan body instituted in 1955 to advance money to individuals for development projects. Already some $20,000 has been lent to men such as Nuar, and by it they have been able to fence in their land and corral their holdings.

Chinese

Murut
Youth

"Carabau"
herder

Bajau
horseman

Sorob has ventured to divide its eggs, and is endeavouring to develop a better type of buffalo as well. This is a far more difficult feat, demanding different experience and needing different soil. The cattle at Sorob roam the hills, while buffaloes stick fast to the soft, muddy, shady banks of the streams. They insist on flat, lush land, and Sorob has little to supply. Nevertheless some one hundred and fifty buffaloes now wallow by the Sorob River.

There are over 100,000 buffaloes in North Borneo, nearly all of them on the flat lands of the west coast, and a considerable proportion of them are on the Tempasuk plains. Although there are so many, to the outside they all look very much the same, slow-moving, lumbering animals, weighing between 700 and 800 pounds, seeking always the coolness of mud or water, and the ability of Dusun and Bajau owners to recognize their beasts is little short of amazing. C. B. Francis, a Chartered Company officer, tells the story in his book *Twenty Years in Borneo*:

'I was riding to a native fair attended by one Mandor, a clever and intelligent Bajau, and as we came to the clearing where the fair was held he pointed excitedly to one of a group of twenty to thirty buffaloes tethered a couple of hundred yards away and said, "That is my buffalo. It was taken three years ago." I pulled up and asked him what his beast's marks were, and he gave me without hesitation a list of four or five whirls in the bristly coat. These were found on examination to be correct, and after the usual case the beast was returned to him. To the ordinary person, even on close scrutiny, this animal looked just like thousands of others, and yet, seeing it quite unexpectedly and among a crowd at a considerable distance, he recognized it in a second, after three years. People say that every shepherd knows each one of his sheep, but would the ordinary shepherd identify a lost sheep among others after three years?'

The intake of buffaloes into Sorob, begun in 1954, has not proved altogether successful. The animals were found very difficult to handle and were very shy breeders, only fifteen calves being born from 55 cows in 1955, for example. Elsewhere in North Borneo the loss of young calves has been as high as 80 per cent. But buffalo breeding constitutes a major business in the territory, and it is now being debated whether it might not be better to establish a separate farm, on more suitable land, for breeding and research. As over 3,000 buffaloes a year are slaughtered for their meat, and some 1,500 exported, yielding half a million dollars, it seems an enterprise well worth consideration.

The Kota Belud Local Authority not only secured with alacrity the services of a manager for Sorob, until a local man was experienced enough (a Colombo Plan scholarship is in the offing for Ashkar to work on an Australian cattle station where there is Zebu stock), but also made great use of the Veterinary Officer in charge of the Animal Husbandry Section of the Agricultural Department. Both were made available to North Borneo in general, and thus Kota Belud in particular, by the Colonial Development and Welfare Scheme, which in this and in numerous other projects is slowly improving the standard of living of the people in Borneo.

The great achievement of the Veterinary Officer, for which the Bajau will be for ever grateful, has been to rid the country of *surra*, the dreaded disease that led to the death in some years of over seven hundred ponies. Throughout most of the Chartered Company days this blood-parasite infection was considered uncontrollable, incurable. It would rise to epidemic proportions, there would be wholesale destruction of dying animals, there would be a pause, a lull, and the disease would begin again. Man seemed helpless, and although it was checked by restrictions on movements and drugs shortly before the war, the disease was merely dormant. It broke out again during the war, and although its spread was checked afterwards, it was not until 1951, when the Colonial Development and Welfare Scheme provided the state's first Veterinary Officer, that hope began to dawn.

There are approximately 3,500 ponies in North Borneo, used for riding or as pack animals, never for draught. They are well adapted to the tropics, and are used extensively for transport in areas where there are no roads. The first tracks that the Chartered Company initiated, the bridle paths of Governor W. Birch in 1902, were designed for these animals, and most of the roads of North Borneo today began life as pony tracks through the jungle.

E. N. Holland, the Veterinary Officer, first tackled *surra* with drugs. When these were employed it was possible to control and finally to stop an outbreak. But when his team moved on from the affected area, and treatment ceased, *surra* invariably broke out again. The section then went to work to keep a register of ponies in various districts, including those which had been affected by *surra*. This involved a comprehensive card index, and it ended with virtually every pony in the country on the files. Routine monthly treatment with drugs was given to all ponies listed as suffering, or to have suffered, from *surra*, and the incidence of the disease dropped rapidly. Two vital factors, hitherto absent, were winning the fight; the right drug to check the disease had been found, and the men to administer it were available.

It was proved that by keeping old cases permanently under treatment the spread of the disease could be stopped. As month followed month and no new outbreak occurred, Holland took the final step. By purchase he acquired all the old cases of *surra* listed on his records, all the ponies his team were monotonously treating, and killed the lot. *Surra* vanished.

Holland had conducted his campaign against *surra* from a compact little centre just outside Jesselton, at Kepaya, built in 1954 from Colonial Development and Welfare funds. Here his files were kept and his experiments made. Assisting him were S. Krishnanandan from Ceylon and an expert made available under the Colombo Plan. In the training of the local assistants under them, and in the routine stocking of vaccines that can be placed in the hands of livestock owners all over North Borneo's 29,388 square miles, as well as in the brilliant veterinary work that preceded this, this team is making a tremendous contribution to the future of North Borneo.

Kota Belud has benefited from another vaccine introduced by this team, the cure for *Ranikhet*, or Newcastle Disease, in poultry. The Local Authority is imposing a small cess on the thriving export of its poultry, some 28,000 head travelling each year in the Land Rovers of Mr. Tan and his competitors to the markets at Tuaran and Jesselton, and now that a vaccine is available for checking the disease that periodically ravaged its flocks, it is hoped to build up this export figure to at least 50,000. Over all North Borneo the owners of poultry have reacted quickly to the introduction of the vaccine. There are perhaps two million poultry in the territory; over a million already have been treated since 1954.

Although the Kota Belud Local Authority is stealing the limelight, and the District Officer is vanishing from his solitary peak to appear instead at the level of a committee table, the Local Authority in some ways has increased, rather than diminished, his importance. It is far more difficult, it requires far more subtlety, to stand back and quietly steer others into accepting responsibility and into making decisions, than simply to take the initiative oneself, and at Kota Belud, delightful residence though it is for a squire, with plenty of riding, walking (at least fifteen days a month are spent walking in the area, visiting kampongs), shooting and polo, it has now become slightly more demanding. There are no signs that the District Officers are not capable of rising to this; if anything they seem to enjoy life even more.

One hoary old chestnut that has been demolished, at Kota Belud and elsewhere in North Borneo, is the old myth that a district officer with a wife was only half as good as a bachelor. The petticoat influence kept him on his own verandah, when he could be yarning in kampongs, kept him at his centre when he could be on safari, and in general kept him aloof from the people he was administering. In fact, the post-war generation has shown that the district officer with a wife is twice as useful as a bachelor, for almost invariably the wife plunges into that aspect of primitive native life most neglected by the male, but most in need of succour, the care and nursing of the women and children, the sick and the pregnant.

The Kota Belud Local Authority lists in its annual report the opening of a Red Cross Centre, and the functioning of a weekly Maternity and Child Welfare Clinic. To all intents and purposes this is the wife of the District Officer. It was a humbling and moving experience to visit this clinic, crowded with minute little infants and patient, trusting (and gossiping) mothers, to watch the tenderness and sympathy with which the Chinese dresser and the young but efficient European dealt with the cases, and to feel the sense of hope and goodwill radiating from this little shack on the hill by the Tempasuk River. The D.O. drove past with some chiefs, in a scurry of dust, off on some important masculine task—the extension of his fifty-three-mile road network perhaps, or the bridging of a stream—while behind him the women, smiling to one another at the boyish activities of their men, turned again to their vital, basic task, of bearing and tending their young.

As dusk falls over the plains and the open rolling hills of the Tempasuk, the Bajaus and Dusuns return from Kota Belud to their kampongs. It is a familiar and much loved sight, to see them splashing solemnly through the shallows of the stream, their buffaloes in single file, plodding home. As you sit in a stilled Land Rover, as the ferry, angled to the stream by an overhead cable, is edged silently across, dusk on the Tempasuk is a moment of beauty. A little later, as you drive along one of the new tracks that now radiate out to coast and mountain from Kota Belud, the beauty is superseded by pure exhilaration. A Bajau, lithe, brown, galloping his pony home, sweeps off his broad-brimmed hat, leans back in his saddle and with a magnificent gesture shouts cheerful *'Tabeh, Tuan'* (Greetings, Sir), and whacks his pony for more speed. At such a moment, and at many others, the District Officer at Kota Belud is a man to be envied, and the Bajau country a place to be long remembered.

4. PENAMPANG

THE Chinese have been moving into South-East Asia as settlers for at least six hundred years. Whereas three thousand years ago China was a patch, no bigger than, say, France, astride the lower course of the Yellow River, by the beginning of the Christian era her frontier had moved irresistibly south over the Yangtse and had reached Canton, and today the tide of her inch by inch expansion continues. While there is an ebb and flow to this tide, the overall impression is of a movement that never recedes. The Chinese shopkeeper perpetually advances, bringing in his train, sooner or later, the Chinese peasant.

For the most part in South-East Asia these Chinese shopkeepers live on the defensive. They are no swashbucklers, they keep behind shutters and bars in 'China towns' that are the counterparts of the ghettos of medieval Western Christendom, fearing but surviving, serving but exploiting the economically incompetent South-East Asian peoples among whom they have settled.

There are now in the *Nan Yang*, as they describe South-East Asia, some nine million Chinese. The bulk of this population was a migratory wave that swept across these southern lands during the last century. The wave has been stopped now, by restraints both in China and overseas, but the two million on Java, the two-and-a-half million in Malaya and the other millions elsewhere have dug in and remain, an essential part of the economic fabric of the countries concerned.

In North Borneo there are 75,000 Chinese, out of a total population of 400,000. Over 55,000 of these Chinese were born out of China, in North Borneo or elsewhere in the Commonwealth, a remarkably high proportion compared with other South-East Asian countries. And North Borneo can claim another unique quality in connection with its Chinese. Whereas in the rest of South-East Asia the nine millions resident there hail almost without exception from the provinces

71

of China south of the Yangtse, North Borneo possesses the one North Chinese settlement in the *Nan Yang*.

This settlement is situated a few miles from Jesselton on the one road leading south-east, to Penampang. From this little village tucked away in a valley of the Crocker Range, ten miles or so from the capital, a track winds into the Interior, to Moyog and over into the Tambunan Plain. It may one day become a road, and provide the avenue of exit the Interior lacks so badly. Even now, although the road ends at Penampang, it is bustling and much used, with bus services, Land Rovers, cars and bikes commuting between Jesselton and Penampang. Points in between are located by the milestone. 'Maxwell Hall, the author? Oh, he's at milestone $2\frac{1}{2}$ on the Penampang Road. The Shantung settlement? There is a track to that at milestone $4\frac{1}{2}$, and another at $5\frac{1}{2}$, but it's difficult to find.'

J. Maxwell Hall, a retired senior officer of the Chartered Company, is one of the very few elderly Englishmen living in the Colony able to provide that quality badly needed in any community, the cautious, sober judgement of maturity, of a life spent in the one country. There were many young men who came to high positions of power in the new Colony after the war who were inclined to scoff at anything that smacked of the Chartered Company, and to sneer at pre-war experience. Old servants of the Company who had survived internment, and who returned to the territory, found their knowledge disregarded, and their legacy of a happy and contented people taken for naught. But this has changed. The hysterics of the post-war pack have died, and the Governor of North Borneo today has often publicly praised the groundwork done by his Chartered Company predecessors. There are not many of them left in North Borneo, and Maxwell Hall is now the grand old man of the territory.

He lives in a two-storied wooden house, sparsely furnished, as befits his Spartan physique, the owner of some fifty acres of land. On this he has built a half-dozen homes, which he rents, with five acres or so of land, to Chinese market gardeners. The area is filled with rows of vegetables, there are small ponds full of ducks, chickens invade your lounge, pigs root beside the house. He lives as a South-East Asian squire, in solitary contentment; but instead of becoming, after fifty years' service in North Borneo, the grand old man of reminiscences, with a memory happily searching the past to recount tales of the good old days, this grizzled old live-wire lives vigorously for the present and future. He is perhaps one of the most wide-awake and pertinent observers of the North Borneo of today whom it was my privilege to meet.

He has written well of the past, in several hard-to-secure books published locally, for he has an historian's bent, and he has contributed numerous articles, in particular to an ambitious quarterly, *Kinabalu*, that could not long survive the rise in costs of the nineteen-fifties. He is writing yet another tale, the history of Labuan. But all this is relaxation; for he is no ivory tower writer, and it is the problems and the possibilities of the present that interest his wide-ranging curiosity and evoke his keenest comments.

Governments of primitive countries sorely lack the spur of an educated and experienced European, and there are brash young men in secretariats who are inclined to resent outside criticism, from which they have been divorced, as something inexcusable, whereas in other circumstances they would realize it was a normal occupational hazard. All the more pity that Maxwell Hall, who writes as keenly as he speaks, does not write acute comments on the future, rather than tales of the past.

One such tale of the past he told me, which filled in some gaps of my Chartered Company knowledge, concerned the unique little settlement of North Chinese, a few miles farther along the Penampang Road, where he took me in his jeep. Owner and vehicle had much in common; ancient but sturdy, and fresh for ventures new. The track to the settlement, though itself obscure, was hard by a shelter in which were a half-dozen beautifully red- and black-painted coffins. On them was the Chinese character *Kwan-chai* ('Rest for a long time'). They were waiting for their owners, then busily tapping rubber, to claim and make use of them. The Chinese see no sense in not being prepared for their next life, and each year, if they are still alive, their coffins are repainted and the characters re-gilded, for one thing is certain: they will be needed one day.

The North Chinese migration was a venture of the President of the Chartered Company, Sir West Ridgeway, who replaced William Clarke Cowie in 1911. Ridgeway made a habit of visiting the territory every two years or so, and on his first two visits, in 1911 and 1913, returned on the Trans-Siberian Railway. He had been in the world's headlines some years before by commanding the small British force that defied Russian moves into Afghanistan, and while Imperial Russia and Victorian England had been on the brink of war, or so it seemed, he had dared the roaming Cossacks to chase him at Pandjah, on the rocky uplands of Asia. As such he was a celebrity; he was not a very good businessman. On his way home in 1913, while in Peking, he heard from the British Ambassador that the mighty Yellow River was on one of its customary rampages, and that millions had been drowned or were homeless. Impulsively he offered to ship them to North Borneo.

'Free of charge?' asked the Chinese Government, its instinct to haggle beginning to re-assert itself, 'With free land? Money? . . .' Ridgeway took refuge in Siberia, leaving the Company's agents to handle the deal, and by November, just before the ice closed Tientsin, a ship had sailed for Jesselton with one hundred and seven families, and the agents, Forbes and Co., had concluded an agreement with the Chinese Government.

This promised them virtually everything except the moon. Free passage, ten acres of free land to be cleared for them, free school, free passage back if unhappy, free tools, free maintenance, free marriage bonus; the cup of charity was drunk dry. 'No doubt you consider', wrote the agents, 'that the terms given to the settlers are extravagant, but you have no idea of the difficulties against which we had to struggle. . . . But the ice is now broken, and if the experiment is satisfactory and the settlers are happy, the news will soon spread in North China. Indeed, I hear that at least one Chinese who wished to go committed suicide because he was not allowed to. This is very hopeful.' Hopeful though it was, the move had cost over £2,500, and all further arrangements were cancelled. The cost was prohibitive.

These northerners came wearing fantastic clothes. Their

jackets were padded with cotton well fitted to keep out Arctic cold. Their felt slippers fell off in the mud of Borneo, and the rain poured through the open wicker work of their baskets, in which they carried clothes and utensils. Their cheeks were still red, coloured by the cold winds of the November north, and many of their women had bound feet, and could do little but hobble. The men towered over the South Chinese, whom they largely disregarded, and even today, over forty years later, the two keep separate and go their respective paths.

In North Borneo they are called 'The Shantung Chinese', or '*Orang Shantung*', while they refer to themselves as people of Tientsin, their port of departure. In point of fact, they come from Hopeh, hard against the Great Wall of China, with the Hwang Ho bordering their lands on the south, one of China's most fertile provinces, the cradle, many say, of Chinese civilization itself.

They were allocated land at the back of Jesselton long ignored by Dusun and Bajau, who scorned its pestilential swamps and its stony slopes. Thick, slow black streams sought a wandering way to the sea; the peaty soil quivered when one stepped on it, and decaying vegetation crashed into the *lallang* grass to moulder out of sight, whenever the south-west monsoon roared over and further eroded the steep hills nearby.

Its one virtue, said the cynics, was that the development of the experiment could be watched from a deck-chair on the Residency lawns, high on the razor-back by Jesselton, which overlooked it. And despite the forbidding terrain the North Chinese occupied, the experiment was a success. They were helped by the Government, in its grant of free tools and free subsistence for the first few months, and by Captain H. V. Woon, the northerner whom Ridgeway had secured to watch over them, and by the friendship with the neighbouring Dusuns. But in the last resort it was their guts that pulled them through, which kept them fighting this soil, draining it, controlling it, until finally their tightly packed rubber trees won through for them.

The Shantung houses, hidden, secluded from each other by dense rubber, are broad and of one storey, with floors of beaten earth. Only a few, Mr. Chung Fu Leong for example, have two-storied homes, and these are people who have usually left the land and are no longer farmers. A surprisingly large number have stayed on their lots, originally cutting down the timber for sale as firewood for the old-fashioned boilers which raised steam to pump fresh water to Jesselton, then growing *padi*, and finally planting rubber. In the process they adjusted themselves completely. The old still remember the days when they had never seen a tall tree or a water buffalo, still yearn for meals of flour and maize, and a cold wind and a padded coat. But the youngsters know nothing of this, and even Mr. Tung Shu Lin, who is now the headman, with eight children, can scarcely remember Hopeh, and thinks of it not at all. He is a North Borneo Chinese, and although he still has the right for his bones to be shipped back to China, they will stay here, in Borneo, in one of the coffins waiting at the end of the track.

A few miles farther along, past numerous Chinese homes and Dusun huts on stilts, winding over undulating country covered in jungle, or crossing flat areas of *padi*, is Penampang. This is the centre of a virile Dusun community and is closely settled. By reason of current developments there, it is one of the most interesting areas in the territory, yet one can search in vain through the books on Borneo for a mention of it; the chief reason for this is that the scanty library on North Borneo is very largely the work of various district officers, and as it is less than a dozen miles from Jesselton, there was seldom before the war a district officer or Government representative in Penampang. It is more surprising however to find no account of Penampang in O. Rutter's *Pagans of North Borneo*, as it is the most detailed work on the Dusuns ever published.

The Dusuns, the main indigenous people of the territory (numbering 120,000) are the predominant race down the whole west coast, grouping most thickly together from Kudat to Beaufort, and in the interior valley of Tambunan. These people figure in early records as Idaans. Both terms are foreign, and the group as a whole has as yet no name for itself. They would appear to be a group of sub-tribes, each speaking a dialect which is more or less intelligible to the others.

Kedazan, Kwijau, Minobok and Mangkok are some of these sub-tribes; there are many others, but no comprehensive list exists. Each sub-tribe consists of a number of separately named villages, and a traditional locality or territory. The story of their development, through thousands of years, may be traced back from Penampang, where an embryonic nationalist movement is beginning, on any journey into the Interior, where they can be observed in the primitive conditions of the late Stone Age, prevalent in South-East Asia perhaps two thousand years ago.

The story of early man is a migratory one, and the Dusuns are no exception. It would seem that they wandered into Borneo from the north, possibly at a time before the last Ice Age ended, when the island was joined to the Philippines and the mainland of Asia, or possibly after, for the long chain of islands that stretches north to China has few gaps of over a hundred miles, and movement south, with the steady monsoon blowing, would be easy. But in the numerous legends of the Dusuns, and in their way of life, there is little to make one think this was the case, and I would consider a slow land migration as more likely.

The most primitive peoples in South-East Asia are the nomadic negritoes, whose descendants now inhabit islands far out in the Pacific, pushed there by the recurrent waves of succeeding migrants that came down from the north. There are no negritoes in Borneo, and it would seem that the ancestors of the Dusuns were the first inhabitants of this inhospitable island. As they continued to arrive over slow millennia of time, they pushed their kinsfolk into the Interior, the latecomers claiming the coast. Here they adjusted themselves by degrees to their environment, those on the coastal plain turning to the cultivation of wet *padi*, and the growth of agricultural villages, those in the interior jungle remaining hunters, growers of dry *padi*, and clinging to the defensive safety of a longhouse.

Slowly the geographical differences of Interior and coastal plain created a general difference between the people. But the differences between the extremely primitive Murut in the Interior and the various types of Dusun on the coast are not racial or fundamental, but local, and what the Murut is

77

today the Dusun was yesterday. Their dress, customs, culture, religion and language all had a common origin, and the variations are due chiefly to environment.

The coastal Dusun has been subjected to many influences, while his brother, deep in the Interior, has lived a life identical to the generation before, and before that. He is as it were a living fossil; in the course of centuries his habits and customs, handed down with rigid conservatism through the ages, can have changed but little. Solitary, he met few others, and then only to flee. With nature he established a compromise, a way of life that permitted him to live in the tangle of jungle, but which forbade any change. He reached a cultural dead-end, and unable to change, remained unchanging.

The Dusun however, once he had made the great cultural change from a semi-nomadic life to a settled life of *padi* growing, found time to spare. He could improve his existence, was enabled to visit and trade by the comparative ease of movement on the plains. As well as imbibing new ideas from neighbouring villages he was brought even more contacts from the rivers and the seas. The Chinese came, perhaps the first, and showed him how to plant *padi*. The Indians same, clawing their way to Cambodia and China. Islam came, spreading round the coasts of South-East Asia; it did not attract him, he had his own beliefs well formed, and he did not particularly care for the people who came with it, the Bajaus and Brunei Malays. But each contact was a stimulus, to accept or resist, until finally the Europeans came, slowly and in few numbers, but nevertheless almost irresistibly, bringing the greatest stimulus of all.

The political boundary of North Borneo is almost an ethnological boundary as well. There are no Dusuns south of the border, no Dyaks north of it. The southern parts of Borneo were occupied by people who moved down Malaya and came up the long flowing rivers that empty now into the Java or South China Sea. At the watershed, which is the boundary, they stopped. This is very largely true, and the three big states of Borneo, Kalimantan (Indonesian Borneo), Sarawak and North Borneo, each have their indigenous peoples. Wandering in the remote central area however, the Muruts, Punans and other nomadic or semi-nomadic peoples cling shyly, unobtrusively to the high headwaters, and know no boundaries but the fearful limitations of their own restricted thought.

The Dusun has been little studied, although he is the major ethnic stock in the territory, and there is little acceptance of the opinion expressed by Skeat and Blagden, in their classic *Pagan Races of the Malay Peninsula* that it is of 'supreme importance to Governments in the tropics to make an intimate study and careful consideration of the peculiarities of the alien and less civilized races committed to their care'. No doubt, however, this will come; first things first.

The district officer or Government official, seeking for information on the Dusun, finds little help in the published material of North Borneo, and is forced to rely on the pages of the *Journal of the Malayan Branch, Royal Asiatic Society.* Since its inception in 1878 this scholarly and informative journal has included North Borneo and Sarawak within its field of interests, and has provided a venue for the observer of the Borneo scene. In its pages can be found the only English-Dusun dictionary in existence, compiled by a Roman Catholic father of Penampang. From its volumes Owen Rutter secured much of his information for his *Pagans of North Borneo,* and to it G. C. Woolley, brother of the archaeologist and accepted Dusun authority in Chartered Company days, sent most of the material that is now embodied by the Government in its moribund *Native Affairs Bulletins.*

Woolley was not alone among Chartered Company officials in suffering from the literary error of incorporating Malay words in his despatches to the Court of Directors in London. The Directors were a patient lot, businessmen with a streak of the romantic, for the most part, but very few of them could speak Malay. So the edict came out from London: 'Use plain English. Do not incorporate Malay words or phrases in official correspondence'. Woolley immediately retaliated by quoting in Greek, and although in his previous letters the English word had been pencilled above his Malay quotation by a member of the Board who spoke Malay, his Greek tags went untranslated. For the Board to have admitted the necessity would have been to admit ignorance, and the lack of a classical education.

The Dusun clings firmly to his beliefs. He yielded the coastline to Islam, but retreated scarcely out of sight of the sea, and even now, when various Christian missions are constantly at work amongst his tribes, the old female priestesses still hold sway nearby. He acknowledges a Supreme Being, and a Paradise, to which entry is gained from Kinabalu. Fifty years ago it was not unusual to kill a slave or a prisoner in order that he might take messages to those already there. In such cases the unfortunate victim was either tied to a tree or confined to a bamboo cage, where he was prodded to death with spears by his captors, who danced round him and accompanied each prod with a message to be delivered to a departed relative. Hugh Clifford, for a short time a Governor of the territory, has vividly described this practice in his *Malayan Monochromes*. Though thought extinct, it was revived for Japanese benefit during the war.

The activities of the Dusun are unduly complicated by his belief in a host of evil spirits by which his whole life is bound as if by chains. There is never a strange tree or hill or rock that is not the abode of some genie or other, and against them the Dusun is forced to rely on charms and offerings. In addition he is as addicted to omens as the ancient Etruscans, and the behaviour of birds, animals and insects apparently affect him at every turn. His life is one long round of prohibition.

The numerous omens are far more scrupulously observed by the hill Dusun than by the Dusun near the coast, who is among people likely to scoff at him, but for all that he too takes his omens seriously, and in this he is perhaps no more ridiculous than are those of us who will not walk under ladders, or who regard Friday the 13th as unlucky. He is not so far from many of us in his consideration of the meanings of dreams, and if the west has studied this more thoroughly, with more hocus-pocus, it is not so far ahead in its assessment of their value.

Perhaps the most interesting aspect of the Dusun beliefs is the veneration held for ancient jars. To the cold, calculating eye of the European these revered objects are of Chinese manufacture, but to the Dusun, and to the Dyak in Sarawak, with whom this belief is shared, each jar has a mythical origin and its own particular history. They are of little intrinsic value, but fabulous prices are paid for them (although they rarely change hands), and the ceremonies conducted before them provide the chief source of employment of the aged Dusun priestesses.

In most Dusun communities, annual rites are performed by these priestesses, invariably widowed ladies of great age, before the sacred jars, and if the jar owners are wealthy the proceedings can last several days. It seems that the full-scale

Dusan priestesses

ceremony, which is expensive, it being in essence a six-day-and-night party for the entire village, is now rarely held; and certainly in my wanderings I heard no account of one. But the evening performance still is very popular, and can be performed not merely annually, but also in time of sickness.

The aged crones come into a room, and squatting on the floor offer up incantations in a language no one else can understand. The jars are given a little food and drink, the house posts are tapped with small ceremonial brass knives, and the priestesses lead a procession around the house at midnight, cutting at the cross-beams, everyone following suit. On the verandah there have been erected a number of young sago leaves. These are slashed down, and at the same time the evil spirits are exorcised. Two bamboos are split, long thorns are attached to them, and they are hung outside the house as a sign that the ceremony has been performed. Finally a fowl is killed, and the witches or priestesses withdraw.

It is now that the night begins. The Dusun above all else is a drinker, and a rough counterpart to his sacred jar serves as his tavern. In long jars he makes his *tapai*, rice alcohol, and at any ceremony, but particularly at a funeral, the amount of *tapai* drinking is prodigious. Whether Christian or pagan, every festivity usually becomes an orgy, with drunkenness, furious beatings of gongs and drums, laughter and sickness until dawn.

Penampang is one of the few places in North Borneo where there is over-population. The flat lands of the valley are heavily cultivated, it is even ploughed by tractor to produce more, but there is not enough land for all. The pressure has forced many to leave their valley; there is a Dusun community now working on the Brunei oil fields, and more Dusuns are working on the timber in Sandakan. Although distant from Penampang they have maintained their links with their valley in two ways; nearly all of them are Roman Catholic Christians, and nearly all belong to the Society of Kedazans.

Penampang has been subjected to western influence for a long time, the pagan element has been pushed underground, and the overcrowded Mission School that stands below the pinnacle on which a stone church surveys a panorama of *padi* fields and rolling mountain side is now educating third- and fourth-generation Christians among its five hundred students. The whole valley is a tightly packed Christian-educated community.

They refer to themselves not as Dusuns, but as Kedazans, and by their efforts they are attempting to replace the derogatory Malay word by which they were labelled by the Brunei-Malay overlords in earlier centuries. Dusun means an orchard, or a cleared countryside, and to be a Dusun was to be a countryman, a yokel. To an educated person this is a slur, and Kedazan as a term of reference is becoming increasingly popular. By a similar movement of revulsion the South Indians of Malaya secured the official and unofficial alteration of their name from Kling, which had derogatory implications, to Tamil, which had not. The labouring classes of the East have largely secured a banishment of the word coolie for the same reason. In North Borneo we are at an interesting stage: Dusun remains, but increasingly, as the sub-tribes realize its insulting undertone, it will vanish. But whether Kedazan, the name of a sub-tribe, will replace it, is more conjectural.

If it does, it will be due partly to the work of the Society of Kedazans, which with Mission encouragement has been formed to uplift the Kedazans, and thereby the other Dusuns, socially, educationally and economically. It hopes to impart a greater racial consciousness to them, and it fears a Brunei or Malayan supremacy over them. Although in my discussions with its young leaders politics were rarely mentioned, it seems to me that here is another South-East Asian nationalist party in embryo.

One of the aims of the Society is to rescue from oblivion those aspects of Dusun culture that are slipping away, and I attended, at Penampang, a combined school sports day and Kedazan culture day which admirably reflected the attitude of the Society. There are some parties and newly independent countries in the world that want to turn their backs on Europe, and endeavour, by looking backward through the mists of time, to re-create the almost mythical state of society that existed before the west came. Fortunately this blind rejection of the west, this looking backward, has not been accepted by the Society of Kedazans. Wisely they look ahead too, endeavouring to assimilate all that they think is useful from the west's many wares, in a manner typical of Japanese nationalism. So we had school sports, Christian prayers and a Kedazan party, in lieu of a garden fête.

One room of the school was given over to *samazau* dancing, which is being revived by the Society. The master of ceremonies was a wizened old rogue in khaki shorts, who had charge of the orchestra, five old men who beat their gongs without ceasing for hours at a time. Round the floor packed the crowd, the hoop-la and other stalls deserted as the big *tapai* jars were broached and drinks were handed round.

Five shy diminutive girls, each clad in a black velvet skirt to below the knee, and a small black velvet jacket, cut to a V-neck, faced us. The jacket was lined with gold edging, and at sleeve and throat, and down the front, thick gold beads were sewn. Round the waist were five or six silver belts, of large Hong Kong dollars. Their glossy black hair was gathered into a gentle bun that rested at the neck. Their faces were finer, clearer, than the rather pudgy Malay, and I could well understand one of the temptations of North Borneo, for here were five lovely girls.

The gongs rang out, and deep inside the excited crowd we began our rhythmic dance. I was wearing the *Sasandangon*, the ceremonial band of Brunei cloth, silver worked, that is carried over one shoulder, and a thick skirt of *attap* with little bells attached (once they were skulls); as the gongs beat we rose and fell on our toes, slowly advancing across the floor towards our partners, facing us.

The thick bamboo floor rose and fell with us, as we moved imperceptibly closer. Suddenly the Kedazan on my left emitted a harsh cry, for all the world like a rooster, and we extended our arms, like wings. Slowly the two lines approached, the women with eyes downcast, the men with fluttering fingers and arms outstretched, until we stood almost face to face.

The rhythm of the dance, the suggestiveness of our approach and the beauty of my partner all caught my breath, and made my pulses beat. She swayed, rose and fell, her eyes downcast, her tiny feet in time with mine. One of my hands went over her shoulder, she swayed and turned away; over the other shoulder I attempted to claim her, and again she turned under the possessive arm. We circled and moved farther away. I approached and attempted to claim again, was rebuffed and continued. Her movements were as delicate as anything on the royal stage of Bangkok, and if the dance was less sophisticated, it was no less suggestive, while her grace and beauty surpassed the ladies of Siam.

The *samazau* dance is one of the tribal or national practices of the Dusuns that is dying out. The traditional clothing of the women is another. The Society of Kedazans, with the support of such pastors as Father Smit, who directs the school, feels that much of the excessive drinking and low standard of living of the Dusuns is due to the fact that while old practices are dying, there are few new interests to take their place. So they are attempting both to preserve what is valuable from the past, and in addition to help the Dusun adjust himself to the future.

One of the leaders of the Society of Kedazans, Joe Manjaji, told me of two objects his Society has in mind. One is education in English and Kedazan, and not English and Malay, as at present. 'Every country that has its education in Malay is Muslim', he told me, 'and comes under the influence of Indonesia. We do not want that here.' Another primary object is the establishment of a Farm School. 'We are an agricultural country, and we are farmers, but there is not a Farm School or an Agricultural College in the whole state, and education is dangerously bookish in bias.'

The formation of a Farm School has been Government policy for many years, and its implementation has been delayed only through the shortage of staff. Manjaji's dream may be nearer actuality than he thinks. His educational hope is rather different. The difficulties involved are tremendous. Malay is firmly established as a *lingua-franca*, and it is not generally accepted that there are political implications in it. But the case for a Dusun at least to begin his schooling in his own tongue is a strong one. He is the indigenous inhabitant of the territory, and he will be increasingly loath to accept this bar to his own language.

The champion of the Dusuns, and the Society of Kedazan's great driving force, is Donald Stephens. Stephens is the editor of the territory's only paper, the *North Borneo News and Sabah Times*, and I had participated in the *samazau* dancing with him. His paper runs a 'Kedazan Corner', a section in Dusun. It is of immense influence throughout the territory, in that it is literally the only printed Kedazan the great majority ever see.

Stephens is a young man, in his early thirties. He began life as a copy writer, that is the writer of petitions and letters for the illiterate. With the accumulation of a small capital he launched his paper in 1953. It is a simple broadsheet, with a circulation of under 2,000, but it is extremely influential, in that to a large measure it is read by the type of person who would read *The Times*. All Government servants, the banks and business houses subscribe; but so too do the young English-educated Kedazans, and the Dusun literate only in his own tongue, and until now without modern guidance. I watched Manjaji and a crowd of other young men crowding round Stephens, keen, alert, enthusiastic; here, I thought, was the mass support that could accomplish many things.

Stephens visualizes a British withdrawal from North Borneo in under fifteen years. At present the prospect does not deter him. 'Look at the President of our Society, Lee Kim Chong—he is part Chinese, part Dusun. My name, Donald Stephens, does not disclose it, but I am part European, part Dusun. Richard Yap, our secretary, is part Chinese, Joe Manjaji is Kedazan. We are all a mixture, and therein is the future of North Borneo. The Chinese are not divided from the indigenous people, as they are in Malaya, by religion or temperament. Rather there is a merger, and the Sino-Dusun is the best citizen any state could wish for. If North Borneo could be ruled by anyone, it could be ruled by the Chinese and the Dusuns. But we need at least fifteen years in which to educate ourselves to acquire the art of government, and prepare to withstand the emergent Islam of Brunei.'

While the aims of the Society, by which the Kedazan is to be uplifted socially, educationally and economically, are to be applauded, I feel that to envisage a stable, independent North Borneo within the foreseeable future is to fly in the face of history and to ignore the realities of the present. Although there is a merger between Dusun and Chinese that is most heartening for any future stability, and which is, in some measure, responsible for the tranquillity of the area today, it is inconceivable that this tranquillity would remain should the linchpin of impartial administration be withdrawn. The Dusun, in the time of people still living, was subjected to the most barbarous tyrannies of Brunei, and Sulu, which he rarely resisted, and should the British withdraw no new state would face the world; rather the vacuum of one would attract irresistibly the powers that now surround her.

North Borneo is not yet a unit, she remains essentially fissi-
parous, and goodwill and racial tolerance have replaced the
maelstrom of eighty years ago only because of British administration.

The outlook of Stephens and others in the Society of
Kedazans, who visualize a sharing of political power with in-
dulgent Chinese seeking mass support, and their estimation
of the date of independence, would have been unthinkable a
few years ago, and even today flies in the face of the
Governor's oft-repeated remark, that he seeks the ever closer
association of the people of the country with Britain in the
government of the territory. He has never mentioned independence, and the speculation of Stephens and others has
been bred merely by overseas developments. But the attain-
ment of independence within the Commonwealth by India,
Pakistan, Ceylon, Ghana and the Federation of Malaya does
not present a true parallel to the case of North Borneo.
Despite the claims of Stephens, anarchy, followed closely by
partition, followed again by tyranny, would come again if the
country secured its independence *within the foreseeable
future*. Within the framework of British suzerainty, however,
the closer association of the people with the Government may
one day reach the stage where the Governor retreats discreetly
into an unfamiliar background and the day-to-day administration of the territory is entrusted to an elected representative
of the people. The constitutional changes forthcoming fore-
shadow such an eventuality, and when this does occur the
man to win the majority support as leader of the Dusuns may
well be Donald Stephens.

A short distance from Penampang, but close to the heart
of Donald Stephens, is the stone slab erected at Petagas, to
commemorate the death of his father, Jules Stephens, Albert
Kwok and others who, having risen in revolt against the
Japanese in October 1943, were captured near Penampang
and massacred. Although the revolt was confined to a small
area in the west coast of North Borneo, there participated in
it virtually all the races of the territory. It was the one rising
of Chinese in occupied British territory in which the communists had no part. Its story is little known, even by many
of the inhabitants of North Borneo, but in Penampang, and

elsewhere, it is well remembered, and an annual pilgrimage is made across the fields to Petagas.

The Japanese occupied North Borneo without resistance early in January 1942. The shield of the territory had been the British Navy. North Borneo had a small police force, but never an army or navy, and the Supreme Allied Commander in December 1941 directed that no resistance should be offered. After a few months all the Europeans in the territory were transferred to Kuching, in Sarawak, North Borneo was divided into two administrative units, east and west coast, and a steady descent into the abyss began.

Although the invasion of the Japanese had been the epitome of efficiency, there was no administrative plan whatever. The territory was exploited, the inhabitants ill-treated, the economy strained to breaking point. Had the Japanese remained in possession of North Borneo for much longer, as with the rest of South-East Asia, the area would have collapsed into a primitive barbarism, with rifle butts perhaps the only sign of the twentieth century.

The antipathy of the people towards the Japanese showed itself from the beginning. On the east coast the imprisoned soldiers brought from Singapore to build an airstrip, were constantly befriended. On the west coast the resistance focussed on Albert Kwok, a Chinese from Kuching, who, after working with the Red Cross in China, settled in Jesselton in 1940. He was a young man, skilled in treating ailments although not a doctor, and after his war service with Chiang Kai-shek fanatically anti-Japanese. In February 1942 he endeavoured to contact the Americans or Australians, but was unable to walk across Borneo, and returned from Pensiangan, in the Interior near the frontier, in June. In April 1943 he was more successful, and he established contact, after an adventuresome sea voyage, with guerrillas in Tawi Tawi, off the east coast. Here American submarines were feeding in arms, ammunition and radios to ship watchers— it was a big Japanese naval base—and to Filipino and Suluk units of the United States Army in the Philippines, which were molesting the Japanese as the American and Australian forces began leap-frogging back.

Kwok had organized on the west coast an Overseas Chinese

Defence Association, and although he could not induce the
guerrillas in the Sulu Archipelago to send him arms—they
asked him merely to supply them with money and information—he visualized a far more active opposition than that.
He began forming a guerrilla force as a branch of the Overseas Chinese Defence Association, firing others with his wild
hopes and optimism. He was helped in this by the Japanese
policy of concentrating the great bulk of its forces in the
Interior, at Ranau, Keningau and Pensiangan, leaving only
small units on the coast. With so few Japanese visible, it was
easy to delude oneself that a rising would be successful, and
the young men of the villages outside Jesselton joined this
new Secret Society.

After another period of service in Tawi Tawi, Kwok
returned again to Jesselton in September 1943, under instructions from Lt.-Col. Suarez, the guerrilla leader there, to collect intelligence, exchange information and to arm the local
populace in readiness for Allied contacts. He found that
although conditions had deteriorated alarmingly he could
raise $500,000 to assist his movement. Prominent among those
who helped him were Wong Tze An, Lim Keng Fatt and
Musah, a former Dusun rebel against the Chartered Company.

By this time Allied intelligence was in touch with the east
coast of North Borneo, and Lim Keng Fatt, who as a trader
visited that side, was instructed to tell Kwok that the time for
revolt was not yet, and that he was to wait. But Kwok was too
impulsive, and too disturbed by the Japanese plans to recruit
3,000 Chinese youths for forced labour, and a large number
of Chinese women for prostitution. He issued orders to his
force, renamed the Kinabalu Guerrilla Defence Force, to
attack Jesselton on the night of Saturday, October 9th, and
thereafter to resist the Japanese by force of arms.

October 9th was the day before the 'Double Tenth', the
great Chinese celebration of the tenth day of the tenth month
when the Chinese Republic was born, and it was hoped that
it would raise morale and stimulate the attack. But the guerrilla force was pitifully small. Kwok had recruited perhaps
two hundred young men round about Jesselton, and an equal
number from the islands. Under his command he had Mr.

Charles Peter at Tuaran, Kong Sze Fui at Menggatal and Hiew Syn Yong, a Deputy Assistant District Officer at Kota Belud. Jules Stephens was the adjutant, and had been responsible for what little training the force had been able to do. At sea the operations were in the hands of Orang Tua Panglima Ali, who had a force of Bajaus, Suluks and Binadans.

The rising was initially successful. Bands of men converged on Jesselton shortly after darkness. There were very few troops there, and as the land and sea parties entered the town simultaneously at 10 p.m. the Japanese administrators panicked. The police station was stormed and captured, the Japanese killed and the armoury removed. With some fifty Japanese dead the guerrillas withdrew, and their hour of victory had gone.

With merciless severity the Japanese struck back. Kwok's main force, camped a few miles north of Jesselton, was hunted by detachments of troops, and kept moving along the foothills of the Crocker Range. Short of arms and ammunition, it was relying on help by sea from Tawi Tawi, and it gradually became more and more dispirited. The villagers around could see no hope in their armed resistance, they themselves were short of food and clothing, and after several engagements Kwok was left by late November with only six followers. He took refuge near Penampang, trying desperately to stay near the coast. The North Chinese, among whom he sheltered, helped him generously. In this hour of need the customary differences between north and south was of no moment, but there could be but one inevitable ending.

It is told by Maxwell Hall, in his *Kinabalu Guerrillas*.

'At this moment an unfortunate but typical incident happened. A gambler staked and lost in an evil hour the money given him to take to the refugees for purchase of supplies. He was an inveterate gambler and he lost the sum of $200 which Chong Fu Kui, a Penampang shopkeeper, had placed in his hands for Lt. Kwok. The man foolishly returned to Chong Fu Kui and tried to force him to replace the lost sum. Chong Fu Kui protested. The man threatened exposure, voices were raised in anger, and a spy in the pay of the Japanese moved a little closer in the darkness of the shop verandah.'

The mischief had been done. On December 19th a hundred Japanese soldiers surrounded the area, and Chong Fu Kui and the headman of the district, Majakui, were given a short space of time to produce the refugees. Kwok surrendered. He had hoped that his defeat would signify an end to the punishments and executions, but it intensified them. Ten days after his capture Lim Keng Fatt arrived from Tawi Tawi, with a quantity of American arms and ammunition, $25,000 in cash and a body of picked men. They returned unobserved to Tawi Tawi, but he was killed later by Bajaus.

He was but one of hundreds who lost their lives as a result of Kwok's revolt. There were numerous executions in the little towns running north of Jesselton, at Inanam, Telipok, Menggatal and Tuaran, while hundreds of suspects, Donald Stephens among them, were transported to Batu Tiga, the police post outside Jesselton, for enquiry and trial. They were subjected to the most brutal treatment and many succumbed.

The leading Chinese of Penampang, Yu Eh, was crushed under stones, his ribs broken, slashed with knives, tortured for two weeks and finally interrogated in his coffin. He admitted nothing and was set free. He had in fact contributed $2,000 to the Kinabalu Guerrillas. Other leading Chinese were not so fortunate, and after constant torturing had extracted their names, it was decided to massacre all of those who had become implicated.

Donald Stephens, who had been tortured and was in prison, saw them marched out, watched his father vanish, and knew he was going to his death. Chinese, Sino-Dusuns, Anglo-Dusuns, Suluks and others, 176 in all, were taken to Petagas on January 21st, 1944, where the soft soil made funeral pits easy, and were there killed. Albert Kwok, Charles Peter, Chan Chan Kong, Kong Sze Fui and Lee Tek Fui, the leaders, were executed, the rest were shot by machine-guns, and dead or alive, were pushed into the open grave. The Japanese sent another 131 prisoners to Labuan, where they slowly perished working on the new airstrip. Only nine survived the war and returned to Jesselton.

Even this did not deter the by now implacable hostility felt towards the Japanese, and two elderly Chinese, Dr. Lau Lai and Cheah Loong Ghee began quiet preparations for a second revolt. A committee of eight was formed, $250,000 raised, and a rising timed for April 13th, 1944. On the 12th the ringleaders were arrested, imprisoned and tortured; no rising took place, and on May 5th another mass execution occurred.

Meanwhile the islanders had suffered catastrophically. There still are islands today where there is scarcely a male inhabitant. The headman of one island near Jesselton is a woman, for there are no grown men. Other islands were completely depopulated. All along the north-west coast, the Bajaus, Suluks and others were chased, caught and executed. Islands and west coast combined, some 16 per cent of the populations lost their lives in this revolt of the Double Tenth.

All this lies now beneath the surface. In 1953 the talk in North Borneo still had centred on the war. The rising and the privations had been favourite subjects of conversation, and had provided favourite excuses for delay or muddle. This is no longer so. Men's eyes and thoughts, in Penampang and elsewhere, are turned hopefully to the future. In such a future I feel sure that no one will play a more important part than the young men of Penampang.

5. PAPAR

TEN years after W. H. Treacher began his service in 1881 as the first Governor of North Borneo, efforts were made by the Chartered Company to conduct a census of its territory. The early belief that North Borneo was somewhat similar to East Africa, with teeming millions of uncounted savages, had already vanished, but it had not yet been replaced with any definite knowledge of numbers. As it turned out, the 1891 census was too hurriedly organized, and a very provisional estimate had to be made, of perhaps 100,000 inhabitants. The Chartered Company tried again ten years later, and again numerous circumstances militated against accuracy. The final figure, of 150,000, was more a guess than a count. In 1911 there were difficulties of staff, and it was not until 1921, forty years after its founding, that the Chartered Company had its fears finally confirmed. In an area as large as Ireland, 30,000 square miles, there were only 260,000 people. The place was virtually empty.

To remedy this deficiency the Chartered Company twisted and turned in its efforts to secure immigrants. It never itself participated, as did the African Chartered Companies, in trade and commerce, it remained aloof from the perils and profits of the merchant and the planter, but as the administering power it did everything possible to attract to its shores a labour force for those crying out for men. In this it was generally unsuccessful.

One of its earliest attempts was a request in 1885 to the Royal Navy, then busily engaged in chasing Arab dhows in East African waters, that it might consider sending the liberated slaves it rescued to North Borneo, where they would be assured of a safe home. It conducted several conversations with the Dutch in Java, and managed to secure for the rubber estates an annual quota of a few thousand young Javanese. These proved poor immigrants, as almost without exception they returned to Java after their service had ended. A bulky file of Chartered Company records bears witness to its un-

availing attempts to secure Indian labour. It was equally unsuccessful with the Philippines and with Japan. In the end
the Chartered Company always returned to the reservoir of
China, and after much trial and error arranged for a satisfactory flow from Hong Kong.

The post-war position of North Borneo is but little different from the past. Polyglot though the population is, it is still
sparse. North Borneo still needs more people. A new element
has been added to it by the arrival within the last few years
of several thousand young Timorese, sent north by their
Catholic pastors to earn a dowry before returning to their
waiting brides. These are birds of passage, as ephemeral as
the Javanese, and welcome though they are, in having
alleviated the labour problem, they are not the answer to the
population question, for without exception they leave the
territory after a few years and return to their womenfolk and
homeland.

It seems inevitable that the Colony will be forced to accept
the lesson of the past, and in this as in much else follow the
precedent of the Chartered Company. The Philippines, Java
and India are still wills-o'-the-wisp. Singapore's surplus is
politically suspect, and for any large-scale increase in population, for any stable additions, North Borneo must still look
to China, to Hong Kong.

There is today a minute trickle of migrants, possibly a hundred a year, restrained by the most stringent of security regulations. Whereas China was previously a reservoir without
walls, and a flow of people could be assured to wherever the
stream was directed, today a bamboo curtain holds back that
flow from China, and an Immigration Ordinance keeps it out
of North Borneo. Between these flimsy barriers patrols the
United States 7th Fleet, heir to the Royal Navy in its mastery
of the South China Sea. In North Borneo, however, the
Chinese community, whether Hakka, Cantonese or Hokkien,
points to the unquestioned capabilities of its kin, and criticizes the restrictive regulations as a slur on its fine record of
the last eighty years. With Hong Kong labouring to support
this ever-increasing population, with a necessity of justifying
to the Chinese in its crowded streets that the free world offers
more opportunities and a better way of life than communism,

with North Borneo crying out for labour, it seems to me inevitable that a planned cautious resumption of Chinese immigration must be permitted if North Borneo is to develop. History provides it with no alternative.

Many see in this not so much a danger as a great opportunity. With such a policy the fertile lands of the territory, now empty, could be developed. New skills could be brought to the towns, new enterprise to the villages, new labour to the jungle. Out of the blending of Dusun and Chinese that would follow, a hard-working community would emerge, and a stable addition to the community acquired. The rigid exclusiveness of the Chinese could be softened, perhaps better here than anywhere else in South-East Asia, and we might, at last, produce here a Chinese unit of the Commonwealth.

While this remains a subject of much discussion and consideration by the bodies concerned, the population of North Borneo within the last few years has now been increased not merely by large numbers of Timorese labourers on the east coast but by a small number of highly skilled Anglo-Indians and Anglo-Burmese on the west, where they have proved invaluable in the workshops and stations of the North Borneo Government Railways. It was in the company of one of them, Mr. R. Gillett, that I discovered again, in the railway workshops, the basic factor of North Borneo, a factor which no new migration scheme must be permitted to destroy. In the workshops I saw North Borneo in miniature, a collection of people from every race under the sun, happily working together. This racial tolerance is worth more than riches; better a poor country than a divided one, and all measures to improve the labour position must start with the supposition that, as Mr. A. Lennox, the Supervisor of the Workshops puts it, 'We have it good; we want it better.'

Mr. Gillett and his apprentice son Peter, working with him, were formerly on a small private railway in Hyderabad, and although the rioting and massacres that preceded and followed Indian independence did not reach their small railway town, it affected conditions considerably. The new terms of service introduced by the Indian Government, and the insistence by it that the Anglo-Indians, a proud and sensitive people with generations of railroad service and tradition behind them could expect a considerable deterioration in their position, decided them, as it decided thousands of others, to leave. John Masters' *Bhowani Junction* reflects the tragedy of their past. North Borneo, Malaya, Australia and elsewhere reflects their dawning hope of the future.

With Mr. Gillett I watched a Murut making steel springs. A Chinese from Hong Kong was working a large pneumatic hammer, ably assisted by a Dusun. A Bajau was repairing saws. A Sikh and a Tamil were repainting old coaches, and another Chinese was doing some carpentry. An Anglo-Burmese was in charge of the spare-parts shop. A new rail car moved out of the workshop, driven by a Sino-Dusun and a Brunei Malay. One old man had worked in the railways since 1905, while several others had an experience of thirty or twenty-five years, and had brought in their sons and grandsons to work with them, when it was time for them to go out to grass. It was an almost incredible collection of different peoples, working in an easy-going harmony that epitomizes North Borneo. If I were the Governor of the territory faced with a V.I.P. who wanted to see the essence of North Borneo in one afternoon, I would either give him a game of cricket in Tawau or take him to the railway workshops in Jesselton.

The west coast railway runs south of Jesselton to Beaufort, the centre of the rubber industry. Here one branch goes inland, up into and through the Crocker Range, to Tenom, and Melalap. Another branch, beginning on the other side of the Padas River, by which stands Beaufort, goes down to the coast, to Weston. Jesselton to Beaufort is fifty-six miles, while the spurs are forty and twenty miles respectively. All in all this is a network, if one can use so grandiloquent a term, of 116 miles, the only railway in Borneo, a lasting memorial to William Clarke Cowie, its founder, perhaps the most controversial and dynamic man in the history of the Chartered Company.

Cowie, a twenty-two-year-old Scot, had come out East in 1870 from Glasgow. Captain Peter Orr, formerly a ship's captain and then a teak trader in Bangkok had bought a small vessel, the S.S. *Argyle*, as a cheap way of returning from leave. She was only 53 foot long, with a nine-foot beam, and weighed only fourteen tons, and he found great difficulty in recruiting a crew for a one-way voyage in such a diminutive craft. Cowie, appointed engineer, was one of three adventuresome youths he secured in Glasgow. The voyage took five months. In the Irish Sea they met a gale. In the Bitter Lakes they passed over the flukes of an anchor which ripped open their eighth-of-an-inch plates, and they sank in three fathoms. In the Red Sea, having patched her up, they ran out of boiler wood, and had to sail (she was rigged, fortunately, as a fore and aft schooner) beating against adverse winds. They left Aden in the height of the south-west monsoon which fairly blew them across the 3,000 miles to the Straits of Malacca, but before reaching it they ran out of matches and the galley fire went out. One last cartridge, fired into a jute sack that ignited, saved them. Five months of adventure, but they made it!

In Singapore the vessel was sold to the Sultan of the Rhio and Lingga Archipelago, and with it went Cowie, as captain. The Sultan appointed him admiral of his fleet, or *Rajah Laut* —King of the Sea, a most extraordinary post for a European, which must have aroused Dutch suspicions greatly. Cowie commanded the *Argyle*, some five large sailing cutters and a number of *prahus*. He was entrusted with the duty of collecting tribute from the petty chiefs of the archipelago, and securing revenue from others.

After some years of this buccaneering life he resigned and entered into a trading partnership with Karl Schomburgk, a Singapore merchant. Schomburgk provided the warehouse, the business contacts, the necessary solid base of an office in Singapore, while Cowie traded among the islands in his schooner, on business as enterprising as any that Singapore ever fostered. Out of this partnership there grew a Company, the Labuan Trading Company, an innocent little title that concealed a smuggling business of great profit, running arms and ammunition from Singapore and Labuan through the pirate-infested waters of the Sulu and Celebes Sea, to Sulu, where the Sultan was busily defending his island realm from the Spanish in Manila. They had been trying to capture the Sulu Archipelago intermittently for three hundred years, and by 1875 they were nearer to success than ever before.

Cowie had discovered a hiding-place at Benkawan, forty miles south of Jolo, the main island of the Archipelago, but it was dangerously close to the patrolling Spanish vessels, and after discussions with the Sultan of Sulu, he moved over to the east coast of Borneo. Here, far from any European power, deep in the immensity of Sandakan Bay, hidden from view and difficult to reach, he established his secret base, trading arms, ammunition and general stores in exchange for the produce of the coast and the islands.

Cowie is Conrad's Lingard, and a picture of North Borneo before European administrators came, when independent traders from the hullabaloo of Singapore searched for profits among the islands, can be found in his *Almayer's Folly* and *An Outcast of the Islands*. Conrad called these traders, who vanished among the islands, 'bold and reckless, keen in business, not disinclined for a brush with the pirates that were to be found on many a coast, making money fast; the acknowledged king of them all was Tom Lingard, he whom the Malays, honest or dishonest, quiet fishermen or desperate cutthroats, recognized as the *Rajah Laut*, "King of the Sea" '.

Conrad knew too, it would seem, of his hide-out.

'He had discovered a river. . . . Into that river, whose entrances only himself knew, Lingard used to take his assorted cargo of Manchester goods, brass gongs, rifles and gunpowder. Many tried to follow him and find that land of plenty for *gutta-percha* and *rattans*, pearl shells and birds' nests, wax and gum-dammer, but his brigs could outsail every craft.'

Cowie collected in Sandakan a group of youngsters as lawless and as enterprising as himself, and in their small craft they slipped across to Sulu. The *Argyle*, renamed the *Tony* after Schomburgk's sister Antonia, was the smallest. She was commanded by a German, Sachsze, and on one trip, when loaded with fourteen tons of pearl shells (at £250 per ton) she was caught by the Spaniards. Cowie was on board but escaped, and sailed back to Borneo in a *prahu*. Sachsze was imprisoned in Manila, and his fate moved the German Government, its economic tentacles then stretching into the West Pacific, to interest itself in him. Its protests secured his release, although he died soon after, and its negotiations with Britain at Madrid, secured the abandonment of any Spanish claim to North Borneo territory.

Above: Government offices at Sandakan. *Below:* H. E. the Governor inspects a guard of honour at the opening of the Legislative Council

Above, left: John Cresswell, the bank manager, whose name is a household word in North Borneo. *Above, right:* The late Philip Lee Tau Sang, C.B.E. *Below, left:* Major Rex Blow, an Australian District Officer who survived the horrors of Sandakan Camp, escaped to the Philippines and became a guerrilla leader there and later in N. Borneo. *Below, right:* A District Officer discusses drainage with members of the Town Board

Above: The playing of Asian musical instruments is part of the curriculum of the Kent Teacher-Training College, near Jesselton. *Below:* A mixed class at the Government Primary School at Tanjong Aru

'The boy's will is the wind's will,
And the thoughts of youth are long long thoughts.'

LONGFELLOW

Malay boys near Jesselton

Two nurses from the Duchess of Kent Hospital, Sandakan. Opened by Her Royal Highness herself in 1952, it was financed in part by a Colonial Development and Welfare grant

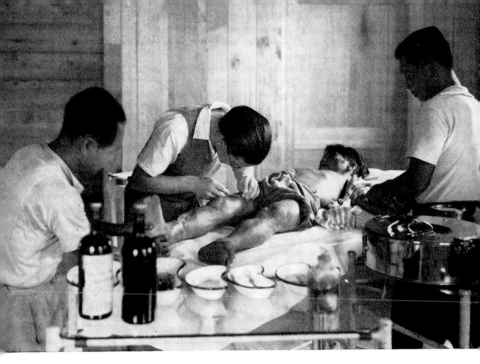

Above: A skin-graft on an ulcer case at Keningau hospital. Ulcers and malaria comprise the hospital's main cases. *Below:* Trainee laboratory assistants are taught to use a modern microscope by an Australian technician on loan under the Colombo plan

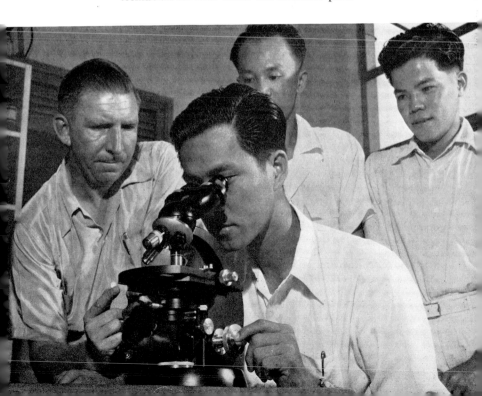

The early morning Chinese street market in Sandakan

The capture of Sachsze indicated that the waters off Sulu were becoming too hot to sail in. Cowie met the American Torrey in Hong Kong, and was momentarily attracted by his cessions, and toyed with the idea of becoming another Rajah Brooke. But Schomburgk refused him capital, and he was still trading for rattans, birds' nests, etc., round Borneo, when Overbeck came in 1878 to acquire a new cession from the Sultan of Brunei. In Labuan Treacher pressed Cowie on Overbeck, as the man most likely to help him in his necessary negotiations with the Sultan of Sulu for the east coast, and together the three paid him a visit, through which the east coast was ceded away.

Cowie quickly fell out with the Chartered Company, and competitors cut the ground from under him. In the 1880s he left the sea and became manager of a small coal mine in Brunei, on the tip of land facing Labuan, where the Government of today plans a multi-million-dollar new harbour. Here, at Muara, he lived a life as autocratic and as free from restraint as the master of a ship. In London, in 1953, I met his widow, who remembers this coal mine well, and who told me tales of her life there, as a young bride, of her daughter born there, Muara by name, the riot of the Chinese labourers quelled by her husband, the lawlessness, the grand piano in the *attap* house, the jungle, the visitors long since dead and the everlasting heat. They left in 1888, the coal mine was sold to Brooke, and Cowie, the possessor of a moderate fortune, returned to London.

He did not, however, relinquish his interest in Borneo. After several brushes with the directors of the Chartered Company he was pushed on to the court by a body of shareholders. He immediately pressed for a revision of their policy, which had been a cautious one of conserving capital. Cowie maintained that no under-developed country could progress against such a break as that. He pointed to Perak, where Hugh Low was spending every penny that came into the revenue, and more, on roads, railways and other public utilities, and he pressed for a similar expenditure in North Borneo.

In particular he pressed for the construction of a railway into the Interior. Cowie, remember, was a coastal skipper, he had never penetrated into the Borneo jungle, all that he knew of it was learned as he bartered in Sandakan Bay for birds' nests and rattan, and he had a fervent belief that in the Interior there were rolling plateaux of fertile land, and at least a million natives. Impulsive, arrogant, stubborn, he carried all before him on the Court of Directors, and committed it to a policy of ill-conceived and hastily-organized expenditure.

In 1895 the Commissioner of Lands was asked for an estimate of the costs of constructing a line from Sipitang on the coast, in Brunei Bay, across the territory to the newly-named Cowie Harbour, near where Tawau is today. The Commissioner, who had never seen the route, had never visited Sipitang, sent back a provisional figure. In strong, confident lines, Cowie drew his railway line across an outline map of the territory. At either end he wrote, 'Deep water port', and along the track, as it crossed country no European had ever seen, he appended such comments as 'Believed rich in gold', 'Very fertile plateau', 'Coffee grows here'. On this basis the court acted, and the decision was taken to build a trans-Borneo railway.

Cowie entrusted its construction to A. J. West, whose previous rail experience had been the laying down of the Labuan track, a few miles of railway across the island. He reported directly to London. The cable had come to Borneo, and Cowie used it to keep all the officials there tied to him, with the Governor constantly being by-passed. The incredible thing is that although he was proved wrong in virtually all his assertions, although it was shown that the territory was empty, that there were shallows and swamps where he said there was a deep water port, although the costs of erection were colossal, and the rewards negligible, yet he retained the confidence of shareholders and court until the end. When he died, in 1911, he was Managing Director and Chairman, and was asserting that he, really, had founded the Company, that it was he, really, who had made North Borneo British.

He was saved in his railway project by a most fortuitous set of circumstances. When it was clear even to Cowie that no adequate port could be constructed near Sipitang, and that deep water close to the coast would have to be sought else-

where, he sent instructions for a track to be laid to Papar
Bay, some distance up the coast. Again Cowie's memory was
at fault. There is no deep water here either, but farther north
still, in Gaya Bay, there was perhaps the best harbour in the
whole of the west coast of Borneo. The rivers between had all
recently been acquired. To Gaya Bay then, came out the
order, Jesselton was founded, and while a firm of con-
structors, Pauling and Co., laid an unsupervised track down
to the Padas River to a town site named Beaufort, after the
Governor, West, who had reached the opposite bank from
Brunei Bay, plunged into the Interior.

This new track, which ran down the coast from Jesselton
to Beaufort, passed through country discovered fit for a new
tropical crop, rubber. Cowie seized his opportunity. No export tax would be levied for fifty years on rubber produced
in North Borneo, he announced, and a dividend of 4 per cent
would be guaranteed for six years on all companies formed
to plant rubber. Some twelve companies took advantage of
this, and purchased land the Government was clearing alongside the new track in hopes of a sale. Without doubt, had
there been no railway, there would be very little rubber in
North Borneo today.

With the advent of rubber the railway had found a staple
in steady demand, and the idle freight vans began to roll.
Despite the high hope, there were no fertile plateaux, no
teeming millions, in the Interior, and the plan for a trans-
Borneo track was quietly shelved. So, too, the Grand Trunk
Road, another Cowie chimera, while the cable, strung across
to Sandakan at great cost, was permitted to collapse after his
death. Rubber alone, however, never paid for the track, particularly as the slipshod methods of construction necessitated
a whole-scale reconstruction after the death of Cowie, and its
running costs, apart from the capital costs of rebuilding,
almost invariably exceeded revenue. Nevertheless it was, and
it remains, the sole link between the populous west coast
area south of the capital with Jesselton. No road, no track,
goes farther south than that to Penampang, and if you wish
to see the stations of the coast, if you wish to visit Papar for
example, you must accept the delay and inconveniences of
this mode of travel and catch the train.

Owen Rutter wrote (in *British North Borneo*) in 1922:

'Though still liable to wash-outs, which dislocate traffic for several days, the State Railway has been improved greatly in recent years. Of old there were few who cared to risk a long journey without a large basket containing two days' rations, and its eccentricities inspired an anonymous bard to sing:

> *Over the metals all rusted brown,*
> *Thunders the 'mail' to Jesselton town;*
> *Tearing on madly, recking not Fate,*
> *Making up time—she's two days late.*
> *See how the sparks from her smoke-stack shower,*
> *Swaying on wildly at three miles an hour.*
> *Sometimes they stop to examine a bridge,*
> *Sometimes they stick on the crest of a ridge;*
> *Sometimes they find the line washed away*
> *And postpone their advance till the following day.*
> *Beaufort to Jesselton—tour of delight—*
> *Taking all day and the best of the night,*
> *Over the metals all rusted brown*
> *Drives on the mail to Jesselton town.'*

This verse is not quite accurate today, although the prose is still a fair comment. As he said, 'It is now possible to leave Jesselton at 8.20 in the morning and to be fairly certain of reaching Tenom, in the Interior, by the same afternoon.' But whereas the timeable is much the same as 1922, the cost of a ticket is very considerably higher. It costs twice as much to travel by rail as an equivalent distance by Land Rover on the road north of Jesselton. Even this cannot force revenue to equal expenditure, and it is perhaps the only railway in the world where a worker's ticket, sold to those commuters who must use it to get to work, is more expensive than the ticket sold after the early morning rush.

In 1956 over half a million passengers travelled on the railway and nearly fifty thousand tons of freight were trucked. As is customary, there was a deficit, this time of over sixty thousand dollars. It is estimated that there will be an annual deficit until at least 1960, but that thereafter, owing to post-war capital expenditure, there will be a surplus. But since the war the railways have had to borrow five-and-a-half million dollars and have had to spend some thirteen million dollars on reconstruction. It is not considered that any surplus accruing after 1960 will be sufficient to meet loan and interest charges on this tremendous expenditure, and the accumulated deficit could be as much as two million dollars in the next ten years.

The decision to reconstruct and improve the utterly devastated track was taken immediately after the war as a step likely to assist in the speedy recovery of the state. The line had been heavily bombed, and every bridge was down. Guerrillas had blown tunnels, the workshops were in ruins, and not one locomotive was available. Very little maintenance work had been done for three years, and nearly all those who were skilled technicians before the war had fled into the jungle. Reconstruction had to begin almost at the beginning, but the Australians, who landed at Weston and who advanced up the line on Jesselton, had large parts of it functioning behind them as they moved forward, and shortly after the war ended, a temporary service was running again.

To overcome the absence of locomotives the Australian engineers adapted jeeps, fitting them with Japanese lorry wheels and replacing the rubber with flat steel tyres. These jeeps were used first as fighting vehicles, and then as locomotives, pulling up to forty tons, and are still in use as inspection trolleys. With Mr. A. R. Wikner, now the Superintendent of Ways and Works, I travelled from Papar to Jesselton in one of these. It had been his responsibility as the Australian engineer in charge of the railway, to adapt these jeeps in 1945, and it says much for his ingenuity that they are still functioning.

As the jeeps were being prepared Wikner's men were simultaneously repairing the track and erecting Bailey bridges. They did such a good job under his command that his services were secured by the Colonial Government, and for some years, until a large capital expenditure plan got under way, Wikner, under the direction of the General Manager in Jesselton, was the only European on the railways, attempting a post-war service in the face of immense difficulties.

One of the difficulties that he faced was the demand made on the line to help reconstruct the flattened towns along it.

Jesselton, Papar and Beaufort had all been obliterated, and a tremendous amount of timber was needed for rebuilding. There were no roads, and jeep-hauled trains had to truck the lot, from various mills along the line.

Even with the best of conditions a jeep could not haul any load up a steep grade without a certain momentum, and Wikner and others have described trips where the train failed to make the grade on the first run and ran back, over a rickety bridge full-speed in reverse, up the opposite rise. Wikner himself was once journeying behind one of their timber trains, and had to throw his jeep very hurriedly into reverse as the train came charging backwards round the corner ahead of him, its driver having failed to make the grade. And as there were no brakes on the old, repaired rolling stock, stopping was almost as big a problem as the grades, with jeep drivers being pushed past their stopping point quite unable to halt their forty tons of timber that had taken them captive.

In 1949 it was decided that the railway was to remain, that a road down the coast would be too expensive, and that if the country were to be quickly developed the railway must be put back into a normal running order. Between 1950 and 1952 the Bailey bridges that had done such good service were replaced by permanent bridges of concrete and steel, that over the Papar River (four hundred feet) being the longest in Borneo, while the different types of rails between Beaufort and Jesselton were all replaced with a strong 60-lb. rail, that being most suitable for a metre-gauge railway. Repaired and, increasingly, new locomotives, replaced the jeep.

The final stage of rehabilitation and improvement is now under way. The post-war rise in costs hit the reconstruction plan severely, and the Government showed great courage in persisting in its efforts to provide a modern, efficient railway. There are now seven Europeans ('one for every sixteen miles of track', say the critics) directing the railway, new railcars have been introduced, a new permanent head office has been completed in Jesselton, together with a new Central Station.

Although small, the railway has always suffered by being not one economical unit but three. The locomotives that run through Papar to Beaufort are too heavy for the light rails up the Padas Gorge into the Interior, and lighter railcars have to function here; while neither are suitable for the track on the other side of the Padas that runs to Weston. This uneconomical division is now being healed, by the relaying of the Interior track, so that freight trains can run from Jesselton to Melalap, and goods loaded in the Interior need not be touched again until the port is reached.

Without doubt the railway today is an indispensable public utility. It provides virtually the only connection between the Interior and the coast, it alone saves the gaggle of rubber estates from isolation, and however restricted and costly its services are, it alone links the coast with Jesselton. Whether a road would do this better, whether it would have done this cheaper, is one of the few subjects of controversy to animate the local Press and the Legislative Council, and one on which a visitor, aware of the sensitivity of those bodies, prepares to maintain a judicious impartiality.

Whether it is a good thing or a bad thing, it is nevertheless a delight to travel on its new diesel railcar, which in the freshness of every morning makes a triumphant journey south to Papar. When the pride of the railways comes into the central station, there are all the friendliness, excitement and best clothes shown by gentle unsophisticated people at a church fête. The stationmaster, in a spotless white suit and topee, looking strangely pre-war, told me the biggest ship ever to edge into Jesselton's new wharf had brought the diesel, and to go for a ride on her has been the joy of the town ever since.

'No, do not sit there, sir,' he said, as I moved into the first-class compartment, 'it is over the box. No one travels first, it becomes much too hot.' A minor flaw, I thought, which could be rectified by changing first with third. The inspector, ticket collector, two drivers and various other officials passed along, everyone of a different race, everyone wearing a proud smile. You were admitted to the club. 'Good morning, sir; to Papar? Sit here, sir, it is cooler.' Without doubt, this was a ceremonious occasion, a farewell, a departure. I regretted the lack of streamers, but the bustling crowd of Chinese, Dusuns and Malays outside the window, the smart police contingent, the small children, the barking dogs, the stationmaster in his suit, the people standing up in the shops across the road to watch us, more than compensated for their absence, as we, the excited élite, moved out on our way to Papar.

The journey of twenty-odd miles takes an hour and a half, not a breakneck race by any means, but a very pleasant ninety minutes in all. The Chinese love a picnic, and flourish in a crowd. Here are both to satisfy them. There is a quiet stretch where you run beside the China Sea, near yellow sand under *casuarina* pines. There are little stations where Hakka women offer you slices of delicious pineapple for five cents, and bananas and oranges. There are *padi* fields, flat, green, and the jungle rolling off to Kinabalu. There are numerous buffaloes (*kerbau*) squatting in the cool mud they need so badly to cover their hairless skins, with Dusun peasants squatting imperturbably on their backs. And finally there is a big brown river, the steam of another train, a crowd of spectators and visitors, and one is in Papar.

Papar is a pleasant place, with little of the vivacity of Kota Belud, but softer, gentler. The *padang* by the station was being mown, and the scent of fresh cut grass was reminiscent of an English village green in summer. Calm, quiet, *padi* fields stretch in all directions, flat and meadow-like, in fallow. It was here that Overbeck deposited H. L. Leicester in February 1878, hoping that he would bring order to this fertile agricultural area then busily fighting its Brunei overlords, and itself. He, and A. H. Everett, his successor, succeeded in this, and Papar became and remained the largest *padi* growing area in North Borneo.

To many the life here is torpid, drowsy, with the solid Dusun a poor contrast to the Bajau, and the few pleasures of the township inadequate recompense for the tantalizing reliance one must repose in the railway. Jesselton is only twenty miles away, but after the daily train has vanished in the heat haze down the line it could be a thousand for all the difference it makes. But Papar has its charm, and an atmosphere that many remember with nostalgia.

For one thing, it is not merely a flat *padi* area inhabited only by Dusuns, with a Chinese township by the river. In the Papar area are also the northernmost kampongs of Brunei Malays, and the southernmost outposts of Bajaus. Eastward, where the flat fields end and the Crocker Ranges rise, are the westernmost huts of the hill Dusuns, a millennium apart from the rice-growing sophisticates on the plains below. There are two rubber estates to add to the complexities of life, and there is the oldest established Christian Mission in North Borneo, at Limbahau, founded in 1881 before the Company received its Charter. All these people add diversity and colour to what might perhaps be a dull agricultural scene without them, and complicate the lives of the young district officers entrusted to their care.

Their lives have been further complicated by the initiation, in July 1956, of a Local Authority. Here, thought Jesselton, was an area large and homogeneous enough to warrant an extension of the scheme being tried out in Kota Belud. It replaced the two separate bodies that until then had been functioning, the Township Authority and the District Team. Both these bodies, devised by Governor Turnbull as a means whereby the local dignitaries were brought into touch with the problems of local government, constitute as it were the first step in the devolution of authority. They met and advised the district officer, and in thereby rescuing him from his previous solitary eminence, and them from their previous mass ignorance, they were and are extremely useful. But they do not control the purse strings, they have no power to raise and spend revenue, and by 1956 it was felt it was high time Papar woke up and grew up.

The Local Authority of Papar is dominated by the Chinese of the township, as they form a solid group of five among the twelve members. Characteristically they have not, as yet, brought themselves to the point whereby they will tax themselves to improve their conditions. They function on a revenue derived in much the same manner as that of Kota Belud. They have the surrendered taxes of the Central Government, a low rating assessment on built-up areas adds to that, and for the rest they rely on the annual grant from the Treasury in Jesselton. Whereas Kota Belud, by means of its various cesses, raised in 1957 nearly $60,000, Papar contented itself with $37,000, and it would seem that although the District Team and the Township Authority have combined, and some administrative tidiness has resulted, no greater responsibility as yet has been accepted.

Papar is one of the places in North Borneo where patience is not a virtue merely, but a necessity. The agricultural heart of the area beats slowly, change comes but gradually, and it is sufficient unto the day that the people have been brought so far when for generations they were left to their economic devices, and the district officer ran the province. Fortunately there are both at the helm of affairs in Jesselton and in Papar men well used to the slow-changing habits of those they are serving, and determined to keep prodding them along. The various committees of the Local Authority are functioning, its files bear increasing witness that people in the villages are turning to it for help, and there is every reason to hope that here, as in Kota Belud, and possibly on a safer broader base than there, the responsibilities of Local Government will come to be accepted.

When searching for the spark that initiated these moves of increased association in the affairs of government by the local people one traces it back through District Officer, Resident, Officer in Charge of Local Authorities until the source is reached in the Governor, Sir Roland Turnbull. It was he who introduced these moves, who formed the District Teams, the Township Authorities, who led them into Local Authorities when the time seemed ripe, and of which Kota Belud and Papar are merely the pioneers, who envisages Provincial Assemblies and finally, in due course, and with all layers below working well, an elected Legislative Council.

Without doubt it is Governor Turnbull who has 'activated' North Borneo, in this and in other ways, has dragged it at last from its war-time mire, and has set it looking ahead, to goals of the future, that were improbable hopes, when he arrived in 1954, but which are now within sight. In reviewing his predecessors, lent by the Colonial Office to the Chartered Company, there are very few indeed I would place alongside him.

Another transformation on the North Borneo scene owing its inspiration to Governor Turnbull is the construction of new roads. The saying in 1882 of W. L. Pryer, the founder of Sandakan, 'North Borneo is a land of infinite promise; all it needs is more people and better communications,' is just as true now as then. The pressing need for the development of

North Borneo, in 1960 as in 1882, is for an expansion of its transport system, particularly its roads. Already it is far better equipped in this respect than its bigger, richer rival down south. Sarawak depends almost entirely on its rivers for transport, and relies on old-fashioned steamboats that seem to have stepped out of the pages of history, and on American outboard engines that constitute a serious drain of dollars. North Borneo has its 116-mile railway, and when Turnbull came it had 300 miles of road. All agreed with him that this mileage, the legacy of Chartered Company tracks and bridle paths and a Colonial Development grant that before the war metalled a road to Tuaran, was puny. Where he differed from them was in doing something about it.

He treated the problem as urgent, and he wisely decentralized construction authority. The P.W.D., solidly based in Jesselton, builds roads to last, carefully calling for heavy equipment which is slow to arrive, sagely surveying the route, and pausing before every river. It does a good job, but it concentrates its resources, and it is slow. Turnbull by-passed it, and shortly after his arrival he initiated throughout the colony a grant for every D.O. to build earth roads.

These roads, equal or superior to the earth roads that are the usual country roads in Africa and Australia, on which every type of vehicle moves, have been maligned in North Borneo with the derogatory title of 'Jeepable tracks', as if nothing else dare venture on them. They do ensure a fairly clear field for the Land Rover, but are, in essence, good earth roads, and were the P.W.D. to concentrate on sealing their surfaces with tar and so eliminating yearly maintenance costs, it would more than justify its existence.

Between 1881 and 1954 some 300 miles of road had been built. Between 1954 and 1957 Turnbull doubled this. There are over 700 miles of road in North Borneo today, over 200 of which are bituminized, and the effect is electrifying. At Kota Belud, for example, the District Officer reported in 1951 that 'There are no metalled roads in this district, and there is no place where motor vehicles can be used.' In 1957 there were over fifty miles of road, scores of vehicles, and the track to Jesselton had been metalled. In Papar it was a similar story, but even more exciting.

With my host, the District Officer, we visited Limbahau, the Mission, in a glorious position beside the powerful river, standing on a high knoll of jungly ground. Over a cool drink with the fresh-faced nuns at the girls' school, on a wide verandah overlooking a panorama of *padi* fields and coconut palms, I was told that until last year it was a day's expedition for them to reach Papar, along a muddy track of six or seven miles. Now they cycle in an hour or so; we in our Land Rover sped over this bitumen road in a few minutes. This road may one day link up with Penampang, and break the railway monopoly.

I went on an even more interesting excursion, on a road that runs east of Papar towards the Crocker Range for ten miles or more. For a time it was metalled, and we drove by the shores of a constantly-fed swamp, several square miles in size. A thin rickety walk ran out over it, to a kampong half a mile away, a most untypical scene, for there are no lakes in Borneo.

The earth road that the District Officer is proudly pushing on, crosses the cleared flat *padi* area, and then penetrates virgin jungle. It is new, so new that the disturbed earth on either side of it has not yet been covered by a decent growth of creeper and vine, and it is still red and naked. Yet already the jungle has been hacked down, and although the track is as yet unformed, settlers have moved in, young rubber is sprouting up, and the Papar Land Office is deluged with applications for land five miles or more ahead of the end of the track.

Two spurs already branch off from this new road, one south to Kimanis, the other north, to reach, eventually, the upper reaches of the Papar River. These are little better than foot tracks, but a vehicle can just push through, and there is a similar scene here, as the land-hungry of Papar move out of the *padi* fields and the crowded shops and seek their fortune in pioneer, back-breaking work. Already an enterprising Chinese is running a Land Rover bus service, and the wayside toddy shop, where weary walkers stopped for a refreshing drink, is losing business, as the buses and cars bump over the railway line into Papar.

These new roads are a feature all over North Borneo, and

credit must go to the Governor who initiated the project. One feature of it, which it shares with the Local Authorities, is its decentralization of authority. The vast new Secretariat in Jesselton has been by-passed, and this, more than anything else, is the reason for its success. In this, as in the new roads, there is hope for the future.

With the new roads of Papar leaving the flat plain, and moving into the hills, the atmosphere of the district will change. Hitherto predominantly a *padi*-growing area, it will

The *padi* cycle

become more diverse, and its crops will begin to rival its inhabitants in variety. The Papar Dusun, however, is wedded to his five acres or so of flat rice land. He likes growing *padi* and despite the general agreement by Agricultural Departments and Governments and experts that *padi* is a depressed industry, that nothing short of a revolution can improve it or assist it in any way, he wants nothing else out of this world than to be allowed to go on as before.

The earliest European records of South-East Asia tell of a scene almost identical to that which you can observe in Papar today. Nothing has changed, neither the implements nor the procedure. It appears as unchanging as the weather, which has ever been, day after day, year after year, hot, humid and very wet. To observe the *padi* cycle is to see one of the world's great constants, one of the underlying motives in Asian history, something probably older than written history itself.

It begins in August, with the assembling of nurseries, planted by women from seed of the previous year's crop. The men are ploughing, with a single-furrow wooden plough tipped with iron. Identical implements can be seen among the carvings at Angkor. It does little more than scratch the ground, but it is light, and a bullock can pull it across a muddy rice field. When the mud has been stirred up sufficiently the Dusun brings out the *sisir*, a framework with a number of hard wooden spokes. This breaks up the heavy lumps of earth left untouched by the plough. Finally the texture of the soil is still further broken by the *ragus*, a kind of harrow on which the Dusun stands, and which his partner, the buffalo, must squelch and splosh round the field. At this stage, with the active work of the men finished, the water lies in an unbroken sheet; from the air, if you fly up the west coast, it is a dull yellow, in vivid contrast to the green all around.

This work takes perhaps a week or ten days. The women do the planting, the harsh glare of the reflected sun of the rice-water forcing them to smear liberal quantities of paste on their cheeks and face. It is a burning, back-breaking job; they are up to their knees in water, bending and rising from dawn to dusk, then going home to cook for idle husbands. In Malaya and elsewhere it is the woman who is leading the drift from the land, and in many cases she is retained there merely by her husband's chronic indebtedness. In North Borneo this does not apply. The Dusun, man or woman, is happy where he is, and finds it difficult to visualize any other existence.

Padi-growing is his life, so it is attended by numerous ceremonies. They correspond very broadly to the agricultural ceremonies performed by simple communities all over the world since time immemorial, and which even the Christian Church has accepted. Before planting the crop, when it is in ear, when it is ripe, and after the harvest (the latter corresponding very closely to the European harvest festival), are the main opportunities for the priestesses to emerge and the long jars to be rolled in, but at any time of the year it is dangerous to visit a Dusun without a strong head, for any excuse, even your humble presence, is enough for a party, for it is a six months' wait after planting for harvest, with little to do except watch for mice or locust plagues, and after the hectic work of harvest in February, when everyone cuts by hand and fills the small baskets, it is another long wait for August again.

The growing of *padi* is one of the few aspects of Eastern life untouched by Western influence. In other matters, small and large, the old East has gone, but in this, the basis of life, it has remained unchanged. Yet even here the signs are all of an impending crisis, for in America and Australia vast new areas are being cultivated by highly specialized machines, and rice is being bagged and sold cheaper than that produced by the peasants of Asia. Will the nineteenth-century miracle of Lancashire cotton goods outselling those of India in India itself be repeated by an even more fundamental under-cut? Although there are signs that this may happen, and the inability of the Dusun to compete, given the present state of society, is yet another factor in convincing the Agricultural Department that it is a depressed industry for which little can be done, and that its efforts are best concentrated elsewhere, it is not imagined that any change will come in the foreseeable future, and that is as far ahead as any planner can legitimately estimate.

Papar is unafraid, unaware, of future problems, and remains by its big brown river, quietly growing its *padi*, watching the pioneers move past it into the hills. It crowds the *tamu* every Sunday, Dusun and Chinese mixing amicably, Bajau and Brunei providing a splash of colour, it pauses by the *padang*, where Police struggle against Railways in an epic game of soccer; and then home it plods, peaceful, calm, in the warmth of a late afternoon, the fields now a vivid green, with all the signs of a record crop. What else could man desire? And the future? What is the future, but another crop of *padi*?

6. TEACHERS AND DOCTORS

IN Singapore today one of the more successful of the businessmen is a young man named Donald Moore. He came to the island after the war with very little money, but with a hunch. He worked hard, as he still does, and he showed the lie to those people who say, like my Chinese acquaintance in the first chapter, that the European has lost his daring, and that you can no longer make a fortune in the East. Donald Moore has become a wealthy man, in ten years of hard work. He found a gap in the business world of the East, and he filled it, as a publishers' agent. In Malaya, Singapore, Hong Kong, Borneo, Japan and elsewhere, individual bookshops were writing to London for a half-dozen or dozen copies of a book, meeting with little success there, and yet unable to deal with any intermediary, for no publisher had an agent east of India. Moore became that link. He imported from his publishers and filled his shelves with books, he pushed them into shops all over the country, kept checking on their sales, and when they had sold them he pushed more and more, and a few others as well.

In particular he sold school books, thousands of them. He came in on the crest of a wave, a demand for education, particularly in English, that has swept the East. Independent governments, however nationalistic, have been almost helpless in the face of this imperious demand. Schools have multiplied, filled by adults and children denied an education by the war, then, increasingly, by children sent by parents with a new standard of living, able to afford an education for their sons. Secondary education and universities have sprung up, and Donald Moore has been there to sell them their books.

Not only has he sold them; he has written them. You may have read them; *The Diary of an Eastern Nobody* is one, *We Live in Singapore* another. The Book Society selected a third, he compiled an anthology of Malayan writings, he wrote a volume of short stories, he became a publisher in his own right, and he sponsored numerous cultural activities as well.

Yet through it all the basis of his endeavours has been the sale of books to schools. I number him among my friends, and I salute him as a Twentieth-century Merchant Adventurer.

North Borneo is a backwater, but no backwater remains unaffected by great tidal changes, and this surge for schooling has swept the territory too, presenting the country with problems and possibilities of the utmost importance. Before the war, when this move for education was just under way, the Chartered Company ended its career with something like 150 schools and 10,000 pupils. The war burnt down the buildings and killed many of the teachers, and by 1945 the country had dropped back in the material scale almost to the beginning, back to 1881. Within ten years (1946–56), nearly 300 schools have been built, and over 30,000 students are being taught. (The growth continues: by 1959 there were 350 schools, and 43,000 students.)

It is a movement that began slowly, as is typical of North Borneo, and it carried the legacy of the war, in the shape of temporary buildings and untrained staff, for too long. It is now at last accelerating, and although many of its features are penny size, they are good. North Borneo is in a most exciting stage, educationally, and to see the various facets of it was one of the most interesting aspects of my tour.

The menace of South-East Asia is Communism. Right-wing extremism, a further problem, is not such a menace, in that however distasteful it is as a régime it does not automatically imply the hostility to the western world of Communism. The days of the great peasant leaders are however over, and whenever a leader emerges in the east today he is an educated man. It is at the schools then that the communists concentrate, and North Borneo, alone among the threatened states, has taken major steps to meet this menace.

The traditional pattern of education in British South-East Asia has rather resembled a broken Grecian temple, or a distant sight of the ruins of Baalbek, a number of unconnected pillars standing close to, but independently of one another. Government education, education by various Christian missions, and Chinese education, all historically justified in the hotch-potch of races and creeds that is the East, have

made up these pillars. They stand now, and lean, at dangerous angles. The lack of cohesion is out of date, and fortunately
North Borneo (and Sarawak) have managed to bring them
together under one roof. For the first time an overriding
harmony is imposed on the three facets.

It is the custom of Colonies, a lazy one, to seek the solution
to a problem by asking the advice of a foreigner, someone
alien to the country, ignorant of its past and indifferent to
its future, while the pertinent criticisms of men on the spot
are rejected or resented. ('The Muruts are dying? Very well,
bring in an expert.') ('We need water-works? What about
W.H.O.?') ('The educational problem is serious? Ask C.D.
and W. for a grant, and get a teacher from Home.') In the
case of the educational problem, the subsequent report in
1955 suggested an answer that would have been feasible perhaps eighty years ago—a tight, rigid control by the Government of all education, with all teachers becoming members
of a single Government teaching service. The suggestions
were hotly criticized by missionary bodies and Chinese
schools, fearful of their independence. Nevertheless the sane
conclusion, that there should be an overriding control, was
accepted, a looser, simpler roof arranged, and in 1956 a Board
of Education was formed.

This Board, a large body on which sit representatives from
all important interests in the territory connected in any way
with education, has become the much needed co-ordinating
factor in all educational activities. As its work extends, it may
come to exercise a marked effect on the youth of the territory,
and be a factor of the greatest importance in producing a
stable community.

By means of a number of committees, the Board plans for
development, supervising syllabuses, avoiding waste in the
duplication of schools. It checks on text-books in Chinese
schools and missions. In association with an enterprising London publisher, covering one of the few territories ignored by
Moore, it is ceasing to depend on books published for English
or Malayan school children, and is having text-books written
with a Borneo bias. The Government examination for all
schools has caused much dust to rise in hitherto complacent
quarters. I spoke to some teachers who thought the examina-

tion iniquitous, but nevertheless it is one of the more important steps taken by the Board in its efforts to raise the standard of education, while the work of the Local Education Committees in the District is also encouraging.

The greater proportion of the pupils at school are Chinese. There are 9,260 of them at Mission schools, of whom 7,500 learn English, and 12,500 of them packed into their Chinese schools, learning basic Mandarin. There are, or were in 1956, 34,250 pupils of all races at school; 21,760, or two-thirds of them, are Chinese. A few Chinese complicate matters by attending a Chinese primary school for six years from the age of ten, and then, as strapping fourteen-year-olds trained in concentrated memorizing and in learning by rote, enrolling at an English primary school, there to sit among boys six or eight years younger. Many others, however, acquire all their education at a Chinese school, and emerge totally different from the other members of the same community.

It is hard to blame their parents for not turning their backs on China, they are not the only migrants who have endeavoured to preserve that which was of their homeland, but it is in some of these Chinese schools that the seed of Communism has germinated. For what is the future of a graduate from these schools? The great aim among all educated Chinese is to become a mandarin, that is to work for the Government. For millennia the educated man has been a servant of the Emperor, the uneducated has been the merchant or the labourer. The tradition is too strong to break. At the University of Malaya, where I work, our graduates, be they doctors, lawyers, engineers, teachers or scientists, turn without question to the safety and prestige of Government service. Firms and businesses tempt them, and indeed the openings are immense; they are ignored, and indeed scorned. The graduate of the Chinese schools feels this pull of the centuries as keenly, if not more keenly, than his brother educated at an English Mission school, but there are few openings, and the mandarin's button is rarely for him. He cannot speak English; he has not the necessary certificates; and Government for the most part remains alien. But then neither can he secure a post in commerce, for the language there is English too. One of the very few openings remaining is to work for the wealthy Chinese businessmen who support the schools, to accept the miserable salary forced on him, and to smoulder in resentment at the unkind fates that have condemned an educated man to the post of clerk in a factory. And so he joins the Party, if he has not done so already in school, for Communism offers him the possibility of a Chinese Government, and a post in that Government, in a clear, graduated hierarchy that he can equate with little difficulty to the pyramid of the ancient Chinese administration.

Small Chinese
girl

Assisting in the spread of Communism in South-East Asia have been the actual inadequacies of many of the Chinese schools themselves, and it is most surprising that a clear feature of the education of the Chinese, a race with stability as its cardinal social characteristic, is instability. This instability begins at the top and permeates the whole structure.

A Chinese school in North Borneo as elsewhere in South-East Asia is formed by a small part of the mosaic that is South China. The Cantonese of Sandakan or the Hokkiens of Jesselton decide on a school. Invariably the funds are raised, and the school so formed is administered, by a school committee. This controls general policy, finance and employment of teachers, but it is a control made less effective than it could be by the very frequent changes in the composition of the committee, and by its emphasis in selecting as members those of the community who that year have been prevailed upon to make a substantial financial contribution, ignorant though they may be of educational problems and objectives.

This question of finance is at the root of much of the instability of the Chinese schools, and Government support is one of the wisest steps that can be taken. The constant need to enlarge the schools to find room for the ever-increasing children, necessitates yearly donations, and levies of doubtful legal validity. Invariably there is barely enough; there is constant anxious speculation on whether the amounts owing will be raised, and no sooner are the trials of one year passed than another presses to the fore.

This instability affects the staff, invariably untrained, for there is scarcely a Chinese Teachers' Training College in South-East Asia. They are engaged at pitiful salaries for the shortest possible time. Their contracts may be renewed, they may be cancelled, they live in hope or despair from day to day, and from day to day their tasks increase, as more and more children are bundled into their room, and when it is impossible to fit in any more, another classroom is built. As it is much cheaper to add a classroom to another than to found a separate school, the *Chung Hwa's*, the Chinese High Schools and the *Nanyang's* of South-East Asia, Borneo included, grow to tremendous sizes.

The result is a school committee constantly changing, a cheaply-built school constantly growing, with an ill-paid and insecure staff, scarcely or insufficiently controlling a mass of students who become graduates with a hopeless future. Nowhere have the Chinese demonstrated more obviously their inability to devise effective institutions, or shown more clearly their fanaticism for that which is of China, than in their schools of South-East Asia, which in scarcely any way whatever assist the student in the environment he has chosen.

Fortunately in North Borneo the Chinese community,

traditionally more prepared to accept Government interference, has not resisted the establishment of a Board of Education, and in most cases has welcomed the advice and help from the small Chinese section of the Education Department. Perhaps half of their students, some six thousand, are in schools aided by substantial Government grants, while every school is assisted in some way, and scarcely a dozen disgruntled teachers have been expelled to China as communists.

In addition to increasing financial support of the Chinese schools, and to other measures designed to lessen the risk of the schools following aims widely divergent from the rest, the Government took the most interesting step, while I was in North Borneo, of forming its own Chinese school. The experiment, for such it is, was made in Sandakan, and follows a successful pre-war Government Chinese Primary School in Jesselton. After months of negotiation with the school committees of three small Chinese primary schools, it was agreed that they would be combined and in future would be financed and controlled by the Government.

The school committees were largely influenced in their decision firstly by the assurance of the Government that there would be no tampering with their efforts to provide for their children's grounding in Chinese language and culture, and secondly by their acceptance of the fact that their financial problems could not otherwise be solved. It is intended, if this is a success, to provide other Government Chinese schools in Keningau and in Tawau in the first instance, and so to overcome the instability inherent in them under the old system.

A further step has been taken, and this is the extension of English education in these schools, producing a bi-lingual youth extremely well fitted to serve the Chinese community as a Government officer, better fitted, because he is bi-lingual, than the very great majority of the officers at present administering the Government. In the course of my wanderings in North Borneo I met only one Government officer who could speak Chinese, the language of the most useful community he was serving. There was no training course whereby officers could learn Chinese, and there was little awareness that here lay a most dangerous gap between governed and governing, which no interpreter, or reliance on a third language such as Malay, could bridge.[1]

If it is considered necessary to develop the teaching of English in Chinese schools, there is an almost equal necessity for it to be developed in Government schools. Nearly all the education in North Borneo at present is primary, that is a six-year course, although this policy too is changing, and in the Government Secondary School in Jesselton, there is an exciting picture of the future. In the Government schools, of which there are nearly a hundred (seven thousand pupils), the instruction is in Malay. This bars the graduate, almost as effectively as the Chinese graduate, from any responsible post in the Government or commerce, and it has never been intended that the graduate in fact would seek or aim for any such responsible post. As with the Government schools in Malaya, the intention was for the boy to return after his schooling to his kampong, or possibly acquire a minor office-boy job at the bottom of the lowest of the echelons of the Government service.

This is dangerously out of date, and the pressure from Local Authorities, native chiefs and village leaders for the provision of education in English is becoming increasingly difficult to withstand. Their requests are being listened to more readily through growing awareness of the new political implications of educating everyone in Malay. Both Malaya and Indonesia have yearnings for expansion, and in Indonesia particularly the claim for all Borneo is made only less frequently than that for New Guinea. Even closer at hand, Brunei is developing a rabid nationalism, and by means of the Islamic religion and the Malay tongue a link could be forged in areas beyond its territories. At the annual conference of Governors of British Borneo in 1957, the need for greater education in English by the Government was stated, and no doubt both political and economic factors played their part in this conclusion. It is at last being accepted that

[1] Since my visit to North Borneo, an attempt to close this gap has been made by the appointment of a Chinese speaking District Liaison Officer, whose task it was to wander over the territory informing the Chinese of the remote happenings of Government. This would appear to be an excellent step.

English, rather than Malay, is more acceptable today as a common language, because it is far more useful.[1]

Until now the teaching of English has been the prime attraction of the Mission schools. These schools, often lumped together as the third independent pillar of the educational structure, are in fact very different in appearance, with different aims and projects, ranging from the world-wide Society for the Propagation of the Gospel, the Church of England's reaction to the Empire, to the little known and Borneo-centred Basle Mission.

The first in the field was the Roman Catholic Mill Hill Mission (St. Joseph's Society for Foreign Missions) which, despite its north London name, is staffed almost entirely by Dutch or Austrian fathers, collectively of a stature difficult to surpass, led by a Bishop venerated by thousands, and admired even by unbelievers. When he was taken prisoner by the Japanese, Monsignor Buis decided that he would learn Chinese. He set himself a target; one thousand characters before liberation. As day followed day, and month succeeded month, he concentrated on his task. Hardships, privations, cruelty passed over him, and are dimly remembered now only to be forgiven. After caring for the sick, and maintaining the faith of all, his spare time was devoted to this intensely intellectual exercise. He had learned 980 characters, he was on the point of success, when he was told he would be liberated the following day. 'Damn!' said the Bishop, or whatever is the Bishop's equivalent, 'now I'll never learn them.' And he never did, and although I doubt if he has concentrated as much again, it is an excellent example of how internal discipline can carry one through years of imprisonment, so that not a scar is left. A rare man.

His earliest predecessor was a fascinating character named Cuareteron, a Spaniard, who at one time was the bitter enemy of Cowie. He was born in 1816, in Cadiz, and came out of Manila at an early age, first as a crew member and later as the captain of a trading schooner. Some of his most profitable, if most dangerous, voyages were to Brunei with a cargo of

[1] Since my visit to North Borneo it has been decided that instruction in Government Schools should be in English, and a cadre of fifty trained teachers is being provided to effect this *volte face*.

Filipinoes, where they fetched a high price on the slave market. Brooke in Sarawak and the British on Labuan were active against slave-raiding, and as a result the demand in Brunei for slaves often was unfulfilled; hence the profit and the danger.

The China Sea is not the deep ocean of its neighbour the North Pacific; it is littered with shoals, shallows and reefs, particularly in the waters near Western Borneo and the Philippines. On one of these lonely reefs, far out of sight of any land, Carlos Cuareteron in 1849 found a wrecked ship, one of the Spanish galleons which for hundreds of years annually sailed to Acapulco, in Mexico, with a load of Chinese silks, returning with a cargo of silver dollars. This vessel had reached Mexico, but had shattered itself on the reef on its way back. It was a fantastic find, a treasure ship of undreamt-of wealth.

He loaded the silver on to his schooner, and sailed away from the dangerous anchorage. By next morning the skies had begun to darken, the clear blue of the gentle swell had changed to an ominous grey, and the wind was whistling through the rigging. It was the typhoon season, and they ran for their lives. In the nick of time, as great waves towered up behind them and lashing rain from low clouds reduced visibility to a few feet, they hove to, but as the typhoon neared its crescendo Cuareteron fell on his knees, and vowed that if God would spare him he would give all the treasure, and devote all his efforts, to the prosecution of Christianity in Borneo.

The storm died away, and they survived. Cuareteron was through with piracy forever. He made his way to Rome, where, after studying for five years, he was ordained priest in 1855, and was appointed Prefect Apostolic of North Borneo and Labuan. He secured two missionaries from the Milan Fathers to help him, and they followed him to Labuan. They found themselves unable to do useful work, and left for Hong Kong in 1860. Cuareteron, who had established himself on Labuan in 1856, continued alone.

By this time he had come to accept the status quo. He had lost his fortune during some troubles in Rome, he was a poor man, and his flash of zeal had died. He figures occasionally in the British correspondence of the period rather as an agent of the Spanish Government than as a representative of Rome, and it was in that capacity that he several times sent information to Manila of the activities of Cowie and his fellow smugglers, who were supplying the Sultan of Sulu with arms in his fight against Spain. It was his information that resulted in the capture of Sachze, the German, and his subsequent death, and it was his presence on Labuan that largely induced Cowie to move to Sandakan Harbour, on the other coast.

It is not recorded whether Cuareteron's efforts secured the release of any slaves, or converted any Muslims or Pagans on the coast of North Borneo, but I doubt it. In 1878, failing badly in health, he returned to Rome, to ask that others might take over his work. Whilst in Europe he fell gravely ill, and in 1880, three days after reaching Cadiz his birthplace, he died.

He had secured a continuation of his work in Borneo, for shortly before his departure from Rome for Cadiz he met Father (later Cardinal) Henry Vaughan. He had founded the St. Joseph's Foreign Missionary Society (the Mill Hill Society), in England, to serve the missionary needs of the native races under the British Crown, and late in 1879 he met Cuareteron and was persuaded by Rome to accept Borneo as a field of endeavour.

The leader of the Borneo Mission was Father Jackson, who had spent several years as an army chaplain on the frontier in India. He and three others arrived in Kuching in 1881. Two remained there, Father Jackson went to Labuan, and Father Kilty was established on the Papar River, downstream from the present mission school at Limbahau, where he moved, and which he founded, a few years later. He had preceded by some months the granting of a Charter in November 1881 to the British North Borneo Company, and the school he founded, not at Papar but at Sandakan, in 1883, was the first in North Borneo.

As time went on the Mill Hill fathers opened more schools, particularly among the Dusuns on the west coast, at Papar and Penampang especially. Many of the young missionaries were (and are) Tyrolese, or Dutch, while the Sisters, who arrived in 1891, have been usually from the United Kingdom or Southern Ireland. Between them they now run forty-five primary schools and eight secondary schools, with over 7,000 pupils, from a Roman Catholic community of nearly 25,000.

The work of Missions in the East often has been criticized as damaging. It is difficult to support this criticism when it is aimed at the Mill Hill fathers, for it seems to me they have done nothing but good. The pagans amongst whom they worked have found in the Christian faith something tangible and worth while, and in the education they have been given they see something of equal, a number say even of greater, usefulness. The same applies to the Chinese in the towns, whose devoutness at the church and concentration at the school are both admirable.

The Anglican Church operates in a much smaller way, with a few schools, albeit of excellent quality, in the main towns. The S.P.G. (The Society for the Propagation of the Gospel) has concentrated its efforts in Africa, and even in Borneo the Anglican Bishop resides in Kuching, far to the south, and North Borneo is merely an outpost of an outpost.

Jostling for a share of souls a new arrival is building modernistic churches, and capturing that element in the Chinese character that adores the neon signs and bright lights of American civilization. The high-pressure salesmanship of the Seventh Day Adventists, who have established four schools since the war, is winning many adherents from the young Chinese in Jesselton and Sandakan. Deep in the jungle to the south, on either side of a little-visited frontier, another newcomer, the Borneo Evangelical Mission, has brought the characteristics of Methodist Australia to the Muruts.

Of deeper root and more lasting substance is the educational work undertaken by the Borneo Basle Self-established Church, usually called the Basle Mission. This Swiss enterprise had been one of the numerous mission bodies from Europe and America attracted to China during the nineteenth century. It had worked, a small band of enthusiasts, among the Hakka people behind Canton since 1846, and when it was visited in 1882 by a Chartered Company officer, Sir Walter Medhurst, seeking migrants to the new land, there were already many converts. A group of fourteen families, some ninety people, from Kwangtung Province, elected to move; they were settled near Kudat, where in 1884 they built their first church, and they became the forerunners of the major proportion of the Chinese population in North Borneo. There are more Hakka Chinese than any other race in the territory today.

It was not until 1902 that the Basle Mission sent a missionary, although the influx of Christian Hakkas, occasionally with their own Chinese evangelist, had been continuing, and small schools and churches had been opening. From the beginning a characteristic of the Church was that the services and the education were in Chinese, and were conducted, very largely, by Chinese.

After the first world war Switzerland and Austria had no finance for their far away mission, and the tenuous link was broken. From 1925 the Church became independent, and entirely self-established. It worked quietly among the Hakkas, numbering many eminent men among the scholars at its schools. The Pacific War brought great destruction to its schools and churches, and death to many of its leaders, and it was very fortunate to find the American Lutherans prepared to help its reconstruction after the holocaust.

The thirteen primary schools and the three secondary schools of the Basle Mission seem to me to offer a greater hope and a chance of longer stability than the other missions, for they have the strength of an indigenous institution. Education is in English and in Chinese, as it should be everywhere. The teachers, the leaders, are of North Borneo. This is their home, where they were born and where they will die. It is in a poor way at present, for North Borneo is not a rich country, and the Hakka is not a wealthy man. Yet in its secondary school in Sandakan there is one of the best science blocks in the whole territory, and a good library, and little known though it is, this sturdy independent Hakka institution may, if developed, well do more lasting good for the territory than all the other missions combined.

All these mission schools are now supervised and their curriculum and development plans discussed, along with the Chinese and Government schools, by the Board of Education. In good time, it would seem, for the literacy rate is still very low (17 per cent of the population over fifteen can read), all educational activities in the state have come under one control. The basic hope is that by this measure, and by subsequent extension of financial and other support, these hitherto independent pillars, leaning in different directions, may be grouped together to produce graduates not markedly dissimilar from each other. The danger before was that the young men, with different outlooks and attitudes from these different schools would threaten and then destroy the structure of the state. The hope now is that they will improve it, and that a common North Borneo outlook will emerge, with all the advantages to the country that that implies.

One of the most important tasks in the community, if this objective is to be realized, is the training of teachers for these schools, and fortunately at Kent College, at Tuaran, a few miles north of Jesselton, there is an admirable Teachers' Training College, outstanding not merely because of its excellent buildings but because it has a small group of young enthusiastic men, led by J. H. Alman, some of whom have already done good work with the few years of their teaching. Alman is a young man with a big job, and after the confusion and slackness of educational institutions in nearby countries it was most interesting to discover Kent College.

Alman now is deluged with applications from students wishing to attend courses there, although many are of very poor quality. A few years ago (it was founded in late 1952), it was difficult to secure any recruits, and women teachers were almost non-existent. Alman quickly built up an *esprit de corps*, but found many problems with the Malay section. Nevertheless, a smart uniform, a neat metal badge, community projects in Jesselton and Tuaran; a well-organized course; good food, plenty of group amusement; all these were attractions that increased the popularity of the college and the prestige of the graduates slowly is rising. The one drawback, its isolation from Jesselton, where it should have been situated, was partly overcome by excursions to the town and by cinema shows in Tuaran village. To go to Kent College will soon become the equivalent in the colony of going to Oxford. It could become the showpiece of Borneo.

Alman has the unique responsibility of arranging two-year courses for all types of schools in North Borneo, Chinese,

English, Malay, and of integrating his various pupils, be they Brunei-Malay girls, or Chinese or Dusun men, each doing a different course. He is succeeding in the face of many difficulties. He is able to build on the state-wide goodwill between all races, he is an intelligent and sympathetic administrator, and he has been most fortunate in many of the staff he has acquired. He and his staff are great believers in practical work, no unrealistic insistence on book-work here, and the first teachers from the Chinese schools, with their traditional means of teaching by recitation and chanting, found it difficult to adjust themselves. So did many Malays, careful hitherto to keep close to a written script and a pattern of lessons, but they too are adjusting themselves and will benefit as a result.

His students have gone to distant parts of the territory to record old songs on tape-recorders, have built models, sporting equipment and a small theatre, and every afternoon they devote themselves to handwork, art, carpentry and livestock or domestic science. There are two hundred of them, two hundred very important people if North Borneo is to develop a common outlook. Alman, by combining or uniting his various groups whenever he sees the opportunity, while not forgetting the customs and the cultures the respective teachers are charged to transmit, is integrating the units as closely as is desirable, particularly by the continual emphasis on English. One day his college may, with the nearby Agricultural Experimental Station, become a University College; until then it must stand out as one of the most attractive Teachers' Colleges in South-East Asia.

This Teachers' College is one of the most effective unifying elements in a community that is by its structure anarchic, and which would collapse into individual units if the administration, which at present holds it together, was withdrawn. Another institution that with great success is employed on this same task of producing a common outlook, of making the peoples become aware that they are all North Borneans, is the Government's Information Department, a title which with typical British understatement does little to describe the activities that it encourages or instigates.

The Information Office in Jesselton to a large extent maintains the local Press, feeding the *North Borneo News and Sabah Times* and the Chinese Press a constant stream of Government news. This was handled while I was there by a Press Officer, an experienced London newspaperman, who contributes to numerous overseas papers and journals as well, but his more important task, as far as North Borneo is concerned, is making sure that the North Borneo people are aware of what is happening in their own territory. Before the local Press appeared, people either knew nothing about anything, or read Malayan or London papers. Under those conditions it was most difficult for a sense of loyalty, for a sense of belonging, to appear, and the Government deserves great praise for its often criticized action in expanding the Information Office, in supporting the independent Press, and in sponsoring the excellent children's paper that the Information Office produces for the colony's schoolchildren.

The Information Office runs its own radio, Radio Sabah, with broadcasts in four languages from a converted Rest House, behind Jesselton's historic clock tower. It has been most fortunate in acquiring talented young men and women to run its Kedazan, Chinese, English and Malay sections, while its monthly programme sells more copies than the daily paper. As it expands its broadcasting time and acquires more equipment, the radio will come to exercise an even greater influence than at present, and it may well play a most important part in the future of the country.

The library maintained by the Information Office is the only public library there is, and so constitutes the only attempt at adult education in the colony. It is being developed actively, for here again the demand for education is pressing, and the need obvious. It is hoped to incorporate it before long, after the manner of the Raffles Museum and Library in Singapore, into a territory museum; at present the Treasury is not sufficiently convinced that expansion in this direction should be financed, but more altruistic thoughts may prevail. Certainly the colony could do with a big library and a small museum, if this cultivation of a North Borneo outlook is to continue.

Assisting not merely the educational efforts of the territory but virtually every aspect of its development has been the

Colombo Plan, the idea first propounded at a meeting of Commonwealth Foreign Ministers in Colombo, in 1950, as a voluntary co-operative effort by members of the Commonwealth to assist the war-torn and under-developed countries of South-East Asia in their efforts to improve their standards of living.

The Colombo Plan helps the under-developed countries in two ways; by awarding scholarships making training available in donor countries, and by the supply of equipment and experts. Both ways assist in raising the standard of living, and both ways have been utilized by North Borneo.

In the Department of Information, for example, the man in charge of training at Radio Sabah was a Colombo Plan man from New Zealand, on loan for two years while a local staff was trained and built up. The veterinary expert who helped in the last stages of the *surra* campaign was from Australia. Dental nurses, laboratory technicians, hemp disease experts, port experts, physical training experts, all come from Australia or New Zealand under the Colombo Plan. The great necessity of these people, if their work is to flourish, is that they be given time to train a successor and the opportunity to create a post. In Borneo as in Malaya, the temptation is for the Colombo Plan man to be assigned a local difficulty and a full-time task, so that when he leaves there is no trained local person to maintain the standard. North Borneo has made over a hundred applications for Colombo Plan aid since 1951; it cannot be said that it has created a hundred new posts as a result.

Of more lasting importance than the outside experts is the training given to selected men and women overseas. In 1957, for example, there were sixty-seven Colombo Plan trainees in Australia alone, and several others elsewhere. There were over a dozen in education, in medicine and in engineering, while others were doing agricultural science and various other subjects, at Technical and Commercial Colleges, Schools and Universities. It is from these men, when they return, that the state will benefit; their long-term contribution to its development will be immense.

In these two ways, and in the supply of equipment much needed but hard to acquire—the small Trade School in

Jesselton was equipped by Australia through the Colombo Plan, for example—the Plan is helping North Borneo subtly but significantly. All the more is the pity then, that there is some resentment by some of the young Englishmen in North Borneo at this very largely Australian assistance, for without doubt there is a far greater admiration by the Chinese than by the English for their neighbour down south and far fewer objections by them in seeking Australian aid. Possibly this stems from the war, when they saw the British retire, and the Australians return; it is a cumulative thing, as more and more Chinese return from their Australian schooling, but it is also a minor thing, a small flaw that scarcely detracts from the success of the plan.

Apart from the Colombo Plan, which is a family affair any- way, North Borneo fights shy of seeking assistance from Inter- national bodies, however attractive the aid, for there are un- avoidable political implications that detract from its value. Countries with little love for Britain could claim that it could not assist its colonies, that it had to seek international help; and apart from that, as anyone who has worked with U.N.O. or its numerous offshoots will confirm, the most back-breaking pile of paper work accompanies all their endeavours.

There is one brilliant and exciting exception to this, how- ever, in the fight currently being waged against malaria. The tropics in Asia today are healthy, for the nineteenth-century diseases that gave the place a bad name, such as beri-beri, cholera, smallpox, dysentery and yaws, are now well known, their origins understood, the preventive steps practised and the diseases themselves either driven from the country or kept well under control. Malaria remains.

In 1956 among those who sought treatment at Government hospitals over forty thousand people suffered from malaria. In most of the districts of North Borneo over 70 per cent of the population suffer from chronic malaria. This one disease, more than any other single factor, is killing the Muruts, and its effect on the rest of the populace, in lost days of work, in slowness of output and dullness of appreciation, must be staggering. If it could be eliminated from the country it would be worth more than the combined work of all the

Colombo Plan experts the colony has ever had; there are hopes that in the excitingly near future, this aim may be realized.

The elimination of malaria from a tropic land was first effectively demonstrated early in the present century in Malaya, and for over fifty years the mosquito has been recognized as the carrier of the disease. It was only in 1938, however, that a young Chartered Company medical officer discovered that the mosquito long known as the carrier in Malaya was harmless in North Borneo, and that the real enemy was an unobtrusive female of the species that appeared only for a few hours in the early morning.

This mosquito, *anopheles leucospyrus Balabacensis*, breeds in the darkness of the jungle. It dislikes clearings and settled places, it shuns the sunshine, and North Borneo's towns and cleared plains, at Papar for example, and Kota Belud, are comparatively free of malaria. But elsewhere it is hyperendemic, and it has been to tackle this major social and economic problem that North Borneo has secured the services of the World Health Organization and the United Nations Children's Fund.

They began work in 1955. W.H.O. supplied the senior technical staff, headed by an entomologist, Professor T. L. Chang, formerly of Shanghai, whom I met slugging across the *padi* bunds at Tambunan, and Dr. I. Santos, from Manila. U.N.I.C.E.F. supplied the jeeps and a great deal of equipment, and the Government supplied its malaria control officer and all necessary labour. The project was conceived by Dr. L. J. Clapham, the territory's Director of Medical Services, and if it is successful he will have done even more perhaps than J. M. Wilson, the Director of Education, in benefiting the territory.

From 1955 to 1957 a pilot scheme was carried out, in an effort to discover whether residual spraying could eliminate the disease from a district. The war saw great advances in spraying as a mass method of controlling or eliminating various diseases, and it developed techniques unknown before. The experts from W.H.O. had two types of spray, DDT and Dieldrin, and while Tambunan was subjected to the former, Tenom received a concentrated blast from Dieldrin. Keningau, in between, where malaria is equally as rife, was left undisturbed.

The habits of the mosquito are well known. She comes out of her jungle habitat in the early hours of the morning, to join the thousands of other species already whirring around your head. She bites you and feeds from your blood, or from your cattle; she is not particularly enamoured of human blood, and research has shown that some 50 per cent feed on buffaloes. If you are suffering from malaria already, then the parasites are developed inside her, and are passed on to some other victim whom she bites later, after a brief rest, while searching for more blood.

After a brief rest. That is the only chance there is. She rests for a brief minute on the walls of the hut, before flying on, and if those walls were sprayed, if every wall of every house were sprayed, would malaria vanish? Clapham, Chang and Santos say (with the usual medical reservations and attempts to be non-committal) yes. In Tenom the infant parasite rate was 16 per cent. It has dropped to 4 per cent. In Tambunan the campaign was more effective, the rate dropping from 21 per cent to 2 per cent in one year.

But the campaign has been waged against various difficulties. In Tambunan, despite the initial success, it has been shown that DDT does not stay sprayed on a wall for over a year, as planned, and that in any case the mosquito is developing a resistance to it. It looks as if all hopes must be placed in Dieldrin, which lasts much longer. In some cases, in far too many cases, Dieldrin in fact lasts longer than the flimsy structure on which it was sprayed, and which to the Dusun or Murut is home.

The *attap* and wood hut that is the main type of house in the Interior, and on the coast for that matter, a simple building on posts, with possibly two rooms and a front room, with a box or two inside, some mats, possibly a mosquito net, the minimum of furniture and adornment, lasts little longer than five years; at times even less. The Tenom team found that after they had passed through a kampong and sprayed it thoroughly a surprise visit some months later would discover several new homes. With unsprayed walls, the mosquito could continue. This is the major problem, and it has made necessary a quarterly check on all housing in the areas concerned.

Despite these difficulties, Dr. Clapham and the W.H.O. authorities think that the pilot scheme has shown that spraying of homes, with supplementary action by local authorities in general anti-malarial precautions, can control the disease, reduce it, and quite possibly, if Sarawak and Kelamantan co-operate on their borders, suppress it. Plans are now drawn up, following the success at Tenom and Tambunan, for a state-wide campaign. It has to be a long haul, for there will be no quick and spectacular success. It will be expensive to the medical department, but the state will benefit enormously, with a fit and healthy community replacing a weak and disease-ridden one, and its long-term savings will more than repay the cost involved. North Borneo is on the eve of a most dramatic new era.

Malaria is enemy No. 1 in North Borneo, but it is a rather simple enemy, with its habits known and its suppression a clear-cut campaign. The other great curse, pulmonary tuberculosis, is far more expensive to tackle, and its elimination can scarcely be foreseen. North Borneo is not wealthy, and it has had to rebuild itself since 1945. Its hospitals vary considerably, from the two general hospitals, a spotless new one in Jesselton and the Duchess of Kent Hospital in Sandakan, down through the five cottage hospitals, smaller institutions equipped only to handle lighter cases, to the twenty-two dispensaries, which almost exclusively treat out-patients. All however share one characteristic; they are overcrowded and understaffed.

Tuberculosis is only one, albeit the most prevalent, of the diseases and ailments that afflict North Borneo, and beds and treatment must be provided for much else. There are only a few more than seven hundred beds in the various medical institutions of the territory; over 1,300 tubercular victims alone were admitted for treatment in 1957, and I saw scores of them, packed together, lying without pastime or occupation hour after hour, responding slowly, apathetically, to treatment given over a long period of time.

The medical department is now spending over half of its annual vote on tuberculosis. In some hospitals the victim has not yet been segregated, and his coughings and spittings carry the grave risk of infecting other patients. The building of TB wards is a major charge that must be hurried on; in Beaufort the small hospital has a small, obviously condemned annexe, packed with iron beds and gaunt victims; in Tambunan the small dispensary has a dozen sick people, with a tubercular man in the middle, in one room; all this is known and deplored by Clapham, who is fighting hard to rid himself of the incubus of war and subsequent shortage of finance and staff. He has a many-sided campaign to wage, and to win a battle in one place he must conserve his forces in another. I only hope that in the long unspectacular war against tuberculosis he and his pitifully small staff—twelve doctors, six nursing sisters, 142 dressers and 82 nurses—may win, and that this curse, so common elsewhere in South-East Asia, may join the nineteenth-century killers merely as another unpleasant memory.

Doctors are in short supply in the territory, and in this, and in other specialized fields, there seems ample excuse for admitting some of the well-trained refugees from China who now cluster hopefully round the Hong Kong wharves. There is a shortage, too, of nurses and sisters, but it is not so acute, and the problem has been tackled by the medical department with a training scheme for local girls. Fighting at first against deeply-ingrained traditional attitudes of thought, which regarded nursing as menial and hence inferior, the Jesselton General Hospital is now training some fifty student nurses and hospital assistants or dressers on a three-year course. They live in a very pleasant Nurses' Home, and the teaching and the conditions have so raised the status of the profession, and so improved the morale of the nurses, that it is now a prized profession, and applicants outnumber vacancies, a most encouraging sign for the future.

The future, then, will provide a satisfactory flow of trained nurses and dressers. Dr. Clapham, like all C.M.O's. however, must think and act for the present as well, and in the serious problem of maternity and child-welfare activities, he has instituted since 1955 a most unorthodox course which despite criticism is already paying dividends, in lowering the infant mortality rate.

Through co-operative village headmen and district officers he has been able to contact the aged crones who at present are the practising midwives in the territory. Apart from a handful of trained women the colony has nothing to offer the kampong mother other than those unregistered, untrained and most illiterate old widows, who largely because they themselves have had a number of children, and are now widowed, have assumed the role of midwives.

A number of these are induced to attend the nearest hospital for three weeks' grounding in basic hygiene. Clapham is happy if all they learn is that it is wise to wash one's hands, to keep the room clean, and to avoid the worse excesses of ignorant native child-treatment. By contacting the traditional midwives in this way, by working on the available material, however imperfect in our eyes, Dr. Clapham is removing present insufficiencies more effectively than by ignoring them and by attempting to begin anew on alien material.

At the end of their three-weeks' stay at the hospital the midwives go back to their kampongs. Their status is immeasurably increased, they are part of the Government, they have a simple bag with a few essentials for child-care, which they can replenish at any time, and they can be called in, now that they are known, for further courses, and Health Visitors can call on them in their own village.

I met one of these old women in the newly-opened Interior Hospital, at Keningau. Clad in a clean sarong and *kebaya*, the few remnants of her once glossy black hair gathered into a neat bun, she was devotedly bathing a minute brown bundle, which I was assured was a Dusun baby. I had pictured a filthy old woman cramming rice into a flea-bitten child; the contrast, so I was assured, is a real one, and it is typical of the transformation taking place as a result of this modest, unassuming experiment.

In health and in education there is a great driving force apparent. North Borneo is on the eve of great developments, and should the nearby countries slide still further down to anarchy, as is all too possible, the territory's health and schooling will stand in ever greater relief to the outside world. In the attacks on malaria and pneumonia, as well as its general health activities, the medical department has established a reputation second to none. Similarly the bold educational reforms, although little noticed, should attract the admiration of the rest of South-East Asia, and do much to produce a united North Borneo. On this safe foundation of a healthy body and a sane, educated mind, the colony could progress, and emerge, perhaps by the end of the century, some forty years away, as part of British Borneo, a new member of the Commonwealth.

7. RUBBER

BEAUFORT was the most incompetent Governor ever acquired by North Borneo. He was a lawyer, sent to the territory in 1895 by Cowie, with instructions to sweep away Colonial procedure and to make the state pay. Cowie had never cared for officialdom while out East, and he saw no virtue in continuing the practice of his predecessor as Managing Director of the Chartered Company, Alfred Dent, who invariably consulted his friends at the Colonial Office and secured the loan of a Malay States administrator whenever he needed a Governor. Cowie would have none of that; he was a practical man who had made money, and together he and Beaufort were going to put the country on its feet.

Between them they nearly put it on its back. Beaufort introduced a large tax on rice, the staple food of the Chinese, who immediately stopped coming. His unimaginative administration provoked the only large-scale native rising the Chartered Company ever experienced; he fell out with European interests, and finally he quarrelled with Cowie, and retired while on leave. Before he did so, however, the railway line coming from Labuan Bay emerged from the jungle to find itself on the south bank of the Padas River. On the north bank Cowie decreed a town, and as the first tree came down he named it Beaufort.

Cowie had bad luck with his town sites. His deep-water ports were mangrovy shallows. His port in Gaya Bay, Gantisan, was useless, and Beaufort, on flat land beside the Padas, is constantly subject to floods. The Padas is constrained and packed together by the rocky fastnesses of the Gorge, which ends a mile or so east of Beaufort, but on reaching the flat coastal plain it meanders to the ocean, spreading out over a vast area of marsh and swamp and delta; Beaufort is where this begins, and when it floods, when it rises thirty feet and spills over its muddy bank, the whole town is awash. This happens nearly every year. After several floods, all the shops have been raised above flood level, and are reached now by a flight of steps. It is common for canoes to be seen in the main street, with business proceeding as usual twenty feet up.

After the war, when Beaufort was a pocket of Japanese resistance, and its shop-houses were flattened by Australian troops advancing up from Weston on Labuan Bay, the opportunity was provided of building again on a more suitable site. Half a mile away was high ground, round which the floods swirled harmlessly. Man being what he is, bound by habit and convention, the new town was built on the ruins of the old, concrete replacing timber as the one concession to progress. The town rather resembles those long-legged Africans, whose limbs have been pushed to incredible heights. To make matters worse, when a suburb was called for, to house the railway employees (for this is a junction, with shunting yards and a workshop), the new houses were put in a hollow, and when it floods here is a lake.

Beaufort has survived all this, in fact it rather glories in its amphibious life, and it is current conjecture that when potential D.Os. are considered, the factor that carries the most weight is the swimming capabilities of the men available. It is certainly a useful asset to any inhabitant.

Beaufort is surrounded by rubber. One would think that it would retard the imagination as fully as it restricts the view, while the dirty little scene of old railway engines, coaches and dilapidated sheds could do little to help. Nevertheless Beaufort possesses one of the clearest-thinking men in the colony, Chung Chao Loong, together with an outstanding Government Officer, Peck, destined to leave his mark in North Borneo.

The problem of Beaufort is the problem of rubber. In North Borneo rubber was planted in economic quantities from 1905 onwards. There was a spate of clearing until 1914, and again, at a lesser tempo, after the first world war. The post-war slump in rubber stopped all planting, and led to the introduction of more economical methods of estate-management, while the Stevenson Restriction Scheme followed by the Depression, when for a while it was cheaper to buy rubber than to grow it, ended all further expansion.

In 1934 North Borneo's rubber acreage was 128,000, the same as today. There has been no growth at all in over twenty years. In 1934, under Government restriction, 11,000 tons were exported, and 20,000 tons in 1957. In 1934 the crop was valued at $4 million. From those same trees the yield of 1956 was valued at $40 million, a tenfold increase. It has been this extreme rise in rubber revenue that has disguised the fact that on the 128,000 acres of North Borneo there grows today an old rubber tree, perhaps forty, at least twenty years old, annually decreasing in value. North Borneo exists on a wasting asset, and production may be expected to drop at an increased rate with the onset of senescence.

In view of the serious prospect of progressive decline in production from the existing plantations, the Government in 1955 introduced an Ordinance which levied a cess of two cents per pound on all rubber exported from the territory. This cess is used to finance new planting and replanting, both for the estates, which constitute slightly over half the rubber acreage, and for smallholders. This cess is administered by the Rubber Fund Board, founded in 1950, a Board representing all rubber interests, large and small, under the chairmanship of the Director of Agriculture.

More than 90 per cent of the rubber in North Borneo, being so old, is unimproved stock. The Rubber Fund Board is taking advantage of the research undertaken in Malaya and Java, and is cultivating nurseries where high-yielding trees are grown. It produces both rubber stumps and budwood, but it is quite unable to meet the demand. The estates, which neglected to utilize this research before the war, and rarely bothered to uproot mature trees in order to plant high-yielding seedlings, are far behind in the race; in fact they are not competing. The future of rubber lies with the smallholder, for the Rubber Fund Board has found that it is encouraging and financing not replanting but new planting, and therein lies the hope of Beaufort.

Its old estates, that now gloomily ring it in, are a sign of the past. If the future is to be a prosperous one, both Chung Chao Loong and Peck are agreed, access must be made for the land-hungry to areas suitable for new rubber. Both consider that such an area lies along the foothills of the Crocker Range, to their north, and when I was in Beaufort all the talk was of the opportunities that would arise when the jungle was pierced and this virgin territory made available, by the headwaters of the western flowing Membakut.

A silent transformation is taking place in these old estates, not merely those hard by Beaufort, but in the rest of North Borneo, and wherever rubber is grown in the East. Groups of Chinese are buying out the British Companies and are dividing up the estates so secured for sale to individual smallholders. The smallholder benefits, by securing trees already mature which will yield him an immediate revenue; the Chinese benefit, by an overall profit on their real estate business; and the Government benefits, perhaps by an increased production of rubber, and possibly by the anchoring of a peasantry to the land, the stable base of a society.

Rubber is an ideal crop for a smallholder, and a few acres of rubber provide him with an indolent and fluctuating living. It seems a tree designed to fit his way of life. In Malaya restrictions prohibit non-Malays from acquiring land for rubber, and production there is constant; but in North Borneo, as the new roads push east from Papar, north from Beaufort, and south from Tenom, the greatest single result will be a rapid spread in rubber smallholders, without exception clamouring for the high-yielding seedlings of the Rubber Fund Board. But as with *padi*, so with rubber; will the scientific methods of America defeat them? Synthetic rubber, or 'manufactured rubber' as America calls it, has shown itself superior to the natural commodity in certain respects, but the fierce competition that now rages between the two is still an undecided fight, and experts see no lack of demand for rubber in the foreseeable future.

Beaufort is connected to Jesselton by the railway. It is a tenuous connection, and if you journey south as I did, on 'the afternoon mixed', it provides a very dull link indeed between the two. Once Papar is passed the railway has done little to develop the land, and there are miles and miles waiting for a road and a population. The jungle is stumpy, the train labours through the heat and dirt of the afternoon to reach an impossible 20 m.p.h., and when Beaufort is reached at last there is a general sigh of relief from weary passengers.

Something of this weariness has come at last to Beaufort. Near the row of new shops, standing back from the river and the railway, is the Beaufort Club, fronting the *padang*. Behind it on a hill is an ancient Rest House; on another the D.O's. pleasant home, and a rambling office. Both overlook, but in no way dominate, the town below, and for the heart of Beaufort you must visit the club.

It is an all races affair, naturally; and in it you will find the economic backbone of the territory, the rubber planter, like all backbones collectively considered, a little rigid, a little unyielding, but individually a weary old man. He has had to endure much, and he has given freely. He has played his greatest role economically, but politically too his contribution to the state should not be forgotten. It has been the constant anti-Government attitude of the planter that has cooled many a hot bureaucrat's cheek, and it has been his salutary presence that has kept many an administrator on the rails. But it has been his economic efforts more than anything that have permitted the erection of the superstructure of a western administration, both in Malaya and Borneo. It has yet to be shown that it can survive his departure.

Maligned in book, play and song, by smart young sophisticates, the eastern planter, already a little out of date, unobtrusively embodied most of the genuine qualities that have made Britain what she is. It would be difficult now to attack him as he was pilloried in the nineteen-twenties. He rarely fought back in print, for while others wrote he worked. But since then he has fought a most bloody war in Malaya, when few others would stand, and he has tackled in his time problems and terrors that would test the finest anywhere. And now he's just a little weary, as he reaches the end of his time. It is not only his end, but the end of an era, and we must salute the passing of a gallant few.

I heard a tale in Borneo which admirably reflected one of the problems of tropical life, and which gave me far better insight into a planter's mind, and a better picture of this impersonal thing called Rubber, than any number of the *Planter's Gazette* or any Government Report. It concerned a planter named Thompson (the name is fictitious, but not the story), and it was told me by the most charming woman I met in all my travels.

He was a young planter, my hostess told me, who had served

five lonely years in North Borneo, and he was going home on leave. He had lived the life normal to the young assistant, of hard work and little play. Every day he had been up before dawn, for the latex flows most freely in the coolness of the early morning, and the tappers must be given their assignment of trees and sent on their way. He had worked in the estate for several hours, and had then returned, day after day, for a solitary breakfast on his verandah, his clothes dripping, the heat and the lassitude of the tropics hitting him already. A shower from cool water dipped from a vast Chinese jar, the water running over a concrete floor to a hole in the corner, the favourite haunt of cockroach and snake, a change of clothing, and then back out into the rows and rows of rubber, for always there was something to be done; weeding to be supervised, a track to be cut, a smoke-house to be altered, a bridge to be repaired; the upkeep of the estate involved an effort as strenuous as the maintenance of a Kentish farm, and without skilled assistance, he must do it all.

Shortly before noon he must be at the factory to watch the latex being brought in by the tappers, to check that it was not diluted with water, to supervise its gradual transformation from its thick milky character to rubber sheet. Chemicals poured into a spotless steel-partitioned trough began the change, solidifying the milk into sheets. The sheets were hung on bars in little trucks, then wheeled into small sheds or smoke-houses where intense heat from fires underneath slowly cooked them brown. Out of the smoke-house at the other end then they were wheeled after five days or so, to the long packing shed, where they were sorted into grades and slapped into a pile. Finally a pressure screw compressed that pile of sheets into one compact bundle, of uniform weight and size, ready for export by rail to Jesselton, by small Straits steamer to Singapore, then bouncing into a *tongkang* to be trans-shipped into an ocean freighter and sent on its way to the industrial centres of the world.

All this passed under the eyes of our young friend. But he saw not the open sea, the ocean-going freighter. For him life was restricted, except for two days a month (which is still the pattern), to the rubber of his estate. In the afternoon, after the tappers had retired to their quarters, he had to begin work again, this time in the estate office, and work through the hottest part of the day on his books.

He was ambitious, and was trying to kill his loneliness by studying hard for the equivalent of his captain's ticket, the Associate Examinations of the Incorporated Society of Planters of Malaya, which from 1924 had a branch in North Borneo. A planter had to pass five phases; languages (Malay was the test in North Borneo), estate practice, agricultural science, elementary surveying, and book-keeping and office organization. A man needed a minimum of three years' planting before being permitted to sit for these examinations, and the study involved could take place only at night, after a very long day's work that ended usually at dusk.

Lady Luck smiled on Thompson, for he passed his Associate, and was offered a managership shortly before he left for London, so that he could contemplate a return not to the rough wooden bungalow, the $200 per month, the poor food and the monotonous routine of the assistant, but the delights of pony-racing in Jesselton, the large annual bonus and the sprawling, airy managers' house. The rubber managers worked hard, rode hard and played hard, and some of their assistants thought they themselves were hard. This would be his life; and with luck he might even plant some rubber.

There was one great drawback. He was not going to spend another five years so damnably lonely as the last. Like many another bachelor sailing home from the East, he set out deliberately to get married. Unlike them, however, he failed. He was by nature, so my hostess told me, rather retiring, somewhat shy. On his occasional days off, when the stout wooden pillars of the Beaufort club shook and shivered under the horseplay of the other assistants suddenly released from their bondage, he felt restrained and restricted. He took part, but quietly, and was happier than most to concentrate on his studies and his reading. So although on leave his mother and aunt produced various young girls, and he felt attracted to some, he never nerved himself to a proposal, and it was still as a bachelor that he boarded his ship to return to Borneo. And then the miracle happened.

Walking up the gangplank the passenger in front of him,

a young woman, dropped her handbag. He picked it up, and by an action as simple as that began another life. It was never the same again. She turned and thanked him, and for a moment the slow-moving mass of people embarking came to a stop as calm blue eyes regarded brown, as fingers met, as a few polite words were exchanged. She was the most beautiful woman he had ever seen, and he fell madly in love with her. He never forgot her as he first saw her, on the gangplank at Tilßury, tall, slim, clutching a big brown coat round her, her fair hair tousled by the wind, and thirty years later he had but to shut his eyes to hear the timbre of her voice.

She was so young, so attractive, that immediately the whole shipload of young men began courting her, and Thompson, never more shy and reserved as when his deepest emotions were involved, drew back. To his immense delight she sought him out, and unashamedly showed the ship her choice. Timidly he suggested that he escort her ashore at Marseilles; with alacrity she agreed, and her mood warmed and lifted his. Together they spent a crowded few hours amid all the colour and clamour of that sun-kissed port.

She spoke French fluently. She had been at school, a convent, in Belgium. She was nineteen, she had lived in Europe, in London and then Belgium, since she was six, and she was now journeying out to her parents in Malaya. The first world war and then the post-war rubber depression had kept them from making the journey back to her, since she had been sent home to Europe, and her slight apprehension at meeting parents who were virtual strangers was the only small cloud on her horizon. But no matter; she had corresponded with her father for over ten years, and she knew all would be well.

Their friendship developed amazingly in the hothouse atmosphere of the ship. She was far more vivacious, far less inhibited, than Thompson, but basically she was as serious and as responsible as he. He found they shared common interests, in music, literature and amusements; and where they diverged they followed each other's point of view, and talked for hours, with pleasure in each conversation, wherever their fancy led them. And all the while, so my hostess told me, Thompson marvelled at the beauty of this incredible child beside him.

Port Said, Suez, Aden, Bombay, Colombo, they shared the East together, each trivial episode in the trip linking them together. As they entered the Straits of Malacca they kissed, as he had wanted to for weeks, and in the most romantic of moments, a tropical night by the rail of a steamer, he proposed. With stars in her eyes, and a look of utter surrender, she accepted, and after some time, quite probably a long time, they talked of the future.

Thompson was under no illusions that life on a Borneo rubber estate, even for a manager's wife, was a picnic. He liked planting, however, he was proficient, and with Governmental control over production there was a good living to be had. He thought an estate in south Johore, near to Singapore, would be ideal, rather like living in the country and coming up to London. She thought that perhaps her daddy could help; he was retired now, living in Singapore, but his estate had been there.

With that settled, they turned, rather shyly, to talk of themselves and their children. Thompson could envisage nothing more satisfying than a brood of four or so, Eton of course for the boys, to follow in his footsteps; he would make enough to see that they could try for the professions, the girls might be as graceful and as talented as their mother, so they would need a town house before they grew up, and they must have a good classical education too.

They talked long into the night. In the morning, on the dockside at Singapore, was the tall, grey-haired father who could not stand the cold and discomforts of Europe. The situation was made clear. In one keen, scrutinizing glance the young planter was judged and accepted. The plans of the youngsters permitted no delay. The small ship to Jesselton—the *Kajang* no less—sailed in two days' time. They wanted to board it as man and wife. The father agreed. Thompson should go to the priest, make arrangements for the ceremony the following day, while he took his daughter home to meet her invalid mother, whom she had not seen for thirteen years, whom she could not remember. Thompson would join them that night for dinner. She left, and he never saw her again.

That evening, when he went to the address given him, an old two-storied house standing in its own grounds, the stucco peeling off the thick stone pillars that held up the porch, heavy trees hanging damply in the lawns surrounding it, it was in darkness, shut and barred. A sleepy watchman who appeared from the back told him the occupants had gone away, no he did not know where, no he did not know how long. Thompson was thunderstruck, bereft. What on earth had happened, what could have happened? He tortured his mind, standing in the drive in the dark.

Next day, after a sleepless night, he returned to the house, it was as before. What should he do? He had made arrangements for the wedding, he attended the church, the priest and he waited, but no one came. At the confessional he broke down and sobbed, man's tears that tore at an aching heart.

The following day the *Kajang* sailed, he had to sail, he had no money, he could not stay, and besides, he did not know what to do. He had asked the neighbours, he had questioned the watchman, he had called at the police, the hospital; no one knew, no one could help. As lonely as when he left Borneo, lonelier for he had been vouchsafed a glimpse of heaven, he went on to the ship, and uncaringly watched Singapore vanish behind.

Six months later a letter came. It was written in France. It was from her. 'My dear', it began, 'I love you so.' It went on to tell him how she had left the ship, and had gone with her father to his Singapore home. Her mother was an Indian, and a complete stranger. Her father had never told her, and the realization that she was a half-caste, a Eurasian, hit her like a blow. She remembered vividly Thompson's talk of children, his hopes for their future and his plans for their careers. What chance would they have, she wondered, with this fatal mixture?

We may smile now, for the Anglo-Indian is an accepted member of many communities. But in the nineteen-twenties a vastly different mental atmosphere prevailed. Unreal, rigid, it condemned far more easily, and snubbed far more than the less intolerant age of today. Her anguish was real, and she proved the depth of her emotion by running away. She convinced her parents; they packed that afternoon and left. She spent a few weeks in Penang, then returned to Europe, and entered the convent where she had been educated. Here, as a nun, she wrote to Thompson and told him she could never bear him half-caste children, and break his heart. This was the better way, for he would soon forget her, marry a nice English girl, and eventually become the proud father of his hopeful dreams.

The tragedy of this tale is that he never did forget her, and he never did marry a nice English girl. My hostess, who would have been a young girl herself then, smiled sadly. 'It was such a waste', she said, 'such a terrible mistake.' After a pause, I heard the rest of the story. Thompson returned to Borneo, the loneliness this time broke him, he took a local girl as his mistress, married her in a quick fit of sympathy, and by her had the half-caste children his only love had denied him. He never left Borneo; he never went to Malaya; he never had much money, for there was nothing much to work for; and now his estate had been sold by its principals in London, it was being divided up for re-sale to smallholders, and he was hanging on arranging the final details.

Yet throughout it all he remained steadily, quietly consistent with himself. He never broke down. He did his work faithfully and well, and after the first year or so he regained his appreciation of the gentle things of life. Post-war amenities, such as long-playing gramophone records, radio and good pocket editions, helped him. Tragedy had hit him, but he remained a calm, determined Englishman, epitomizing the strength inherent in the rubber planters of today.

Another tale, of vastly different texture, but which equally illustrates the courage and the problems of the rubber planter was told me by a veteran, Kingsley Pallant, managing the Borneo Abaca Estate outside Tawau, on the east coast, perhaps the one place in the Commonwealth where first-class manila hemp is grown. He had come there in 1954 from a rubber estate in Malaya, on which he had lived throughout the emergency.

He told me of the constant, unceasing watch on one's tongue, and actions that was necessary. In South Johore, where his estate was, the communist terrorists were particularly bad. Their effectiveness was greatly increased by the very large army of supporters, people who willingly or unwillingly supplied them with food, with ammunition, with

information. It was against these that one had to measure
one's remarks; it was against the terrorists watching in or near
the estate that one had to watch one's actions.

Day after day the constant battle for survival went on, for
the planter was in the front line. He was their target. There
was one solution that never dawned on Pallant, and the others
who stuck it out, and that was to leave. The communists
could kill them, as they did, but they were killed at their
posts. Pallant said: 'If I told the foreman that I would check
the south-west section in the morning, I never went near that
section. If I drove away from the office on the road going
north, I got on to the south road as soon as I was out of sight
of the office. I never stuck to a routine, I deliberately kept
myself from making a decision on what to do until the last
possible moment. I never travelled except in a reinforced
van, I always took with me my special constables who walked
well away from me, in the rubber, and on their holidays, or
at meal-times, I never drove away from the estate. I stayed
in my house and kept inside. I do not think that in all those
years I made an unguarded step; and yet they got me just the
same.'

A few days before he was ambushed he had visited a new
road, which eliminated a long swinging U of a track. It went
across an old clearing, through a cutting, to join the old road
just beyond some new rubber. The communists reasoned
that he would come again, they positioned themselves, they
waited three days, and they got him. The only mistake they
made was that while Pallant had driven on the first trip on
the new road, the second trip was managed by Pallant's
driver. He was an elderly Malay, it was a narrow cutting,
and he proceeded with care. The communists had reasoned
that if they detonated a land-mine when he passed point X,
it would explode directly under that car at point Z. But it
exploded just ahead of the car, raising a cloud of dust, and
they survived.

Everything happened at once. The communist placed at
the rear, to fire into the back of the van, rose to spray tommy-
gun bullets into the aperture between the bullet-proof sides.
He was shot and killed as he rose, by one of Pallant's specials,
the other having leapt from the van and hidden by the side

before the pall of dust began to settle. In front a squad was firing at Pallant, who had lowered the armoured bullet-proof vizor, and at the side another terrorist rose, to lob in a grenade. The special, lying under the bank, killed him with one shot. After a further burst of firing the remainder fled.

Pallant had been saved by the training he had insisted on with his specials—the drill of car-ambush being but one of many they had practised constantly—by their courage, and by the failure of the mine to blow up. That same night he heard from the police of Johore Bahru that another planter, a nearby friend, had been killed near the estate office. 'He had a rifle, and he did not take it. He had two special constables, and they were not with him. He had an armoured car, and he did not use it. He simply walked down the road, and they stepped out from the trees and killed him.'

Pallant survived, as he deserved to, and his strength of character, no less than Thompson's, can be taken as typical of the successful planter. Somerset Maugham called them sixth form boys who never grew up. It is a slur that has stuck; in the Beaufort Club on one of their two days off a month there is a wild escapism evident, but it is as unjust to judge a planter by that behaviour as it is to judge a war-time bomber crew by its behaviour in the Mess. Had Maugham stayed in Borneo for just a little, he would have met not sixth form boys, but men recruited, as the pioneers were, from the best types of Assam and Ceylon tea estates, and from the Sumatra tobacco plantations. And those that followed, seasoned World War I officers, were of equal calibre, their names equally well remembered. Men such as Lease of Sapong, Anderson and Cooper of Tenom Borneo Rubber, Halliday of Jimpangah, Rex Carew of Lingkungan, Tuxford of Beaufort, Lutter of Tuaran, and Hardwick of Membakut, were solid, hard-working men, on whom the economy of the state depended. There never was more than a few score; within five years it is doubtful if there will be a European rubber planter in the whole territory. Let us honour them while we can.

8. THE INTERIOR

A JOURNEY into the Interior of North Borneo can be undertaken in various ways. From the east coast the vast rolling expanse of virtually uninhabited jungle can be penetrated at present only on foot or by launch up the long rivers, whereas from the narrow west coast one can move in by rail, air, and possibly by the time this is printed, by car as well.

High hopes are held for the journey by air. This is a new means of transport, and the men behind it are young, enthusiastic, who laugh to scorn such prosaic things as roads, who regard you as a century out of date if you mention the railway, and who maintain that the only way to open up the Interior, quickly and economically, is by air.

The Department of Civil Aviation is one of those thin, gossamer-like threads of co-operation that link North Borneo to Sarawak down south. It is staffed, and its planes are flown, by enthusiasts such as Jock Holliday, who see the present boom in aviation merely as a beginning, and who regard the small modern aircraft as the answer to the pioneer's prayer. A strip in the jungle costs possibly $100,000, and Holliday would like to see a half-dozen, or better still, a dozen more strips placed in the Interior. From each strip roads would radiate out; it would serve as a focal point, it would transport goods and supplies, and bring in materials and men.

Already the Department maintains strips at Labuan, Jesselton, Kudat, Sandakan, Lahad Datu and Tawau on the coast, and at Ranau and Keningau in the Interior. A subsidiary of Malayan Airways (which flies the daily DC-3 from Singapore to Jesselton), named Borneo Airways, flies an internal feeder service to these strips. It is immensely popular, and services are constantly being increased, but even the enthusiasts would agree that air transport has not yet been extended far enough inland, on a wide enough system, to open up the Interior as much as it helped to develop the coast.

Borneo Airways, founded after the war, was yet another

enterprise that I encountered in the throes of a typical transformation, changing from its long chrysalis to a bright new
butterfly. It has struggled along with surplus war material
and its planes were old De Havilland Rapide biplanes which
bore testimony to the quality of their British construction but
which had a small pay-load and which, being of wood, were
unsuitable for the tropics. By now it will have discarded these
veterans, and round the flanks of Kinabalu will be swooping
and swaying its new all-metal monoplanes, Pioneers, able to
land on a handkerchief, and able to carry five times as much
for virtually the same cost as the Rapide.

The tall Australian pilots who run a daily service from
Labuan to Keningau in the Interior, then back across the
Crocker Range to Jesselton on the coast, up north to Kudat,
down the east coast to Sandakan and on to Tawau, covering
unconcernedly and without incident territory that late-
nineteenth-century explorers hacked through for months, are
loud in their praise of the new aircraft, and optimistic as to
what it will do. The slow, ancient journey of the decrepit
spur-train line, from Weston to Beaufort, is marked by one
outstanding feature; the demand from the peoples along the
track for fresh fish. Youths, hanging precariously from the
solitary woebegone carriage, bring these fish from the sea,
and the cost rises every yard they penetrate inland. Yet the
demand is intense. In Sarawak the shortage of fish in the
Interior, and the resulting iodine deficiency, is a serious
problem. A Pioneer could bring several tons of freshly caught
fish from Labuan to the Interior in a matter of thirty minutes
or so, and could return (*will* return, say the enthusiasts) with
fresh meat for the Brunei oil fields, that same day.

Without doubt this new aircraft will assist in the development of North Borneo. Strips at Tenom, the most rapidly
expanding town in the Interior, and at Beaufort, will be an
asset to both places. Additional services to towns already
served will be utilized. But no country in the world, with
the exception of New Guinea, has been developed solely by
aircraft, the role of which appears to be to assist administration and to encourage expansion already occurring. It is improbable that it could begin it.

The feeder service is used by Government officers, by

Chinese towkeys and by European businessmen, the young representatives of the great Singapore houses of commerce. It is less frequently used by the natives of the country. Ranau, linked to the coast only by track and by plane, has a flourishing tobacco industry. The native can sell his tobacco to the Chinese in Ranau, who flies it out, or he can walk it out to the coast. In practice very little comes out by air; the Dusun prefers the laborious lug to the coast, where he is assured of a good price. When the road comes to Ranau from Tamparuli it will develop the area more in one year than Borneo Airways has done in ten, because it will be used extensively by the indigenous peoples of the territory. Their lords may still fly over them, but their goods will go by road.

At present, access to the populous interior valleys that run north and south behind the Crocker Range is confined to the daily plane, and to the railway. It is the tightest bottleneck in the territory. The light metre-gauge railway which runs up the Padas gorge from Beaufort, through the Crocker Range to Tenom, is quite unable to provide the necessary blood for the pulsating heart of the Interior, for here a boom is under way, and this one-track line is its sole link with the coast. It runs into Tenom; a track there links Tenom with Keningau to its north, and runs on to Tambunan, farther north still; three emeralds on a single thread, emeralds already of great value to the State, emeralds already attracting many to make their homes here, three emeralds that will give way to a dozen once an all-weather road joins the three to the open world at Jesselton.

The journey up the Padas gorge, for all its economic futility, is a fascinating trip, typical in many ways of North Borneo. A petrol-driven railcar is used, and until the light pre-war rails are reached a considerable speed is maintained. By 1959, after several years of work, the whole track will have 60-lb. rails, and powerful steam trains will be running direct from Jesselton. The gorge itself, by means of which the Padas has worked its way to the west coast, the solitary swan (for all other west coast streams are puny in comparison), is a spectacular sight, and the railway must have provided West with many anxious moments during construction.

But what made the trip typical of North Borneo in so many

ways was not so much the scenery, striking though that is on occasions, as when a broad river roars over immense granite boulders, and cuts into the steeply-sloped hill on which the line is poised, but more personal things, the people and their attitude. It was the mixture as before; European, Eurasian, Chinese, Indian, Dusun and Brunei-Malay, with various combinations of these basic elements thrown in for luck. All accepted one another, everyone was doing a different job, and if there was a serpent in the Garden of Eden it was not in this ark as it rocked and swayed through the jungle up the gorge.

Three times out of five, I was told, the railcar breaks down, and break down again it did. With great goodwill we all turned out and pushed it until it ran backwards to the nearest shade, where the jungle met overhead. Here, happily enough, for what was an hour or so of delay, we waited; there was only one track, so if anything came along it would have to do something for us. Sure enough another railcar appeared, pushed us a little way, and then, thanks to the joint efforts of the crews, we were started again, and raced off up the gorge.

The Padas River is rather similar to a beautiful virgin; it is attractive, but it is unexploited. It is a wasted economic asset, for it provides a powerful and constant generating force, and the gorge an ideal dam site. This was recognized after the war by British capital. Comprehensive surveying and prospecting established the fact that a dam could be built across the Padas shortly below the point where it began its exit from the Interior by plunging into the Crocker Range. With such a dam a large-scale hydro-electric scheme could be developed, and various mineral enterprises undertaken. Government consideration of the scheme froze all life on the plain behind the proposed dam for several years and as this included the town of Tenom, and thousands of acres of fertile land, all of which would have been flooded, there are many who cheered when the industrialists decided that the chronic shortage of labour would jeopardize their endeavours, and turned instead to the Volta River in Africa.

With their departure the town began to boom, and it was at a bustling little station, full of bags of cement and sacks and crates, and a small horde of humanity, that we stopped.

Chinese

Sikh

Old Malay

It is a town that owes its origin again to the European. There was a small kampong by the Padas at the gorge when the railway came through, but the District Officer was established at the present site, his presence attracted the Chinese, and a small township grew. It had a European name at birth, but it was never anything but Tenom, and quietly though it had lived its fifty-odd years, it is the centre now of exciting dynamic developments that make it the town, second perhaps only to Tawau, with the most attractive prospects in the territory.

There is a strange, pleasant feeling of remoteness in Tenom. One knows that over that green range of hills to the west lies the coast, that in a day one could be in Labuan boarding an ocean steamer or a Super-Constellation aircraft, yet there is that same Shangri-la atmosphere that one catches in Ranau. Ranau is immeasurably more isolated, backward and primitive than Tenom, half a dozen wooden shops facing, across grass and peaceful chickens, another half-dozen, while Tenom is solid concrete, with two cinemas and innumerable cars and Land Rovers, a town with a population of over a thousand, but it is there all the same. You say to yourself, 'I am in the Interior of Borneo', and even if you are drinking cocktails and discussing your holiday of the previous week in Southern Italy, enough of the magic remains to convince you that you are miles from anywhere, in an area incredibly remote.

Possibly the clean dry heat helps, so different from the humidity of the coast. It is a non-tropical heat, more the heat of South Africa or Australia, where you can walk awhile without immediately perspiring. It is hard to believe one is almost on the equator. The horizon helps, too, the long valley going north and south, the green-blue Crocker Range to the west, the Witti Range to the east. It is a landscape in colour and clarity again different from the coast, reminiscent to many people of the timbered slopes of Australia's Blue Mountains. Again, it is hard to accept that one is a few hours from the South China Sea. Particularly do the evenings help this illusion of remoteness, for they are cool, a blanket is often necessary, and in the morning there is mist banked against the hills and settling over the Padas.

This Shangri-la feeling has not deterred the Chinese, Sino-Dusuns and others who have poured through the bottleneck of the gorge from hard work; and the rows of shops, as well as the new schools, cinemas and banks, are the result of their endeavours. Sitting astride this plunging horse is the D.O., with all the complexities of a rapidly growing town to control, playing the roles of mayor and rural board chairman at the one and the same time.

The growth of Tenom merely reflects the growth in the countryside round about. South of Tenom, new settlers, many fleeing from Beaufort, 'the doomed city', have found fertile land by the banks of the Padas, as it ends its long northward descent from the central massif of Borneo. There is ample land here to support thousands more, and an old Chartered Company bridle-track shows them the way up the river valley; small outposts among the jungle, at Paal, Kemabong and Tomani, where a shopkeeper or two exists miserably on the scanty produce brought him by the Muruts, may one day be thriving settlements.

I watched this southward penetration through the courtesy of the manager of Sapong Estate, one of the two large rubber estates in the Interior, through which the main road incongruously runs. It is a private estate road, yet it is used by all, providing ample excuse for argument about maintenance responsibility. Just south of the estate, in fact on land sold by the estate, the new settlers have dug in. Where a few years ago was scrub, *lallang* or jungle is now intense cultivation. In particular coffee is growing here, the new settlers neglecting rubber to a certain extent, and with the assistance of the Agricultural Department cultivating in the approved manner (that is under shady trees) a glorious crop of coffee.

We passed hut after hut, and then, near the end of the inhabited area, near signs of very recent occupation, we came on what is a very typical scene among these Chinese pioneers. They had reached stage two. Stage one consisted of clearing the land, growing a crop, building a house. Then immediately that was done, stage two began: the building of a school. We watched a group of these farmers busy with saw, spade and bucket; one was mixing cement, cheap but good Japanese cement for the floor, another was nailing cross-beams to the roof, some children were digging a hole for the basket-ball post. By community effort these poor people were striving to preserve for their children some minute part of their ancient culture, something they as peasants possibly could only vaguely remember, but something which to them was as precious as the land they had at last acquired.

Sapong, which was formerly one of the showpieces of South-East Asia, and which is still a very fine estate, lies hard by the entrance to the gorge, where the old native kampong, Tenom Lama (old Tenom), once stood. Between it and the railway is the Padas. A little upstream it is joined by its powerful tributary, the Pegalan River, which flows down from the north, while the Padas, coming from the south, skirts the boundary of the estate.

One crosses to Sapong by an antiquated ferry, an outboard engine on a *prahu*, that pushes a flat barge diagonally into the current. People have drowned from this ferry, and there is crocodile danger too, even this far upstream. The more typical method of crossing streams, by a steel wire, cannot be used here, for when the Pegalan and Padas come down in flood, and their combined mass smacks the entrance to the gorge, the stream rises forty feet or more, and spreads for hundreds of yards. At such times it is a navigational hazard, and already it is considered unwise to rely on this crossing as the main feeder route for the southward penetration.

However, I crossed without incident, and heard rubber tales stretching back to the semi-legendary days of Lease himself, the tobacco planter who turned to rubber at the beginning of the century, and who became the uncrowned king of the Interior. Sapong has preserved a continuity of manager-ship rare in rubber estates; each manager served for some time under his predecessor, and no new man was brought in. But although there has been continuity in management, there has been little continuity of thought. The attitude of Lease and the beliefs of Williamson are poles apart, and if Sapong today stands as an exceptional estate, with an excellent labour reputation and conditions of output, and efficiency second to none, much of the credit must go to the young manager there now, who like so many others feels the cold breath of sale and partition over him.

On all the estates, in all the enterprises of North Borneo, labour was and is the great problem. Lease tackled this in the autocratic way that made him notorious. His labour, secured largely from China on contracts to work for three or five years, was constantly slipping away to the coast. If the labourers absconded they could be charged, as was for example Thin Sie, who ran away from Sapong on June 24th, 1904. He was caught, the case was heard on the estate, he was given ten strokes of the rattan cane and sent back to the labour lines. He was lucky; Beh Tam was caught trying to commit suicide. He claimed that the overseer's cruelty and the hardness of the work had driven him to it. He was sentenced to six months' gaol in chains. Lim Tan, caught absconding, received a flogging of ten rattan strokes, and spent a week in the stocks.

Labour laws followed those of the Malay States, and contract labour, flogging, the stocks, chains for prisoners, even estate gaols, all vanished. Remaining on Sapong Estate, however, was the whipping triangle, kept until 1941 as a reminder of what might happen. Lease was a firm man, as the cases above bear evidence, but it does not seem that he was alien to his age, and there are many stories that indicate that he was far tougher to his European assistants than to his labourers. Two instances will suffice, and they should give some picture of life on Sapong in the first twenty or so years of this century. All assistants had to wait, in spotless neck-to-ankle white uniform, at the foot of his bungalow in the blazing heat, while he finished his breakfast and cigar. At his convenience he called them in from the sun and gave them their orders. If that was cruel, what of this? He would not permit his labourers or his assistants to marry, and as far as his assistants were concerned he personally selected and assigned to them their mistresses for the tour, usually newly-arrived Javanese. There was no argument, no discussion; you took her and you loved her, or else you got out.

The labour problem on Sapong now is tackled in quite a different way. The Chinese have vanished, the Javanese, except for a few, have long since returned to Indonesia, and in their place Williamson employs Muruts, over 400 of them. Scattered throughout the thousands of square miles to the south of Sapong are a few thousand more of these primitive people, perhaps less than 18,000 by now, but they live in small groups, possibly two or three clan houses comprising the entire population of hundreds of square miles, and Sapong boasts of the largest single Murut community in existence.

A Murut

Williamson is the sole planter in North Borneo who relies on these indigenous people for labour, and his use of them presents him with numerous problems. They come seeking work as a group. You either employ them all, or they all leave. They come and go as they please. They are on a monthly contract, and if they feel like it at the end of a month, or actually at any time, with or without their pay, they will vanish back into the jungle. They have a wanderlust, a desire 'to go bush', 'to go walkabout', as strong as the Australian aborigine, and Williamson wisely lets them go. As he says in his annual report to his slightly incredulous Directors, 'The regulation of arrivals and departures was again extremely difficult, and for the greater part of the year there was a surplus, 150 at one time. So long as the major tapping force is Murut, this occasional labour must be given work, otherwise whole clans move off.'

Near the head office, smoke-sheds, and central quarters of Sapong, stands an old storied wooden house. Sapong was a Japanese headquarters during the war, and it was so badly bombed that nearly everything is post-1945, but this house remains. It is allocated by Williamson to new Muruts, and when I was there a party of a dozen or more, having trekked from deep in the Interior, from the fastnesses of Indonesian Borneo, arrived on the estate. They had never seen a European before, never seen a rubber estate, or a car, or even a box of matches, surely the most travelled object in the world.

The house was completely shuttered, and I climbed some filthy wooden stairs in a gloomy silence. Suddenly over my head was the sound of scuttling, as the minute Muruts, tiny little people, fled from their cooking hearth to a far room. Here I found them, a small, timid, motionless group carefully watching these strange giants, their hair matted, their limbs naked, clad only in the *chawat* or loincloth. Hanging on the wall were their *parangs*, a *bongon* or two, little else; they knew of metal, but apart from that they could have come from the Stone Age.

As they stay with Williamson he moves them by degrees to other quarters. In their third visit or so they may be wearing shorts and a shirt, and they may even wash it occasionally. They have learned to use a latrine, and forsake the hole in the floor. They are a little cleaner, personally, and less timid, with a few more interests than the *tapai* jar. They are even useful on the estate, and justify their $2.50 a day tapper's wage. It is an amazing advance they make, on Sapong, and it is a pity that there is not a greater effort to reach this unique concentration of nomads, and to show them some of the benefits of government; medicine and education in particular.

The Muruts are among the more primitive of the peoples

of South-East Asia, and they are among the more pressing of
the problems of the Government of North Borneo, for they
are a dying race. They are of the same stock as the Dusuns
and as with the Dusuns they have no name for themselves as
a whole, and merely name themselves as members of a sub-
tribe. Timoguns (around Tenom), Nabai (Keningau area),
Baokan (in the upper reaches of the Sook River) and
Semambu (in the deep south) are amongst the groups represented on Sapong. Their dialects are mutually intelligible,
and bear an affinity to Dusun.

Until some fifty-odd years ago the Muruts lived in long-
houses, a practice still observed among the Dyaks of Sarawak.
It is largely a defensive measure, and the habit has died out
in North Borneo since the establishment of District Officers
shortly before the turn of the century, which brought peace
to the Interior. They live still in a large house, with a number
of other families, each with its own hearth, but not a longhouse, so-called. The change is still continuing, and Williamson in Sapong, when he provides single family huts, is merely
following the habits of the Interior. But whether this is due
to peace, or to depopulation, it is hard to say.

The Murut lives very largely on shifting agriculture, as
do primitive peoples in the equatorial belt all round the
globe. Dry rice is grown in the jungle, in clearings made by
an annual slash and burn. Domestic meat is rare, but scrawny
chickens abound; tapioca is almost as important as *padi*;
sweet potatoes and maize are common, and much use, of
course, is made of the wild fruits of the jungle. Simple though
his diet is, the agricultural part of the Murut's life is involved in most complicated ritual and ceremony, and the
annual round of tasks connected with its production is the
framework for all other village activities.

Hugh Clifford, who was the first Governor to visit the
Muruts, has described them most disparagingly in his book
In Days that are Dead. Fifty years later his fulminations at
their consumption of alcohol and their generally depraved
state are seen as typical nineteenth-century scorn of 'primitive savages'. Today we are more prone to accept them for
what they are, not blame them for what they are not.

Politically they have no paramount chief, their whole

Above: A Dusun girl goes fishing with her fish-trap on her head
Below: A Murut girl from Tenom

LAND OF MANY PEOPLES. *Top, left to right:* Malay driver. The old and new in Murut dress. Hakka labourer from Jesselton. Dusun village headman. *Below, left to right:* Dusun student-teacher. Sikh laboratory assistant. Bajau women rubber workers. A Suluk from an east coast island

Left, above: This print of a Borneo interior was published in 1853. *Below:* The modern photograph is of a Bajau hut and shows women weaving and mat-making. *Right:* A Murut aims his blowpipe while another holds a dart in his mouth

Above: The manager of a rubber estate talks with some of his employees.
Below: Old shop-houses of the Kongsi type, which are rapidly being replaced by 'the approved P.W.D. model'

Above: An evening football match on the Sandakan *padang. Below:*
Coffee-shop scene at Tuaran. The essential refrigerator burns kerosene

Spear-fisherman with his catch, at Semporna

environment is against any link larger than a single community, although sub-tribes can be held together, and it is traditional for there to be joint leadership, for consultation among a half-dozen seniors, men and women, and for a final decision, based largely on group consensus, to be made by the leader. For the most part they are left alone to make their decisions, and to form their plans, and there is very little Government contact with them at all. The attention of the Interior officer is largely taken up with the rapid development of the townships, with the settled agricultural life at Tenom, Keningau and Tambunan; at best he can find a fortnight or three weeks to trek over the everlasting razor-backs south to Pensiangan, and meet perhaps a few hundred Muruts *en route,* at worst he can send an assistant and a dresser. But the time on tour is largely taken up with the hardships of the journey and the hectic atmosphere of the traditional entertainment in the various houses. Administration by patrol is usually ineffective, as the Australians in New Guinea are discovering. Personal interchange is brief, as ephemeral as an address to a luncheon group, and in the period since the war only Ian Peck seems to have acquired a good knowledge of Murut language, customs and attitudes.

The Government is considering a suggestion from an anthropologist, sent into the south to investigate Murut depopulation, that it appoint a Protector, and that all aspects of this problem of the Interior be brought under his control. Malaya, whose administrative techniques reflect all that is best in British government in the Far East, has long had its Protector of Aborigines, and through him a tremendous amount of good has been done for the primitive tribes that ride the watercrest of that peninsula. In North Borneo the Muruts, a greater problem than the Senoi, come under the Departmental care of many, but they are on the fringe, there is so little money and so many demands, and the old pattern of indifference continues.

The Muruts once challenged that indifference, and to the amazement of all who said they could never combine, rose in revolt. The Rundum Revolt of 1915 was the last virile, vigorous gesture of a people denied their traditional head-hunting, people who knew not the west or anything else except their jungle, and who listened to the stories of a remarkable man who promised them victory. The whole south, from the border, Rundum (now an empty valley, but then a Government post a week's walk from Sapong), Tenom, Pensiangan, Sook, burst into revolt. It was squashed, the ringleaders were sent to Kudat for a few years, and never again did a Murut say 'boo', except at the end of World War II, when his head-hunting habits helped to slaughter several thousand Japanese, marching to Tenom to surrender. But as I stood in the filthy house on Sapong, and saw the Muruts, terrified, regarding me in a huddled silence, not knowing what I represented or what I wanted, I felt I could understand their attitude, and I sympathized with their fate.

There have been three accurate censuses of North Borneo. In each the Murut population has declined, from 30,355 in 1921, to 24,444 in 1931, to 18,724 in 1951. There are no signs that the trend has altered. By the end of the century the race may be extinct.

Following the pre-war research and report on Murut depopulation by Dr. A. J. Copeland, a Chartered Company medical officer, the Colonial Government sought overseas advice. In 1953 from Malaya came a doctor experienced in social medicine among the aborigine. After a three-month tour he confirmed earlier reports and stated that the Muruts were certainly dying, and that a detailed study should be undertaken to discover the relevant reasons. So he came back for a further tour the following year. They were still dying, he reported, and what was more, they were not having any, or many, babies. A woman doctor needed? In 1956 then a woman doctor, Mary Saunders of the Government of Singapore, was brought in with him, she was able to question and examine the Murut women, particularly on Sapong Estate, although despite the importance of the task no woman interpreter was supplied, except for two weeks, and she was able to unearth at last, from the shy, timid Murut women, some explanation for their declining numbers.

Dr. Saunders began her investigations of Murut women on the supposition that they have never conceived as they have no children but it gradually became clear that the majority of the women have had at least one conception, although not always recognized as such. Of those who have had pregnancies, none of the children have lived. They have married young, usually by the time of their 'coming of age', before the full functioning of the reproductive system has developed. They suffer from malnutrition, debility, and in particular from malaria, which almost invariably precipitates a miscarriage or a premature birth.

Murut
Woman

The pattern is inexorable. The premature birth of the underfed baby is followed by pelvic infection, of a type that could be expected to prevent further pregnancies. One of the main ways of transmitting this infection is by the filthy and primitive 'assistance' at birth rendered by the aged crones of the community. Another way, growing increasingly common, is the new habit adopted by Murut women in contact with the outposts of civilization, of wearing pants, pants they never wash, and rarely discard.

With the young woman now infected and sterile, her child soon dies, owing to his premature and weak delivery, and to the gross lack of knowledge of the care and feeding of infants, assisted by malaria and dysentery. The conclusions she drew, at the end of a horrifying tale of a dying people, was a simple one. The main cause of their depopulation is disease. This is preventable.

Between Mary Saunders and the shy young women on Sapong there grew up a bond of sympathy, and she was consulted by them in large numbers for various complaints. Towards the end of her stay she witnessed what must be taken, except for the ending, as a normal birth; it illustrates the supreme necessity of an extension of maternity and child welfare service in the Murut country. Dr. Saunders writes:

'In the course of our investigations we had heard descriptions of the conduct of Murut labour, which we were most anxious to witness for ourselves.

'One day I heard of a woman who had just started in labour. I went to her quarters, and found a young *primipara* of about sixteen years in early labour. She had not been examined by us antenatally.

'On our arrival the girl was sitting on a bamboo log about six inches in diameter, facing the corner of the room. A loop of rope was suspended at a convenient height for her to rest her arms upon when required. A cloth was bound round her waist above the bulge of the uterus; this did not appear to be unduly tight or uncomfortable. By her side was a bowl of water and plates containing boiled rice, ginger root and a piece of bark. The rice was for food and the ginger and bark to rub on her abdomen to stimulate pains. Most of the time she was supported from behind by another woman in whose arms she could lie back and relax.

'The floor of the house was made of planks and was filthy. It was covered with débris of food, cigarette ends and other litter. No attempt seemed to have been made to clean it for a long time. Throughout, men, women, children and dogs came and went freely. Everyone, including the patient, spat frequently on the floor.

'From time to time the girl was examined internally by one of three old women, crouching down in front of her. The hand was inserted without any preliminary hygiene, such as washing, having been performed. As labour went on the examinations became more and more frequent. After the sixteenth I lost count. On our arrival, pains were occurring about once in ten minutes. These gradually increased in intensity and frequency until they were occurring once every three or four minutes. After about four hours I enquired if the membranes had ruptured and was told that they had not. After about another hour no progress seemed to have been made, examinations came thick and fast and the patient began to appear exhausted, although she had never uttered a sound. The husband also was getting worried, and asked me to take a hand. I therefore examined the girl, and found that there was a pulseless prolapsed six-inch loop of cord protruding from the vulva, and an arm presenting in front of the head, so that it was impossible for the child—now dead —to be born. It was, in fact, an early case of obstructed labour, a condition which, though easy to recognize, had been completely missed by the women.

'I told the husband that the child was dead and that the mother would die too if she did not come into hospital. This she rather un- willingly consented to do eventually. In pitch dark and pouring rain, we made the rather hazardous journey, which involved crossing a river by ferry, and we arrived at Tenom hospital about midnight. The mother was attended to, and the child delivered, after manipu- lations, with forceps. Recovery of the mother was uneventful, and she returned to her quarters ten days later.

'An incident which impressed me occurred next day. Another woman on the estate enquired after our patient. On being told that she was well, but if she had not come into hospital she would have died, she replied, "Of course—we know that." The complete acceptance of death in childbirth as a natural consequence was frightening.'

*   *   *

If Tenom is a pocket dynamo, bustling with new energy, Keningau is a spacious, restful town, the administrative head- quarters of the Interior Residency, calm, assured, without any of the roughness of its upstart rival, a society matron sur- veying through her lorgnette some *nouveau riche*. It is reached from Tenom by a dusty track badly in need of bridges that heads north up the broad valley formed between the Crocker and Witti Ranges, and which, after passing Melalap, where the railway ends in an anti-climax (it stops abruptly in the gloomy middle of a rubber estate), gives refreshing glimpses of wide horizons and spacious views.

The Interior Residency of North Borneo is dominated by two rugged monoliths, Mount Kinabalu and John Dingle, the Resident. The Dusuns of Keningau and Tambunan wor- ship both, but the latter commands a wider reputation than the mountain among the other communities of the territory. Native chiefs of Sipitang, close to Brunei, Chinese traders of Kudat, in the north, Europeans in Tawau, in the south-east corner, all regard John Dingle with awe, and while relegating Mount Kinabalu to their Christmas cards commit his exploits to legend.

He is of a dying breed, one of the few survivors of the Chartered Company, and one of the few—Chartered Company or otherwise—who refuses to let the worries of administration deny him the simple pleasures of living. He is a great sportsman, again in the old tradition. The few books of North

Pensiangan Murut

Borneo written by Government officers in the past all dwelt on the enjoyment of outdoor exercise; but not so today. One feels that the complexities of work play too predominant a part in officers' lives, and the time is not far distant, I fear, when assistant-secretaries will write a chapter on their career concerned with the difficulties of administering the Colombo Plan or other dreary subjects.

Dingle's father was the Senior Medical Officer of the Chartered Company, and the boy grew up in North Borneo before returning to Scotland for schooling. He came back to Borneo, entered the Government Service, and was interned in

Kuching during the war. He is now forty-five, and can retire. There has been a Dingle in North Borneo for most of this century; should he leave, the country will be the poorer for his going.

He has captured the affection of the Interior people again in the old tradition, by getting out amongst them, not as a duty, but because he wants a group to play polo against, or he wants a partner at tennis, or he wants a horse heavy enough to hold his frame. He has the build of Aneurin Bevan, and the ponies of North Borneo, game little things though they are, are not quite built for a hectic *chukka* with John Dingle.

In London several years ago I met the late Sir Neil Malcolm, the former President of the Chartered Company. I asked him how he chose his officers. It was quite simple, he told me, and it provided an excellent corps of administrators who quietly and efficiently governed a peaceful, happy country, a feat to be envied in South-East Asia today. Sir Neil's habit when a post fell vacant (and there were not many, perhaps fifty all told) was to circularize the Appointments Board of Oxford and Cambridge. When the various applicants came to Old Broad Street in the city, the Company's offices, for interview, Sir Neil recalls that the crucial question he asked was, 'Play rugger, m'boy?' If he did, he was in; if he did not, he was considered of no use. John Dingle, and the others long since gone, as well as the few remaining, bear witness to the efficaciousness of this simple procedure.

Apart from John Dingle there are two features of Keningau that rather give the lie to its gracious lady pose. These are the new roads that are spreading out from the town, and down which new migrants to the Interior are pouring, and its resettlement scheme for wandering hill Dusuns. Both reflect the pulsating life of new North Borneo rather than the placid, flaccid existence before, and both are destined to play before very long a significant part in the development of the Interior.

The earth road grant to Keningau is being applied to widening a track that the Chartered Company made, along the pad-path of the natives, swinging south-east to Pensiangan, almost on the Indonesian border. This hamlet of a few huts deep in the jungles of the south is the most isolated Government outpost in North Borneo. It is a week's walk to get there, up and down never-ending razor-backs. The present intention is to make this track a road, at least as far as the powerful Sook River, twenty miles from Keningau. It is twenty miles of heavily-timbered territory, extremely fertile, almost completely empty.

I was taken out along it, heading east from Keningau. Formerly the vehicle transport could go no farther east than a mile or so, where flows the Pegalan River, coming down from the north to the Padas at Tenom. This is now crossed by a wooden ferry, angled by steel wire to the current, and on the other side the new road runs on. A bus service is functioning now, and a new community of three or four hundred Chinese has established itself some two or three miles from the river, in what was a thickly-timbered area. Forest giants, with immense girths, and heights of 80 to 100 feet, were burning as we drove through; obviously the first stage of clearing was not yet over, but the jungle was being pushed back, vegetables were being sold in Keningau, a community leader or Capitan China had been appointed, and the A.D.O. had one more responsibility on his hands.

The problem that faces Keningau, and Tenom too for that matter, is that the roads being pushed out from them will provide, are providing, lands for people who demand far more than the isolated Interior can supply. As Sapong said in its annual report, 'The railway became more congested, and at times great difficulty was experienced in obtaining necessary supplies. Building materials were long delayed, and to obtain low priority goods from Jesselton we often had to wait for months after placing an order.' Dingle and others are aware of this bottleneck which increasingly will retard development, and plans are being made for another road, not east but west, west over or through the Crocker Range, a road that will link the Interior with the coast from Jesselton. This is not far off; when it occurs, the boom will really begin.

A few miles north of Keningau is the small Dusun village of Bingkor, lying on a flat scrubby plain, with the Crocker Range rising well to the west, and the Pegalan River flowing down a few miles to the east. Before the war Bingkor was the scene of the Chartered Company's attempt at a Local Authority, and this isolated community was the first centre in British South-East Asia to be entrusted with authority over its own finances. The pioneer experiment had been only partially successful, for there had been no strong indigenous leadership, able to discuss and decide. There had been only one chief of any strength, Sedomin, and the weight of the Local Authority rested entirely on his shoulders. Now retired, and living outside Bingkor in a two-storied wooden house showing many bullet holes from low-strafing R.A.A.F. aircraft, Sedomin is still a power to be reckoned with. Sundang, his younger brother, is the Assistant District Officer under Dingle, and as such is the Government. But when visiting this tough, hard Dusun chief, he is still the younger brother. Sedomin struck me as being the strongest Dusun in the country, as tough as a Chinese towkey, reserved and non-committal, correct but cautious. Should the European ever go, I thought, here is one who will adapt himself without much trouble.

Bingkor today is the site of a most successful resettlement scheme, undertaken by means of a Colonial Development and Welfare Grant. In the Tambunan area, north of Bingkor, the plain is extensively cultivated, and the hill peoples are unable to move down. Their semi-nomadic shifting cultivation too is intense, in some places the cycle of crop rotation being cut down to two years. The result has been the degeneration of large areas to bracken, serious erosion on the hill slopes and landslides.

Their problem was investigated in late 1952, and it was found that many of the Dusuns would like to move, but simply lived from hand to mouth, and just could not migrate. The Government marked out blocks of land on the flat at Bingkor, beside the Pegalan River. Each family wanting to settle there was given fifty dollars to pay for the long trek. Free *padi* seed was supplied them for the first planting, and provided that their work was satisfactory, that the blocks were cleared, fenced and bunded, a small allowance was paid them for the first six months.

By late 1957, when I visited the settlement, over five hundred people had taken advantage of this free land and seed, and the settlement was a most encouraging sight. Sundang told me that the early families had walked in, skinny and disease-ridden, their children mere bags of bones. I saw them, splashing and swimming in the Pegalan nearby, healthy, happy youngsters. The benefits of the move to them were obvious. Leading a settled life, on a plain, by a road, they are at last able to benefit from the Government's medicine and education. The Government benefits by the relief in the strain on the land in the Kirokot area of Tambunan, the increase in wet *padi* production, the addition to available labour in the Keningau area, and the permanent anchoring of a previously wandering community, with all the chances of improving its lot that that implies. It was a small scheme, carefully thought out and flexibly and gradually applied. It was a great success, and it may be the forerunner of more attempts at helping the hill peoples to move to the plains.

Tambunan, the third jewel of the interior (we are excluding Ranau, still farther north, as it is not linked to this pendant), was formerly as isolated as Ranau, for before the war it could be reached only on foot or by pony from Keningau in the south, or from Jesselton, on the other side of the Crocker Range, to the west. It is still unconnected to the coast, although I was driven into the range and shown the beginning of the trail that wound through to Moyog and Penampang, only twenty-odd miles away, but the Japanese with forced levies of labour built an interior road from Keningau northwards across the flat valley through Bingkor to Apin Apin, a road as straight as the Nullabor railway in Australia, and this was carried across the intervening hills to Tambunan after the war by Sundang, so that one can now drive from Tenom north to Tambunan, and if the twenty-odd miles to Penampang was completed, one could reach the coast.

Sundang's achievement was most meritorious, as it was built very largely by voluntary labour. He explained to kampong after kampong how they would benefit from a road, that it would bring doctors and help lower costs, and when he had convinced them of its worth he allocated each group to a section of the pony track which they were to widen and drain.

He had been allocated $3,000 for this road; it was meant only as a gesture, so that it could be begun, but with over

1,000 volunteers, and the vote spent largely on tools, the hills were crossed and the Interior linked up.

There are over 10,000 people living in the Tambunan valley, only 2,000 less than the Tenom area and 2,000 more than Keningau, but its centre is very considerably smaller than either Tenom or Keningau, being nothing but a small village. Here no new economic pulse is throbbing and no administrative machine is whirring, merely the slow, steady beat of an agricultural community closely in tune with nature. With Papar, Tambunan very largely is a rice bowl, and in this more literally than the flat fields of the coast, for Tambunan terraces its small fields as they rise up the slopes, holds back the water by bunds mounting the hillsides, and if you stand outside the Rest House in the cool of the evening the tinkling noise of innumerable falling rivulets is your charming introduction to Tambunan, rice bowl of the interior.

It is intensely cultivated; there are small kampongs everywhere. The whole valley is cleared, in active production, and the jungle long since has vanished. The people are Dusun, divided into two sub-tribes, the Tambunan and the Tegaas, farther north up the valley, and there was a time at the turn of the century when this peaceful valley was the scene of carnage, and these two tribes fought one another and government almost indiscriminately, in the concluding stages of the Mat Salleh revolt.

Lucky countries with scarcely a war tend to exalt the few they have, and to pay excessive attention to them. It is so with Mat Salleh, who will become soon a national hero as he led the only major revolt against the Chartered Company. He was a minor chief on the east coast, who after various disturbances there was declared an outlaw in 1894. After being hunted rather spasmodically and certainly unsuccessfully for several years he crossed to the west coast and sacked Gaya Island, then the chief post, was pursued to Ranau, and was unsuccessfully attacked there. Cowie appeared from London and pardoned him, his action causing most of the west coast administrators to resign. He was given the Tambunan Valley as his private estate, a valley which at that date the Company had never penetrated, and whose people were left well alone.

From here he both harassed the coast and oppressed the Interior, the Tegaas Dusuns siding with him, the Tambunan Dusuns allying themselves with the Government Officer at Keningau. War again broke out as Cowie washed his hands of the affair, and Salleh, after building forts all over the valley, was killed by a mountain gun. It took several more years for his chief lieutenants to be caught, but the fire had gone with his death, and nothing that came after, not even the mad month of the Muruts in 1915, ever shook the Chartered Company again, or interfered with the layers of peaceful administration it was spreading over the people.

I had studied Mat Salleh in detail before visiting Tambunan, had read through all the Chartered Company correspondence on him, and had written in detail of his revolt, with all the paraphernalia of scholarship, in the *Journal of the Malayan Branch, Royal Asiatic Society*, and in my book, *Under Chartered Company Rule*. What I had not done, and it was this that made the trip to Tambunan so fascinating, was to investigate it from the local's point of view.

Europeans have been writing histories of Asia for a long time, basing their work largely on official records, which by the nature of things are European. An entirely new slant is given to our knowledge and understanding of Asia when Asians begin to write, not Europeans, or when we use Asian sources. In a very small way I attempted this in Tambunan. Sundang, who drove me there, was the son of chief Gunsanad, who had been the chief native ally of the Government against Mat Salleh. He told me tales his father had told him; his chief complaint, which came oddly from a Government officer who had spent two years in Exeter, doing a course on local government, was that the promise of the chief of police to give Gunsanad Mat Salleh's head was not honoured. I gathered it would be the central piece of attraction in his house today if his father had secured it. Chief Teliban, who had fought against Salleh as a youth, in 1899 and 1900, when asked what he thought of him, said, 'He was a foolish man, building forts in the centre of the valley, and not hiding in the jungle; and he was unlucky. But he was not a bad man.' Foolish and unlucky, but not bad: I had not thought of Salleh like that, but it is not difficult to see his point of view. Others I questioned throughout the valley agreed with Teliban, and added small pieces by which I built, I hope, a new mosaic of understanding, and so equipped myself for a new interpretation of this revolt against the west.

Mat Salleh's revolt, in a blind, inchoate way, reflected the nationalism then stirring among the countries of the East, and the response of the government of the day, to stamp on him, reflects the outlook then prevalent. Today the reaction has changed completely. Nationalism is a tidal wave you cannot stop, they cry; you can do nothing against it whatever. True it is that you cannot stop a tidal wave, but you can channel it, you can direct it to wide, broad streams, and its force can be used in co-operation, not in blind opposition. Nationalism in North Borneo is bound to grow, but to throw up one's hands and to shout 'This is the end!' is as stupid as wheeling out the guns. Both are extremes, and the sensible path for North Borneo is to see that this tidal wave of nationalism is directed and influenced from the beginning, from the moment the swell begins to rise. Otherwise there will be a far more chaotic and bloody Mat Salleh, and anarchy will be our legacy to the future.

9. MARUDU BAY

ON even the smallest map of Borneo some space has to be provided for the immense indentation in the extreme north, which is Marudu Bay. Kudat, small town on the north-west side of this bay, is its administrative centre, and holds in addition a fourfold importance economically. It exports the three products of the area, rubber, copra and livestock, and it has a flourishing barter trade with the islands to its north as well.

Before the Chartered Company came, the small inlet by the side of the bay was uninhabited. A settlement was founded through the enthusiasm of William Pryer, the first Resident of the East Coast, who urged that it be established, so that small ships sailing up the flanks of Borneo, and threading their way southward through the islands, would have a terminal point where ocean-going liners would collect their produce and proceed to Europe. Treacher, the first Governor, swallowed this theory so well that he made a clearing here and named it the state's first capital. It has always been a little embarrassed about that ever since, for it quickly became not the bustling emporium of Pryer's dreams but a sleepy hollow of coconut growers, and as such, as a backwater of little importance, it is not regarded at all highly by the more pushing of the North Borneo community, who are inclined to ridicule it and pass it by.

To see Kudat in a true perspective, however, one should not take the customary route, either by air from Jesselton, the feeder-line aircraft flying north up the coast, close to Tuaran and Kota Belud, and then along the length of the arm of the western peninsula that divides the bay from the China Sea, or by sea, an overnight trip northwards round the tip of Borneo that brings you to Kudat by early morning, but preferably by small Chinese-owned *tongkang* or *kumpit* from the north, from the lawless, ill-administered and grossly inefficient islands such as Balabac, Bugsuc and Palawan, that are becoming through necessity more and more self-sufficient

with a low standard of living, and which look to Kudat, southwards on the horizon, as a new world.

If you approach Kudat from the north, as I have done, you
thread through the islands, and then cross an hour or so of
territorial water, the last island behind you, the coast of
Borneo ahead. Already you will be able to see Kinabalu
towering up; you move into the clear blue water of Marudu
Bay, some twenty miles wide and forty feet deep, and por-
poises will race to intercept, then gambol a foot or two from
your bows, their symmetrical forms clearly visible in the
depths. On your starboard you pass a dazzling white beach,
and behind it rows upon rows of coconut trees, light green
and graceful against the dark-coloured jungle. The occasional
kampong, small huts wading into the water, as if to dodge
the rainstorm behind, and groups of sailing *prahus* on the
sands, help you on your way.

Nearing the small inlet on the point of which stands Kudat
you turn round several buoys and beacons, signs of organized
stability unknown for hundreds of miles north to Manila, and
as you approach the small wharf, with the little town drawn
up behind, the district office, police-station and dispensary
all clearly visible, you immediately perceive the smart young
policeman waiting for you, the bustle of Chinese-owned
trucks on the inadequate wharf, the collection of *kumpits*
and launches, and overhead the flag fluttering in the tropical
heat, the Union Jack. It is then, when you set foot safely on
shore, when you speak to the policeman and are treated with
respect, when your papers are examined efficiently, and you
know that here stands law and order, that you really
appreciate Kudat, and the men who make it work.

This law and order, these blessings of civilization, were
introduced into Marudu Bay not without a struggle, and they
are maintained there not without effort. If you stand among
the trees on the nearby ridge, on which rests the bungalow
of the District Officer, the view of Kudat on its flat little point
can be encompassed without moving the head. It is a tiny
town by the side of an immense bay; the white sand of the
beach is hot, the breeze is salty and smells of the open sea,
the air is pleasantly warm; it could not have needed much
effort, you may think, to build those half-dozen go-downs,

those few rows of shops, to plant those shady trees and to level a *padang* by the rough sea grass. Appearances are deceptive; an outpost of civilization is not installed and maintained by inanition, but by constant vigilance and much hard work.

Fifty years ago the struggle to survive was exercised mainly on the mainland, as Kudat itself was raided by the remnants of the Mat Salleh rebellion, and only saved from complete destruction by the stupidity and avarice of the raiders, who insisted on sharing the loot before the opposition was defeated. The administration suffered then the consequences of slackness; it would be the same today, it would pay the same price, although the danger is not now from a contented mainland but from an envious collection of barbarians beyond the northern frontier.

A hundred years ago the barbarians were within the bay itself, for while the east coast of North Borneo was controlled more or less by Sulu, and the west by Brunei, this northern area was the pirate haunt *par excellence*, with fierce independent Sherips (chiefs) leading an amphibious life, slave-raiding and attacking every ship that passed, and sweeping with the monsoons as far as Singapore and beyond, and then lying up one of the many small rivers that flowed into the bay, where they stored their loot and repaired their *prahus*.

One of these rivers, the Langkon, was the haunt of the most predatory of the lot, Sherip Osman. He was allied with Pengiran Usop, the Prime Minister of Brunei, and the two of them were working, in the 1840s, for complete control of the whole west coast. Opposing them was a frightened Sultan, supported by Rajah Brooke, who had arrived in Borneo a few years before. From Sarawak, in the far south, he was spreading peace and order northwards, stamping on lawlessness and seeking the British Navy's aid against west coast pirates.

In 1845 he secured undreamt-of support; not just a frigate, or a few jolly-boats of marines, but a squadron of eight warships, commanded by the Commander-in-Chief, Rear-Admiral Sir Thomas Cochrane. It accompanied Brooke to Brunei; Usop was put to flight, and subsequently executed on the Kimanis by erstwhile followers. The squadron then sailed north, and entered the pirates' haven, Marudu Bay, in the innermost recesses of which Osman waited.

Langkon today is a small kampong at the base of the peninsula on which stands Kudat; a foot-track winds over the hills to Kota Belud, and so to Jesselton. From Langkon it divides, one track running north to Kudat, another skirting the bay, keeping clear of the mangrove and slush of the shore itself, to the Bengkoka River in the east, another old pirate haunt. This track will be a road soon, and in less than a decade one will drive there; at present it is primitive, isolated and incredibly quiet. It is impossible to imagine, as you walk or bicycle along, and pass cheerful, friendly faces, that a hundred years ago it was a fanatical slaughterhouse, where violence ruled supreme, and licence and savagery were unchecked. Yet it was here that Usop had his forts, protecting his kampong, here were his thirty-two guns, eighteen- and twelve-pounders, commanded by his ten Arab captains, and here his double-boom stretched across the river, enormous tree-trunks bolted together with large iron plates, and bound round and round with the iron cable of a pirated ship, defences he defiantly challenged the Navy to take, and which protected a vast array of loot and slaves.

It was the scene of a desperate attack by Cochrane's men, in August 1845, in which the courage and ardour of the pirates were of no avail. Hundreds of them were shot down by the sailors, or killed in hand-to-hand encounter, as cutlass clashed with kris. Large quantities of ships' stores and merchandise were secured, a half-dozen large war *prahus* sunk, and Sherip Osman and his wife were killed. The entire fort area on the Langkon River was razed to the ground after a hot day's fighting. I am told that a few charred stumps can still be seen, and that near Langkon rubber estate the grave of Sherip Osman and his wife, of the Sulu royal family, is clearly marked by white pebbles and a headstone; but I did not see them, and there was no one to guide me.

Despite the death of Sherip Osman the instincts of piracy prevailed; it never became the uncontrolled menace of the days before James Brooke, and with the advent of the steamer the curse was contained, but Marudu Bay remained throughout the nineteenth century a place for sailing vessels to avoid, or to hurry past; on naval charts it was marked with the word 'Pirates', and it was not until the coming of the Chartered

Company in 1881 that tales of piracy and slavery died away.

In the late-nineteenth century the little rivers that flow into the bay became sought after as sites for growing tobacco, as planters from Java and Sumatra, short of good land, and controlled excessively by a paternal Government, flocked to North Borneo to participate in a land boom. The long east coast rivers, Marudu Bay, even the islands off shore, all were investigated and found desirable. Tobacco estates, nearly all staffed by Dutchmen, sprang up on the Bengkoka, Langkon and other Marudu Bay rivers, and bales of high-class wrapper leaf chugged across to Kudat in little launches commanded by imperious rotund Dutchmen.

These tobacco planters lived an incredibly tough life, drinking vast quantities of rough gin (there was a vague theory which said it kept malaria away, but I do not think the Dutch concerned themselves unduly with that) and eating tremendous North European meals, totally unsuitable to the tropics. On top of that, as I have been told by unfortunate people who had to work for them, they worked at a tempo that would kill a giant, took the risks of a madman, and paid the wages of a pauper.

They have vanished almost without trace. A few of their estates have survived, Langkon is one, Sapong near Tenom is another, converted from tobacco to rubber, but they changed hands in the process, and the names that once filled the *British North Borneo Herald*, Vorwarts, and Fleming, Van Dyk and De Jong, for instance, are known no more. I doubt if today there is a Dutch planter in the territory; a live one, that is, there are quite a few of the dead. Here is the inscription, taken from the headstone of one. It needs no translation.

'HIER RUST ONZE LIEVELING
CHRISTOFFEL ANTON DANIEL BOOM.
GEB LINKUNGAN ESTATE, 10 JULI, 1916,
GEST 13 NOV., 1918.
SLAAP ZACHT, ADESTIE.'

'Here rests our darling', how poignant are the mother's words; 'Sleep softly, little one.' Death far from home is always sad: there is an added feeling of sorrow when a small child is involved, for there remains the thought that possibly in a gentler clime, in his own country, this sacrifice might have been averted.

The waters of Marudu Bay are peaceful today, but death still lurks in its charming depths. The Rest House of the town faces the long white beach of the bay; you have merely to stroll from the verandah across the road and you are lazily swimming over a firm sandy floor. Shortly after I had swum there I heard that a few weeks previously a small boy, the son of the highly respected and greatly popular doctor, had been stung by one of the Portuguese men-of-war which drift to the shore in great numbers. The pain from their sting is intense; it killed the boy, who died on the beach, in his father's arms. 'Sleep softly, little one.'

The long, trailing tentacles of these almost transparent jellyfish detach themselves, and appear to wrap themselves round whatever they encounter. The *Serang* of the large Government launch based at Kudat, a tough, wiry Malay, showed me thick weals on his leg, and arm, caused years before by an inadvertent encounter with a Portuguese man-of-war, and he told me the pain was so severe that it could drive a man to madness. Yet in appearance it looks harmless, a midget transparent octopus.

The *Serang* showed me his wounds on the way to Balembangan Island, three hours out from Kudat, an island I had wanted to visit ever since the time when as a schoolboy I had read the life of Captain Cook, and the events that led up to his discovery of the eastern coast of Australia. For the man chosen originally to make the journey was not Cook, who knew nothing of the southern seas, but Alexander Dalrymple, of the East India Company, whose explorations, map folios, and writings, had established him as the British expert in these Dutch-monopolized waters, and it had been the representations of Dalrymple that had led the East India Company to establish a new settlement in South-East Asia—the first for over a hundred years—on this green island we were rapidly approaching. Before we anchor, let me tell you the story.

Alexander Dalrymple, a Scot, of good but impoverished lineage, came east to Madras, as a fourteen-year-old writer in the Company's service, in 1750. He worked in Madras, under Lord Pigot, to whom he had been commended, and was chosen as assistant to the Secretary. Madras had become the great centre of the 'country trade', ships under the Indian flag that traded illicitly with the islands of South-East Asia. It was illegal, in that it contravened the East India Company monopoly, but since it dare not risk a war with the Dutch East India Company the merchants of Madras were permitted to continue, in fact they were encouraged, for as the East India Company slowly found itself changing from a trading company into an administering government, it found also that government paid no dividends. All its trading profits, and more, were being swallowed up by the costs of ruling India, and it was only able to continue by the mounting profits of its trade with China, in which the country trade assisted tremendously.

The Company had traded with China throughout the sixteenth century, in a puny sort of way, for almost immediately after the first contact it was made clear to the Europeans that they had virtually nothing to offer in exchange for the silks and other luxuries of China. Whatever they offered, China had it already, or did not want it. The Company turned to India. But in the seventeenth century the position changed, in three ways. The rival English Chartered Companies combined to form one great company; sufficient strength was acquired to conquer India and to make the long haul to China. The people of England acquired a taste for tea; the trade changed as a result from an intermittent one for luxuries, to a steadily increasing one for a staple in great demand. And Britain obtained at last a base in China, at Canton.

One difficulty remained. Whenever the East India Company brought a cargo of tea to London, it made a tremendous profit. But it could have brought a dozen more cargoes, if only it could find a commodity the Chinese would accept in exchange. There were two commodities only that China would consider; silver and tin. As the expenses in India during the eighteenth century continued to mount, and the profits from China became ever more necessary, the East India Company became constantly more susceptible to suggestions that it return to South-East Asia, from which Dutch pressure had forced it to retire in the previous century, in the hopes that by trading there it could secure the tin (from the Malay Peninsula and the islands south of it), and the silver (from the Philippines) which it needed so badly, rather than rely on the country trade. It was in a receptive mood then when Dalrymple made his appearance.

Already he had made his mark in Madras, where he had learned both Spanish and French, and had acquired a considerable knowledge of seventeenth-century trading activities in South-East Asia, before it became the closed preserve of the Dutch. He thought that a trade could be resumed there, and magnified to something far greater than before. He also maintained, and it was here that he first achieved fame, that it was quite incorrect to believe that the 'factory' at Canton, subject to all manner of restrictions and controls by the Chinese as it was, of necessity had to be isolated for six months of the year as well. The Company, faced with a north-east monsoon which blew directly down the China Sea for six months, had accepted the geographical impossibility of sailing directly into it, and ships reached Canton only on the southerly, which blew during the other six months. Dalrymple, from his study of records and logs, said this was unnecessary. Ignore the China Sea, sail east from the Sunda Straits or the Straits of Malacca, go out into the Pacific via the Celebes, or the east or west coasts of Borneo, and then head north-west for Canton. This was attempted, it succeeded, and henceforth contact was maintained with Canton throughout the year.

For nearly a decade after this success Dalrymple escaped from the steamy, stinking writers' quarters of Madras and took to the sea. He wrote voluminously of his travels, constantly urging his employers to move into South-East Asia. Between 1759, when he secured his first command, and 1767, he wrote a score or more pamphlets and books, and edited, with exceptional clarity and neatness, various folios of charts, taken from the logs of earlier ships.

His persistence bore fruit when in 1762 he accompanied the small force from Madras which, as one of the last acts of hostility in the Seven Years' War, captured Manila from

Spain. He was able to bring about the release from prison of the aged Sultan of Sulu, whom the Spanish had captured some years previously. He took him back to Sulu. In gratitude the island of Balembangan was ceded to the East India Company, and Dalrymple returned to London, to acquaint the directors of its possibilities.

While he was in London, his maps and other writings (in particular *An Account of Discoveries in the South Pacific Before 1764*, which was published in 1767) brought him a national reputation, and in 1768 he was asked by the Royal Society if he would journey to the South Seas for them, and in the clear air of the Pacific, perhaps at Tahiti, observe for them the transit of the planet Venus across the sun. He was on the threshold of greatness. Already he had postulated the theory of a vast southern continent, and that there was a Strait between New Guinea and it; without doubt he would have sailed into the eastern flank, precisely as did Cook. But his moment slipped from him.

Throughout his life he was arrogant, stubborn, impetuous. Numerous actions of his bear witness to this, and his portrait substantiates it. He insisted that he be given command of the Royal Navy ship assigned to the expedition. He refused to be merely the leader of the Royal Society team, he wanted all power in his hands. The Admiralty refused to allow the command of one of its ships to any but a Royal Navy officer, and the Royal Society, to solve the dilemma, accepted the Admiralty proposal of a naval officer to lead both parties.

The position was offered to a forty-year-old Lieutenant, James Cook, the son of a farm labourer, who had risen from being a scullion on a Whitby coal barge, and then an Ordinary Seaman in the Navy, to be one of its best hydrographers. He had sounded the St. Lawrence off Quebec, he had guided Wolfe to the Heights of Abraham, he had charted the coasts of Newfoundland, and he had written a paper for the Royal Society. Thanks to the petulance of Dalrymple this was his big chance, and in a ship built for the coal trade he made his observations of Venus and discovered the fertile east coast of Australia.

Dalrymple was slightly more successful with the East India

Company. It decided to reverse a century-old policy, and to attempt to re-open trade among the islands of the Malay Archipelago. The advantages of Balembangan, its remoteness from the Dutch, its closeness to China and the Philippines, outweighed any disadvantages, and a settlement was decided on. Dalrymple was appointed chief of the new factory, and immediately by inordinate demands and bad-tempered disputes, ruined his prospects here too. He was dismissed the service, and the command was given to another, to Mr. John Herbert.

Herbert arrived at Balembangan in 1773, having taken nearly two years to reach there from Bombay, as he paused to sell and buy, to his own great profit, all the way. On Balembangan he disposed of cargoes sent by the Company without informing them, and news trickled back of an island where graft and inefficiency held full sway, as the factors built up their own fortunes.

In other respects, too, the settlement was a disappointment. Remote from any trade route, with nothing to tempt the native peoples or the Chinese to sell or buy, barren and brackish, the factory languished on an uninhabited island. In 1775 it was decided in London to abandon it; but the matter had passed out of the hands of the Company, and its decision came too late.

The island had been secured from Sulu, and Suluk traders were among the few who visited the settlement. Herbert was active but tactless, and he had the stupidity to insult the Sultan's cousin, Dato Tating, and to place him in the stocks. This was unforgivable. On the nearby island of Banggi, in league with his cousin, the Sultan, he collected a large body of men, and led them at night across the narrow stretch of water into Balembangan. The settlement, which faced Banggi, was protected by a stockade, sixty yards in from the steeply-shelving beach, with some nine guns mounted on it. Behind it, stretching up a low hill, were the Sepoy Barracks (some one hundred men supplemented by Bugis did garrison duty), several go-downs, the military officers' houses, and on the peak, the assistant factor's house. Mr. Herbert, for some reason, lived outside the stockade, some seven hundred yards along the beach.

The rear of the settlement faced the jungle; only the beach side was defended. The path of Tating and his Suluks was obvious. On March 5th, 1775, as Captain Forrest relates in his fascinating book, *A Voyage to New Guinea from Balembangan* (London, 1779), a voyage he undertook in a small *prahu*: 'During the night, strict watch was kept all over the settlement. At dawn the gun as usual announced the morning; and for a few moments tranquillity reigned. A house at some small distance suddenly fired, proved to be the signal to the Sooloos. They rushed into the fort, killed the sentries, and turned the guns against the Bugis' guard. The few settlers, lately rendered fewer by death, were fain to make their escape in what vessels they could find.'

Complete panic was created by the amoking Suluks. None of the officers stayed to fight, but fled to the two anchored brigs. Herbert was first on board, from his house on the beach, and although it was not until well past midday that the Suluks turned their attention to it, he never returned. Was he a coward? Or was he, as many suspect, prepared, and was there nothing left in his house that warranted a return?

With the settlement blazing behind them, with the Company suffering a loss of £500,000, and with the Sepoys and Bugis being led off into slavery, Herbert sailed away. The experiment had proved a complete failure, and the lesson the Company drew from it was that if it wished to trade in the Eastern Seas it must first establish its post on or near a great trade route, and then see that the Navy was there to protect it. These considerations led, a decade later, to the despatch of Captain Forrest to the Rhio Archipelago, just south of Singapore. Forestalled here by Dutch vigilance, he returned to London to write his book of travels, while the suggestion of Captain Light, that Penang Island be acquired, was acted upon, and a settlement was established there, in 1786. Singapore, in 1819, another uninhabited off-shore island, followed as a matter of course.

Balembangan was occupied briefly by the Navy in 1803, in its campaign to protect the China convoys from Dutch, French and Spanish attacks. Trafalgar, in 1805, perhaps the most decisive event in British nineteenth-century Far Eastern history, by which it substantiated its claim to Malaya and the waters before and beyond, made any such post unnecessary, and it was withdrawn that year. It was never occupied again, and it was, I thought, off a green, deserted island, tucked alongside the far more massive Banggi, that we anchored.

I was wrong. As we anchored, and then clambered into our small dinghy, we discerned through the bamboo and scrub which lined the sandy shore a small hut. With a rifle over our knees, and the Government flag fluttering behind, we investigated. A small group of devil-faced men came to greet us, clad only in *chawats*. They were Banggi Dusuns, still pagans though living on the coast, growing a little dry rice and securing a few fish by primitive methods. They showed us the way to the old settlement. The dinghy's powerful outboard-motor roared over the calm bay, deep blue water of eleven fathoms close to the shore, as we sped towards the Dusun group that had crossed a point and was waving to us by some *casuarina* pines. Suddenly, right on the beach, the bottom rose up, eleven fathoms, nine, eight, four, and we hit a sandy bay.

There is nothing standing of the East India Company settlement, but its site is clear to see, for the jungle is kept back, in a scrubby clearing 400 by 100 yards, and there are old red bricks and Chinese porcelain scattered over the whole area. There is a legend that there is treasure here, that the Suluks never secured the 14,000 Spanish silver dollars of the settlement, and that it is buried in a well; and there are several half-hearted holes here and there. For my part I collected a piece of Ming ware that the devil-faced man gave me, thanked my lucky stars we had not met on a dark night, and shared a rather odd meal with him, of bananas and rice, and some bottles of beer from the launch; it was fascinating merely to be on the site of Britain's first attempt to move into South-East Asia, for a few weeks later (August 1957) I witnessed the independence of Malaya and with its *Merdeka* saw the wheel turn full circle, and the end of that same British endeavour which had begun there.

We returned to Kudat that afternoon, passing 'Pirate's Point', as the northernmost tip of Borneo was called for centuries, riding easily over a light swell. As we neared the township, the Union Jack quite visible, a powerful speed-boat, with two 50-h.p. outboard engines, roared past us. 'Dato Mustapha', said the *Serang* proudly, and at once I was back in the present, aware again how constant must be the struggle to maintain that Union Jack, for should that man, Dato Mustapha, now whirling round us in a lather of foam, elect not to support it, such is his strength and power among the islands and round the coast that the most determined effort would be needed to keep it there.

O.K.K. Dato Mustapha Bin Dato Harun is perhaps the most powerful chief in North Borneo, a member of both the Legislative and Executive Councils, with an authority ranging farther than any other and an influence extending beyond the boundaries of the state itself. He is young, not yet forty, a small dark dagger of a man, a Suluk only a generation or two removed from unchallenged paramouncy.

Dato Mustapha can remember when piracy was common; his grandfather was one of the bravest, and the life was an honourable and adventuresome one. He does not want to see piracy come again, and he does not want to see the British depart. 'My people are not ready for it. We could not govern this area as once we ruled it, by force of arms and fear; that is out of date. We would be no match for the Chinese, and we must be educated so that we can stand up to them. Perhaps by A.D. 2,000, in forty years' time, we will be ready.' For the present he is prepared to remember his grandfather, and seen at Government House, a slim, shy figure in white slacks and shirt, he attracts little attention, but on his own element, the sea, the tameness disappears, and all the strength, virility and independence of the Suluk stands out in clear relief. I saw him once from a Straits steamship, riding out a storm in a small Government launch. He was completely in his element, and there was something primitive and dynamic about his lithe form that made me realize that the tameness was but skin deep, and that here indeed was not a Government officer so much as a Suluk chief. Daggers are meant to be thrust; is it only his charm that causes the Chinese of Kudat to court him so?

10. SANDAKAN

BETWEEN Kudat and Sandakan stretches an aircraft's flight or a ship's voyage around the tip and down the northeast coast of Borneo. It leads through the Malawali channel into the Sulu Sea. I sailed on the S.S. *Marudu*, which was forced to swing constantly, turning now to port, now to starboard, as it dodged the innumerable islands and cays in its path, like some lumbering and aged rugby three-quarter. I shared the ship, by great good fortune, with several youngsters, to whom every island was a pirate haunt of some kind, and who saw above every sail we sighted, although it was indistinguishable to me, the black flag of the skull and crossbones. Their childish dreams were not far short of reality, for pleasant though the trip was, and calm the summer day, this Treasure Island Sea with its miniature islands of palm trees and sandy bays is murderous and malevolent, and that nearby coastline dangerous and deserted, as Suluk pirates menace again, as they did a hundred years ago, the whole eastern edge of North Borneo.

Sandakan in the freshness of dawn; on board ship the crew are hosing down the decks, and the rattle of derricks being prepared and hatch-covers coming off mixes with the harsh cries of the sea birds, as they swoop for refuse. It is a good time to take your morning tea and banana on deck, for as you enter the great bay through the narrow heads it gives you an opportunity of admiring Berhala, the island in the entrance, sheer red cliffs rising two hundred feet over an idyllic bay of coconuts and white sand, and to pity the lepers who live there, not quite without hope, but desperately short of succour.

Down in the well of the ship the deck passengers are folding up their sleeping-mats, packing away their gear in their cases and paper bags, and crowding the rail. They are largely Chinese, smart young girls, aged men and women; there is a small police detachment, in khaki, transferred to the east coast, and the occasional Muslim, in his best sarong. All is cheerful laughter as they dodge the derricks and help remove the hatch top on which they had been sleeping.

Softly the calm sea slips past, and the morning mists recede into the folds of the ridge that runs down the northern shore. Here clings Sandakan, and there looms her quay. Some half-dozen large freighters are loading timber some distance up the bay, but the quay, the territory's biggest, holds only a small coaster, and the *Marudu* edges alongside.

The great new wharf, recently completed, is the showpiece, the heart of the town. In Jesselton the wharf is tucked away at one end of the capital, rather like a poor relative, and the most outstanding building is its bloated Secretariat, its arms turning in on itself. Sandakan, expansive, throws wide its arms to the commerce of the world, and glories in its quay-side, and the ships that come alongside. In particular are ships from Hong Kong welcomed, and even our small vessel had a crowd to meet it, a bustling, cheery, early morning crowd that was to a man Chinese, Chinese to whom Hong Kong is home.

The East Coast is little more than three Chinese colonies, Sandakan, Lahad Datu and Tawau being three small urban conglomerations of Chinese set in an uninhabited jungle, and hard by long rivers that wind back for hundreds of miles to the Interior watershed. In these three centres, and particularly in Sandakan, the only heartbeat, the only impulse, is economic. There is little culture, less politics; only the stimulus of a wholehearted, intense striving to make two dollars grow where only one had grown before; and even that, even the economic urge, is confined to trade in timber and copra. In the west the urge to build new roads is apparent everywhere; Sandakan feels no great need for roads, for the great rivers and the calm sea are all that is needed for the timber and copra industries, and Sandakan sees little beyond that.

Its one and only road has been extended little since the war, and the jungle presses close behind. Sandakan faces the harbour; the harbour *is* Sandakan, and while its few administrators solemnly rearrange the go-downs and shops on the narrow flat, everyone else goes to work, fights for a living all day and then goes home. It is a bad place for claustrophobia, Sandakan; even to stand on the ridge and look out to sea, or gaze across the immensity of the bay is to feel a prisoner, hemmed in. No wonder people meet the ships, no wonder there is cheerful waving to friends on board, for the prison door is opening, and here comes the outside world.

Sandakan, as much as Singapore, is European-inspired. A hundred years ago there was nothing but jungle pressing down to mangrove where Sandakan now stands, and scarcely a kampong anywhere in the bay. In the 1870s Cowie and his gun-runners had established a hidden base, far up the bay, behind a protecting island and reached only with difficulty, and it had attracted a few natives who settled there. Outside the bay, and near the entrance, Suluk, Balignini and Bajau pirate fleets attacked every kampong within sight, in their pursuit of slaves, and the whole coastline was in anarchy.

In 1878 William Pryer was deposited at Cowie's old station, 'Kampong German' as it was called, and while Overbeck and Alfred Dent busied themselves in London he was left to reduce this anarchy to order. Almost unaided he slowly extended a circle of peace and profitable trade, until the pirates had been driven from the bay itself and then from the neighbouring coastline and rivers, until his sure possession of the territory was recognized by Spain and Holland, and the country was in the safe hands of the Chartered Company.

Pryer founded Sandakan. His base at 'Kampong German' was unsuitable as an administrative and economic centre, remote as it was, and when it was burnt down in June 1879 he collected the chief men of the village and told them the pirates had been dispersed sufficiently, and the villagers were strong enough, for a move to the harbour entrance. His drive, more than anything else, made the jungle and mangrove a thriving settlement, bigger in three years than any other post in North Borneo.

He was a likeable, hard-working enthusiast. Here is a typical day, taken from his diary: August 12th, 1879.

'Kept the three gangs at work clearing, killed a twelve-foot crocodile, sent the boat to Balhalla to collect *rattans*, settled two or three matters with Hadji Omar and sent off the gig to Kg. German for more planks. Found a ridge of rocks, very thinly covered, right across where we were making the *Jimbatan* and had to pull down all the posts, and start a new place.

'Slopped about in the mangrove and water for at least two hours and got stung by a medusa, superintended planting a lot of broken bottles round the fort pagar, changed my coat twice and my trousers three times in the course of the day. Sat down to a dinner of first-rate fish, partridge of probably a new species, and roast pig and apple sauce, no vegetables, brandy and water, bed at 8 p.m.'

Pryer worked furiously in these years, settling disputes, attacking pirates, encouraging the jungle trade in *rattans*, birds' nests, *damar* and camphor, inducing natives to settle in the bay and Chinese to trade with him from Singapore. His efforts succeeded, and after the Chartered Company was formed, in 1881, and following a two-year choice of Kudat, Sandakan became the capital city.

A rather vivid picture of the man of 1883 was written anonymously in the *British North Borneo Herald* some forty-odd years later.

'Dr. Walker lived a little out of the village, and beyond him again, approached by a bridle path, was Pryer's *attap* Residency. Some half mile beyond that again was Pryer's experimental "Beatrice" estate, in charge of F. G. Wickam, whose abode consisted of a wooden platform on high posts and an *attap* roof—cool and airy, but unsafe for sleepwalkers, there being no side walls.

'Pryer, a busy and enthusiastic soul, would periodically enliven us by rushing in excitedly with his latest "discovery" in Borneo's assets. He was a very charming and likeable man. An ex-amateur champion boxer, utterly fearless with man or beast; a magician with snakes, the collection of which he made a hobby, he once seriously upset the nerves of a party of officers of H.M.S. *Magpie* he had taken for a walk in the jungle after lunch. He was leading us, talking, when he suddenly dived into some undergrowth, shouting "Grab his tail!" While we started, he immediately reappeared plunging about grasping a twenty-foot python by the neck. Its horrible wide open mouth and dangerous aspect chilled us stiff, until Pryer's Malay orderly, pushing past us, hurriedly seized the monster's tail, and Pryer, gasping out, "Lend a hand!" partially restored our senses, and we flung ourselves on the brute's tail. Then the orderly rushed to the other end and hacking away with his *parang* at the brute's head and jaws reduced it to impotence.

'On another occasion, when walking along a bridle path with him, I noticed a pretty little fern growing at the mouth of a hollow in the side-cutting, from which a boulder had dropped or been washed out. It was above my head, and reaching to pick it for my flower pots, I sprang back at a sharp hiss and the elevation of an ugly, squat snake's head with angry eyes. Next moment I was further startled by Pryer pushing me aside as he sprang up and, quick as a flash, seized the reptile by the neck and calmly holding on to it as it writhed furiously around his arm with its three feet of muscular body, poked it under my nose while he endeavoured to point out to me the form and number of scales on its lower jaw to denote its classification among poisonous varieties of reptiles. I was an indifferent pupil and kept well away from him as he strolled along with the horrible thing which he said he was going to send to the London Zoo, alive.'

Pryer, the rugged individualist who had carved Sandakan out of the jungle, the only Englishman on the east coast of Borneo, found the presence of other Europeans restrictive. Living cheek by jowl on the ridge overlooking the harbour by 1883 were the Governor, Colonial Secretary, Treasurer-General and various others. They were cooped up there, and friction developed. Pryer left the Government in 1892 and began growing a variety of crops outside the town on the Byte and Kabeli estates. He married a woman who adored him and whose diary is one long tender love-story. The natives kept coming to him for redress of grievances, although he had left the service, and even Mat Salleh asked for his intervention to settle his problems, when he threatened Sandakan in 1895. Unfortunately, Pryer was on sick-leave, in Sulu; it is possible his understanding of and authority among the natives might have solved the crisis before the rising reached serious levels. His years of slogging through the mud, of unremitting work in the jungle, took its toll in the end. He left Sandakan, a very sick man, in 1898. He died on the way home at Suez, at the age of sixty, and was buried there. His wife came home alone, to write her *Decade in Borneo*. There were no children, and today his name is unknown, even in the town he founded.

Eighty per cent of the population of Sandakan is Chinese, the highest proportion in any town in North Borneo, and yet the most powerful institutions in this Chinese town are those of British commerce. There are innumerable Chinese concerns as well, but there appears a fatal flaw in their business techniques, which restricts them to a maximum size. One Chinese company owns a third of the town area, with timber concessions, copra interests and general importing agencies as well. It is possibly the biggest Chinese company in the territory, yet it is infinitesimal compared with the European. It appears virtually impossible for the Chinese, despite their single-minded pursuit of money, to advance further than the family concern. The blood-tie is the only substantial link in commerce. That is why nearly all the largest Chinese firms, in North Borneo as elsewhere, remain as family businesses, restricted by the size of the family, and the need for tight parental control.

Pre-eminent among the European business houses in North Borneo is Harrisons and Crosfield. For nearly forty years it has been the major economic concern in the territory and it has built up an unrivalled concentration of power. This power has not gone uncriticized, and its monopolies by some are resented; yet it is a power that has been wielded with acumen and restraint, and were the Quaker founders of the firm alive today they could not but approve the activities of this, their remotest offspring.

Harrisons and Crosfield was founded in 1844, when three Liverpool merchants, Daniel Harrison (aged 49), his brother Smith (26) and young Joseph Crosfield (23) combined, with a capital of £8,000, to enter the tea trade. The East India Company had lost its monopoly rights for the importation of tea from the Far East in 1833, and the great market was open to individual enterprise. Each of the three Quakers worked hard and efficiently, and a sound, solid business emerged. At the end of the first year the partners' balance-sheet showed assets of over £50,000, with liabilities around £40,000; a profit exceeding £3,000 had been earned.

In 1857, just over a hundred years ago, Smith Harrison opened a branch in London, in Great Tower Street, and it soon became and has remained the head office of the firm. Content for some time to build on its tea business, it expanded tremendously following the addition to the firm, in 1894, of two of its most brilliant employees, Heath Clark and Arthur Lampard.

Clark laid the foundations of the trade in blended tea, and occupied the managerial chair during the first World War and after; Lampard not only achieved fame as a pioneer of planted rubber but was primarily responsible for the establishment of offices of the firm in Ceylon, India, Malaya and the then Netherlands East Indies.

The first overseas branch was established in Ceylon, in 1895, and the first tea estate was purchased there in 1899. Lampard moved into India in 1900, opening in Calcutta. Canada and the U.S.A. were now figuring prominently as customers for tea, and offices were opened in the U.S.A. in 1904 and in Canada in 1905. At the same time Lampard was launching Harrisons and Crosfield into the almost untouched rubber business, being attracted to Malaya by an employee who had been approached by an old Malayan hand, W. S. Bennett, who wanted to sell his 2,000-acre coffee and rubber estate. Lampard formed a syndicate, the Pataling Rubber Estates Syndicate, Ltd., and managed in 1903 after some struggle to secure the capital needed, Harrisons and Crosfield supplying £1,000, to this, one of the first public companies floated in London for the purpose of growing rubber.

This proved a tremendous success. In 1910 dividends aggregating 325 per cent were paid, and whereas the Pataling Company had been floated with much labour, there was an eager rush to other issues floated by Harrisons and Crosfield, both in Malaya and Sumatra. The success of their estates was partly due to the policy begun by Lampard, who saw clearly that the talents required of a first-class planter were not always combined with the qualifications of an accountant and an all-round businessman. The policy he adopted then was to engage the best planting talent for the management of the estates, and to give them the support of an outstanding and experienced planter as Visiting Agent, and the assistance and co-operation of the firm's own office in matters of business finance and accounting. An office to implement this policy was opened in Kuala Lumpur in 1907, and, to assist its tea estates, in South India as well.

The following year the old partnership of 1844 was replaced by a limited liability company, a change made necessary by the vast commitments and the need for adequate finance. Harrisons and Crosfield, Ltd., capitalized at £307,500, made their bow. A new epoch had begun, for with ample new capital, subscribed in 1910 and 1911, Lampard initiated moves that increased its tea and rubber interests and moved it into general trading activities as well.

Its expansion into North Borneo occurred in 1918, shortly after Lampard's death, by the acquisition of Darby and Company. At that time W. G. Darby was the uncrowned king of trading and shipping in the territory, and with Lease was the most prominent unofficial in the state. He had come to Sandakan from Hong Kong a quarter of a century before, had secured numerous agencies, had managed a timber company, had built an ice-works and had instituted the Sabah shipping service of coastal vessels. All this was sold to Harrisons, who formed, as was their custom, a local subsidiary, Harrisons and Crosfield (Borneo), Ltd., to continue the expansion. In 1920, together with the Chartered Company, it formed the British Borneo Timber Company, with long-term concession rights. It expanded into the estate business, as in Malaya, and it secured the Straits Steamship agency, by which it secured a percentage on everything shipped in or out on this lifeline of the territory.

In North Borneo today the Company has offices in Sandakan, Tawau, Jesselton and Labuan; in Brunei; and in Kuching, Sarawak. It has interests in the British Borneo Timber and the Bakau and Kenya Extract Companies. It has the importing rights for the products of over forty great firms in the United Kingdom, Europe, Australia and America, ranging from Ford cars to Nestlé's milk. It is the agent for over twenty shipping lines, for four air lines and for nine rubber estates. It handles all types of insurance, it exports copra and jungle produce, and it is fostering yet another subsidiary to handle the growing engineering work in the territory.

It is a flourishing, if minor offshoot of the giant London concern. Eric Millar, the present chairman there, went on the first board, in 1908, and he has guided its development since he was elected to the chair in 1924, inserting it into new opportunities, carefully husbanding reserves and directing developments in its numerous subsidiaries in the United Kingdom, North and South India, Ceylon, Malaya, Java and Sumatra, North Borneo, China, Australia and New Zealand, Japan, Canada and the U.S.A. He, no less than Lampard and

the three founders, reflects that rare combination of unobtrusive shrewdness, cautious yet imaginative, sound but
daring, that embodies the Quaker business virtues. The
parent firm has a paid-up capital of some three million
pounds; a small sum considering the vast assets it controls.

This colossus is now being challenged in North Borneo by
other firms from Hong Kong and Singapore, but their competition is not thought so dangerous as what Mr. Jones, the
Jesselton H. and C. man described as 'The major post-war
economic development in North Borneo'. This is the growing custom of the Chinese firms of dealing with London or
Sydney, and not through the intermediaries, such as
Harrisons and Crosfield. In a friendly discussion with Chinese
and Europeans, it seemed clear that the former were slowly
making less use of H. and C., and that the general importing
business would gradually decline. However, in all the H. and
C. buildings I visited, with the wholesale crates, sacks and
bags on the ground floor, trucks backing to the door, and the
various departments above, shipping, insurance, general business, etc., the scene was always a most animated one. The
manager, in the post-war uniform of the European businessman, slacks and shirt, long-sleeved and tied; the dozen clerks,
Chinese, in open shirts; the fans whirring overhead, the type-
writers, the pretty Anglo-Dusun girls in gay skirts and
blouses, the papers in the *rattan* In and Out trays, the heat;
everyone doing a job, the young Europeans in particular
holding responsibilities and taking decisions far heavier than
their counterpart in grey old London. There was no sign of
slow death here, nor even of middle-aged sickness, which
some critics point to; Harrisons and Crosfield (Borneo), Ltd.,
has all the signs of vigorous young life.

Harrisons and Crosfield, the North Borneo Trading Company and the other European-controlled firms in the territory maintain themselves because they have links overseas
unknown as yet to the numerous Chinese businesses, and
because they are reputable. When more Chinese competitors
come to acquire these two assets the inherent advantages will
vanish, and there will be clear-cut competition.

Untroubled by such prospects the two great British banks
in the colony face each other in Sandakan on opposite corners,

their new head offices in contrasting architectural styles, but each offering to the commercial community of North Borneo a similar safe service. The Chartered Bank (formerly the Chartered Bank of India, Australia and New Zealand) and the Hong Kong and Shanghai Banking Corporation, have no rivals whatever; there are no Chinese banks in the territory, and the two share the business between them, not in any complacent manner, but in a fiercely competitive spirit, that by its nature makes that business grow.

Banks to many people are dull. I find it hard to understand this. I still wonder at the oddness of seeing so solid a British institution among the jungles of South-East Asia; it is a matter of great pride to see the amazing collection of individuals who push into its air-conditioned hall, and who deposit their money trustingly within it. I watched a Chinese labourer cash a cheque, Indian and Chinese merchants, the most charming of girls, her exquisite *cheongsam* betraying a visit to Hong Kong, the Paris of the East, and many others all making casual use of the bank. Here is something that can be trusted; it is as simple as that. It applies in reverse, too, as Mr. Marshall, the manager of the Hong Kong and Shanghai Bank (the 'Honck and Shank') epitomizes; here is something that trusts you. Between Chinese towkey and English bank there is a close understanding, and, I venture to think, a greater respect, as between equals, than exists between Government, aloof on its hill, and businessman in the town.

The actual working of a bank is fascinating, and so, often, is its origin. The history of the Chartered Bank appealed to Compton MacKenzie, whose *Realms of Silver* tells in clear close prose the story of its founding, in 1854, by James Wilson, who had founded the weekly *Economist* a few years before. As with Harrisons and Crosfield, it was the end of the East India Company's monopoly in China and India that attracted Wilson, and in the hundred-odd years since then it has continued to expand in Asia (Australia being denied to it), until it has become, although never changing its constitution or losing its independence, perhaps the greatest bank east of Suez, rivalled in East Asia only by the Hong Kong and Shanghai.

Although in 1888 it secured the services of Sir Alfred Dent, the founder of the British North Borneo Company, and although he remained a director for nearly forty years, it did not venture into North Borneo until after the Pacific War. Neither did its great rival, which had been founded in Hong Kong itself in the 1860s by Chinese and European businessmen who regarded the Chartered and other concerns as more interested in India, and inclined to treat their requirements as secondary; both came to North Borneo in 1946, which until then had existed on a State Bank, and their new buildings, in Sandakan and Jesselton particularly, and their adventuresome spirit, have added much to the increasing development of a new colony.

Banks and business are not the full story of Sandakan, although there is little more to tell. Along the northern shore of the bay, clinging precariously to the slope, are the timber mills and the *cutch* works that combine with re-export of copra to keep the wheels of commerce turning. The labourers for these concerns live in large five-storey buildings, like wooden prisons without a surrounding wall, that strike an anachronistic note; 'coolie lines' have long vanished from estates, to be replaced by family units, but here the old remains. The *cutch* works, one of the oldest businesses in Sandakan, boils mangrove wood in immense vats, extracting from the bark a dye. It ends its tour of the grim, dark factory a solid toffee; it is bought largely by American firms, and competes with other dyes and tannins in the leather and clothing industries.

Like all concerns in North Borneo, the *cutch* works suffers from a lack of labour. So, too, does the nearby mill of the British Borneo Timber Company, the H. and C. subsidiary which on its formation in 1920 was granted a monopoly of timber-exporting rights in the territory. It was a sweeping concession necessary in 1920 to attract overseas capital. It was out of date, however, after the Pacific War, and following discussions between the Government and the B.B.T. it was revoked in 1952. The contract clause insisting on a mill was retained, however, and imposed on all new timber-seekers, despite the labour shortage, and the distance from the market; no mill in North Borneo works now to a profit, and the whole east coast is hoping that the mills may go where they belong, hard by the large consumers, in the United Kingdom, Hong Kong or Australia (the three largest buyers), where requirements that are constantly changing may be catered for by immediate alterations in output, and where skilled labour can be easily secured.

A timber mill is perhaps the only assembly plant where one unit comes in and a multitude goes out, directly reversing the general pattern of a factory. In the B.B.T. mill, completely rebuilt since the war, 120 different types of cut-wood are produced, from a minimum of two different species, by eight grades. If any one of those types is replaced in popular choice or housing decree, or planner's whim, in the far-away market, it takes weeks for that decision to reach the mill; that is why the most impressive thing about the mill is the row upon row, the stack upon stack, of cut-wood for which there is no demand. As the chairman of the Company said in his 1957 report: 'The position has been reached in which the quite reasonable profits on logging are offset by losses on sawmilling.'

Sandakan above all else is a port for the export of logs. In 1952, the year when the British Borneo Timber Company surrendered its concession, the territory exported 3·1 million cubic feet of timber, compared with the five million of 1940. In timber as in everything else the heavy nightmare of the war had hung too long. In the following five years it was thrown off. Exports in 1956 were 15·7 million cubic feet, an unprecedented boom, in which Sandakan and the east coast generally participated.

The waterfront commands the attention of all eyes, and the development going on behind the town is little noticed. There is one road, the metalled version of the track Pryer began, the Leila road the prisoners-of-war marched down in 1945. Then, as now, it faced the jungle; but since 1945 the crowded Chinese of the town have climbed the ridge in unprecedented numbers, and have settled along it to such an extent, in new smallholdings of rubber, with little rubber mills, in vegetable gardens and such like that the 1951 Census Report listed it as one of the six most rapidly developing areas in the colony. There is an undoubted land hunger among the Chinese in Sandakan, and it is a pity that this ex-

pansion inland is not encouraged, and the diversification of
its economy assisted, by the provision of feeder roads and
'Jeepable tracks'. But the attention of the local authorities is
on the waterfront and the new town rising over the ashes of
the post-war fires that have conveniently destroyed the temporary wooden buildings. It was in a hired taxi, alone that I
visited the bustling area behind the town, and it was with
some astonishment that I heard (having seen what the west
coast and Interior had done) the lack of roads attributed to a
shortage of P.W.D. equipment.

North of Sandakan there stretches an undeveloped and
little-visited coastline; for a short period in the 1880s there
were one or two tobacco estates there, but ever since, as for
long before, it has remained a virtually uninhabited tangle of
jungle. There are two big bays, and two long rivers, the
Labuk and the Sugut, up which there are one or two minute
kampongs. At one of these, Beluran, at the entrance to the
Labuk, there is a Government station where resides the
Assistant District Officer, the one European in the whole
area.

He watches over this native area with the minimum of
fuss, and the minimum of staff. He must travel constantly if
he is to do his job well, not merely in Government launch
up the coast and out to the numerous islands, but in *prahu*
up river, and on foot as well. Many of the natives are Bajau,
and such is the lack of research into them that there is as yet
no English-Bajau dictionary, and the district officer must rely
on Malay, while compiling, if he is sensible, his own list of
common words. Some of the kampongs up river are Dusun,
still pagan; others are Muslim; all are very primitive, and the
main activity, and the little wealth that exists is on the coast.

Here amid idyllic surroundings, the unspoilt Borneo, of
native kampong over a calm sea, coconut tree and flaming
flower of the forest, laughing brown urchins splashing and
diving in the water, watched by tall white herons, it is his
task to supervise two native-controlled activities, the collection of turtle eggs and of seed pearls. The little islands where
the turtles lay are well known, and the collection efficiently
organized. From July to October, the main months of this
seasonal venture, the huge lumbering turtle waddles up the

beach in the dark and lays a large collection of eggs. Unknown to the mother the cascade is being collected behind her by a Bajau who has tendered as much as $4,500 for the privilege. Over half a million eggs are exported, at $2.50 a hundred. Well over a million are consumed locally.

The seed pearl beds, apart from one brief Japanese interlude when Mikimoto endeavoured to cultivate them, have remained a native preserve, and the sea-borne Bajau has attached to their collection certain ceremonies and customs that have been little recorded. The young students of Kent College, I believe, are hoping to record some of the songs of the Bajau, while Dr. Polumin of the University of Malaya has filmed some of their dancing; but they remain largely unknown to the anthropologist, their customs and their language waiting to be studied.

A pioneer in this field is Pike, who for several years was the D.O. among them, and who was invited to participate on the island of Tetabuan in the ceremonies performed before the seed pearl crop was harvested. The ceremonies are two: a *berongsai*, or three unbroken nights of dancing round a pole, a phallic symbol, for this basically is a fertility rite, and the *berubat*, or ceremony at sea after the *berongsai* has ended.

The dancing consists of a very simple step, the women holding on to the pole and going round it in a group, the men holding hands on the outside. Pike writes:

'They sing practically all the time from dusk to dawn their *pantums*, which are usually impromptu verses to a set rhythm and time; first the men and then the women answering them; there is usually one man who sings the main *pantum* and the rest join in a sort of chorus. It was all in Bajau, so I could not understand it very well, but judging from the ribald laughter they sailed pretty close to the wind. Amongst these people it is a characteristic that on such occasions you can sing practically anything you like without giving offence, but if you should take a lady's hand you commit a sin.'

Following the three nights of dancing, during which no one is permitted to sleep, there come three days in which no one is permitted to sail; finally the fields are visited. Pike sailed out with the Sherip and amid much noise and fluttering of flags revolved over the bank three times, and then landed

Seed pearl ceremonies

on a shelf of rock, known locally as the *keramat*, or place of miracle-working.

'The Sherip vanished ashore with some rice and some flags, and while he was absent on his holy mission the *kulintangan* (a series of gongs struck with wood) and drums ceased playing. On his return the main flag was planted over the pearl bed, and then everyone after some prayers took a handful of rice and scattered it on the water, and then returned to the kampong to the accompaniment of gongs and drums once again.'

Pike further records a rather strange sequel:

'On the way back a little fish jumped into our *prahu* (there were twenty people on board, with a freeboard of little more than two inches, so it was not difficult) and made its way back to the stern, flipping and flapping all the way. No one would touch such a good omen; it passed me, and stopped at last before the Sherip. He picked it up, said a few words, opened its mouth, spat into it and threw it back into the sea. It was, he said, the first time a fish had jumped into his boat while he was conducting the *berubat* ceremony. It was an excellent omen, he added, that it had happened when I accompanied them. They have such a way of paying a compliment that one almost believes they mean it.'

The pearls on these sheltered banks are collected by Bajau divers. The water is warm, the depth insignificant; so too are the pearls they recover, for fifty would fit on your finger-nail. They go to China with the birds' nests from Goman-ton, to satisfy another unique Chinese demand. They are crushed into fine powder, and the powder is then bottled and sold to the herbalists throughout China and South-East Asia, to become an indispensable element in many a Chinese medical prescription. All manner of queer and expensive things figure in the prescriptions of Chinese doctors, and are kept for them by the herbalists in their peculiar shops. The teeth of the Peking man were found in one shop, the tusk of the rarest Malayan animal, the rhinoceros, and the long-extinct dinosaur in others. But it still seems bizarre that amongst them are pearls dived for by Bajaus in a remote corner of Borneo, to satisfy a 2,000-year-old prescription. Do they do any good, I wonder?

11. PIRATES

IMMEDIATE CHIEFSEC JESSELTON FROM RESIDENT, SANDAKAN. OFFICER LAHAD DATU REPORTS SEMPORNA RAIDED PIRATES LAST NIGHT. SEVERAL DEATHS INCLUDING POLICE AND ASSISTANT CONSERVATOR FORESTS. RAIDERS BELIEVED FILIPINOS IN TWO KUMPITS. AM PROCEEDING SEMPORNA WITH POLICE.

WITH police. . . . The Police of North Borneo always have had a difficult task, and post-war piracy has added to it. Not only have they had to maintain law and order among widely diverse peoples, to whom the Penal Code is an alien commodity, but they have had to be ready, at all times, in the absence of any other military force in the colony, to undertake punitive expeditions against rebels, or against pirates and raiders from other countries. They have to be the police, the army and the navy of the territory; yet all these engagements are being fulfilled admirably.

It is the more difficult for them in that there is no competition. The spick and span, the efficiency, of any single army unit comes in part from a determination to surpass the standards of a rival unit. Each destroyer of a flotilla strives to excel her neighbour, and no police force in Britain is unaware of what is happening in the next county. North Borneo is a long way removed from any such external spur to efficiency, and in the territory itself no internal encouragement is visible. The emphasis, in business and in government, as in the home life of most of the constabulary, is largely on comfort and ease. Men dress in a casual fashion, and act in a casual manner. *Tid'apa* (do not worry), the Malay equivalent of *mañana* (tomorrow will do) has become a universal attitude and a common saying; slackness and slovenliness are only just removed from the standards considered satisfactory, and the manners accepted as desirable.

Standing four-square opposed to this, functioning with a smartness and efficiency that must demand a constant effort to maintain, in the absence of all outside stimuli, and in complete contrast to everything around it, the North Borneo Police Force welcomes comparison with any of the battle-tried army units I have visited in Malaya, and far surpasses any of the police forces in the countries surrounding it.

This efficiency and smartness, which I witnessed in a number of unrelated incidents in my tour of North Borneo, is not an inhuman, impersonal standard. The relationship between the 1,000-odd men and officers of the force is friendly and unaffected; a welfare clinic run by the officers' wives at the Marina Barracks, the Jesselton headquarters, is symptomatic of the attitude. The refresher courses for old retired members of the force, who are still serving as village constables, feel like home-comings. It struck me very forcibly that here was an integrated team, that the officers and men, far more than any other department I visited, were one unit doing the same job, as efficient and as mobile as the Royal Navy.

Piracy, as instanced by the cable that began this chapter, is no new thing to North Borneo. It has a history far older than the European in these waters, and it has never been completely suppressed. The Chartered Company began and ended its days with lawlessness on the east coast, and the peoples off shore, whether Bajau or Suluk, Balignini or Illanun, have been regarded always as pirates first and traders later. During the twentieth century, the Chartered Company, the Royal Navy and the American administration of the Sulu Archipelago, eliminated the nineteenth-century curse of slavery, but could not altogether suppress piracy, and with the departure of the Dutch and the Americans the islands and territories to the east of North Borneo, in particular the Sulu Archipelago, reverted to a considerable extent to the nineteenth-century anarchy; but with one significant difference: the pirates possessed twentieth-century arms and methods of marine propulsion.

Rex Blow, who is now the District Officer of Jesselton, served in these islands during the war, fighting with the Suluk and Filipino guerrillas. He, and a few others, had escaped from Berhala prison camp. Blow came back into the Philippines, and as *One Man's War* by H. Richardson bears witness, well-earned his D.S.O. He and the other guerrilla groups were fed lavishly by submarine with American small-arms; rifles, automatics, machine-guns in particular. A great quantity of arms remains there today, and it is this, plus the powerful motor-boats, that make these pirates the menace they are. What has saved North Borneo from more of the raids that have devastated Semporna and Tungku, for instance, is that the people of the southern Philippines (including the Sulu Archipelago, which stretches to the North Borneo horizon) are Moro and Muslim. Those in the north are Filipino and Christian, and luckily for the colony the two are constantly clashing. It is only in the brief moments of peace, when the dozen or so naval units from Manila have returned north, for example, that the territory fears for its outposts, and the *kumpits* coming eagerly across with their copra are eyed with additional care. For it is then, as it was in March 1954, that death strikes the east coast.

The attack on Semporna has been so far the most bloody post-war affray. It is typical, however, of what might happen again. It was completely unexpected. At about 5.30 p.m. on 29th March two black-painted *kumpits* came alongside the jetty of Semporna, which extends to a reef some two hundred yards out. It was a peaceful afternoon, and the arrival of *kumpits*, tear-shaped boats with a raised cabin aft, and a voluminous hold for'ard was quite normal.

Gerald Chong the Customs clerk was sitting on the jetty with Bajau Chief Jaji, watching the bright-coloured fish among the piles, and pleasantly discussing the end of another lazy day. They both got up to check the boats and to question the occupants. From less than twenty yards' distance the Suluks opened fire with automatics and rifles; a second later and the two on the wharf were running for their lives, through the small Customs shed that straddled the jetty, and then down the two hundred yards of planking to the land. Jaji dived into the sea and swam out to some motor-boats; Chong kept running until he reached his home. Both were unharmed.

Close behind Chong followed the raiders, firing as they ran. They were in some sort of jungle-green uniform, probably surplus war equipment, and nearly all of the twenty had white half-masks over their faces. They came level with the collection of launches tied and moored half-way down the jetty. Mr. T. Barnard, the young English Assistant Conservator of Forests, was fishing from the deck of one at the time, and he dived inside, fetched his rifle, and began firing. He was shot several times, fell back, the launch was leapt upon and he was overrun, to be slashed to death by *barongs* (heavy Suluk knives). A youth, Manak bin Ganap, who was also fishing, was likewise killed, and all the motor-boat engines were smashed.

The pirate force, minus one, killed by Barnard, now divided, and part of it re-boarded a *kumpit*. The small shop centre of Semporna was about half a mile away, along the coast past the police-station, and while one group advanced on it by land, the other quietly crossed the water and landed in the rear, on the other side of the town. This tactical move won them the town.

Semporna possesses one of the few pre-war buildings in North Borneo, a venerable old blockhouse, built at the turn of the century as a strong-point in a turbulent area. Two-storied, built of *billian*, a local wood harder than mahogany, with thick shutters, it was once the scene of a mad episode told in *Land Below the Wind*, when a long-term prisoner found himself alone inside it, and kept the police at bay for several days. He showed, and so too did the Suluks, that block-houses are only effective if they are not surprised. The Sergeant in charge of the small force, Sagar Singh, was playing soccer. On hearing the firing on the jetty he ran to the block-house, and began firing at the force moving up from there. Behind him, unobserved, came the Suluks who had landed from the *kumpit*. The front door was open, a burst of automatic fire killed him and two constables, and the station was overwhelmed.

At much the same time small groups had attacked the small dispensary, destroying a wireless there, and as the transmitter at the police-station was smashed Semporna was cut off. Some of the shops were now looted for several hours. In particular the Capitan China, Wong Mui, a goldsmith, and Hassan Gobra, an Arab, suffered big losses, although many of the others were not touched. The raiders, who spoke Suluk and

Bajau, and who knew the town well, made the people carry goods to the *kumpits*, which were run ashore as in the minor raid of 1952, below the shops.

Almost all the inhabitants of this little settlement had fled when the shots first were heard. The Capitan China and Lee Po Tat, another shopkeeper, who delayed their departure, were fired at but escaped, but a tailor, Pan Chee, was killed in a lane behind the shops. Altogether eight people were killed, thousands of dollars' worth of goods were stolen, and over five thousand rounds of ammunition, two Owen and Bren guns captured, all for the loss of one man. Jubilantly the raiders left in the dark, and quietly vanished among the maze of islands. By the following morning they were outside territorial waters, and were back in the Sulu Archipelago.

They left undestroyed one motor-boat, moored some distance away from Semporna, which they had not seen. This set off for Lahad Datu, on the other side of Darvel Bay, which it reached at 8 a.m. Forces from here left immediately for Semporna; another force left Sandakan a day later, to bury the dead and to begin an investigation that is still proceeding.

Successful piracy is difficult to keep quiet; the raiders of Semporna, by their bragging and their loot, were soon known among various circles in the Sulu Archipelago, and the identity of the ringleaders quickly established. They did not slip back into some remote kampong and merge themselves into an inconspicuous background, but ventured after more loot instead. Ten of them were caught in August 1955 by a Filipino gunboat when attacking a village near the ancient settlement of Zamboanga, for centuries the southernmost base of the Spaniards. Jamiri Musa, the leader, was a notorious pirate. He, and Imam Issa, and the eight others, were found guilty of homicide, robbery and rape. In addition, they all admitted of their participation in the Semporna raid the previous year, and stated that the rest of the band were all dead.

One alone survives, and that is partly the reason why a new concrete blockhouse is rising alongside the old *billian* one in Semporna, why the look-out at the top, wedged between sandbags, scans so closely the sunlit panorama before him, of sea, islands and sailing craft, why his loaded Bren-gun traverses every *kumpit* that chugs across to the jetty, and why unceasing contact is kept with Sandakan; for Abdul Kalil, the Suluk still at large, was the leader of the Semporna raid, the brains behind its success, and he may well return, to kill and loot again.

Abdul Kalil is a name that keeps occurring, when piracy is discussed on the east coast today. Speculation is equally as rife concerning the whereabouts of one particular *kumpit*, the *Ailsa Craig*, which leapt into prominence in March 1957.

Tungku is a small village on the north side of Darvel Bay. A hundred years ago it was itself a pirate haunt of great notoriety, the Royal Navy attacking it, and the Chartered Company destroying it as late as 1883. It was largely to control its piratical depredations that Lahad Datu farther up the bay was established, followed by Semporna. Before that the Bajaus of Tungku had acquired Borneo-wide reputation, and had attracted to their kampong the Illanuns defeated by the Navy and by Brooke on the west coast.

Seventy years of Chartered Company rule had tamed the settlement considerably, and it had become a peaceful place, with Chinese shops straggling along the coast just a few yards in from the beach at high tide, living on its fishing and its coconuts, when on March 21st, 1957, it received back some of its own medicine.

At six-thirty in the morning, shortly before high tide, a dark-red *kumpit* came right on to the beach at the edge of the village. A group of twenty-three armed men jumped out and opened fire. They quickly split up into groups, and guided by the shouts of a man with binoculars, who stood on the *kumpit's* cabin, moved towards various objectives. One group of four ran for the small police-station in the middle and to the landward side of the village, firing as they ran. One village police constable, who was washing, ran to the village shouting the alarm. The other rushed to the station, arriving a few brief seconds before the raiders; he grabbed his rifle, but was unable to get to the box where for security reasons he kept the ammunition. As the pirates burst in he threw his rifle into some bushes outside, and surrendered.

With the police taken captive the *kumpit* was loaded with goods taken from the shops at the eastern end of the village. It then backed out on the still-rising tide, and moved to the

Above: Mt. Kinabalu from Kota Belud
Below: Taking fish from a fish trap net at Tawau

INDUSTRIES, *facing page, above, left:* A Cantonese 'receiver' grades tobacco leaf
Right: Malay worker with manila hemp fibre
Below: Water buffalo grinding copra
This page, right: Tractor logging at Kalabakan
Below: Mangrove bark going into a factory to produce cutch, used for dyes and tanning

Water-buffalo plough

i Padang Papar

Rubber from seedling to slab:
Above, left: A new bantam hoe being tried out at Tuaran Agricultural Station
Left: Tapping. A new incision sends latex into the cup
Above, right: A plantation
Below, right: Bajau boy lifts latex slab from the coagulating tank at a factory

OIL FROM THE SEABED

Right: A tower for underwater boring. *Below:* "The Orient Explorer", a mobile oil-drilling platform, is towed away on a three-months' voyage from Southampton to North Borneo. Constructed to withstand a 100-m.p.h. wind, the platform has a helicopter landing-stage and air-conditioned living-space for 56 men

centre of the shop-houses, and finally made a third landing at
the western end, as the villagers, under the watchful eyes of
the armed Suluks, carried out their goods and loaded them
into the hold of the *Ailsa Craig*.

When it pulled itself off the beach, the tide just beginning
to ebb, it was half-past nine. In three hours it had collected
nearly $50,000 worth of loot, including four powerful out-
board-motors, $10,000 worth of jewellery, $9,000 in currency
and numerous bales of cloth and goods of all descriptions.
The pirates had destroyed the police-station and the office of
the Government clerk, but had harmed nobody.

Like the Semporna raiders, they were armed with Garand
rifles, carbines and pistols, and were dressed in dark-green
slacks and shirts, with cloths over their faces. It had been a
well-planned raid, and the moment and manner in which it
was executed showed excellent local knowledge. Bajaus, still
living in their *prahus*, their hair burnt brown by the salt and
sun, and Suluks, inhabit the coast. Their loyalties are not to
the Chinese- and European-controlled settlements of North
Borneo, but belong to the water which unites them to other
islands almost within sight. In both cases Muslim shops were
spared, and the planning that will go into the other raids of
the *Ailsa Craig* undoubtedly will take into consideration the
Muslim community in the proposed attack area.

In June 1957 an R.A.F. Sunderland tried to discover her
as she proceeded south, later to sack a village in Indonesian
Borneo, south of Tarakan, killing five, but it was a fruitless
mission, and the *Ailsa Craig* still pursues her piratical path.
She confines herself, as do her sister ships, largely to the
islands that stretch from the Philippines to the Celebes, where
virtually a state of anarchy prevails, and where there is not
the fear of capture or retribution that might come were
North Borneo attacked.

The North Borneo Police have organized a Marine
Division to combat any raids that might be contemplated,
and its deterrent value is playing a significant role in maintaining peace. The Tungku raiders, for example, were extremely lucky to slip away that March morning, for the news
of the raid, brought by a villager to Lahad Datu (for some
unexplained reason he went past another wireless post,

Kennedy Bay, that could have flashed the information earlier) just failed to catch a patrolling launch when it was in a position to intercept. By a hair's breadth those raiders escaped; the next may not be so lucky.

The Marine Division, with its headquarters in Sandakan, is led by Inspector J. A. Stephenson. Where does he, or the force as a whole, turn for inspiration, for competitive imitation or initiation? What other police force in the world is fighting armed piracy? Indonesia? Will he learn anything there? The Philippines? He has established the closest unofficial contacts, and there is a very much appreciated exchange of information, but its methods are not his, and as with 'Chips' Plunkett in Jesselton, the driving force for his planning and for his efficiency must come from within himself, and from the *esprit de corps* of the force he leads.

Under him there are eighty sea-police; some are Dusun, who have adapted themselves very well to their marine life, while the others are locally-recruited Bajau, being paid for what they love, hunting men at sea. Their equipment is constantly being improved, and the bad days of the early post-war period, when a few heavy old launches were all that were available, have long gone. Stephenson has four fast *kumpits* and three large launches constantly at sea on a systematically unsystematic patrol. They are all in radio touch with the land, where the force keeps constant watch. There are high-frequency sets that can transmit or receive from the craft at Tawau, Semporna, Lahad Datu, Sandakan and Kudat, and at Jesselton as well. Ready for immediate co-operation, the R.A.F. in Singapore maintain a Sunderland flying boat for sea-patrolling.

The Marine Division guards not merely against piracy but undertakes the work formerly done by the Preventive Section of the Customs, and in its patrolling it is constantly on the watch for other raiders, not pirates, but Filipinos who race across in slim craft powered by 25- or 50-h.p. outboard-engines, to strip the coastal mangrove of its bark. This bark makes *cutch* in Sandakan; in the Philippines it makes liquor, and the Division in its attempts to stop this illegal massacre of a North Borneo asset has steamed 52,000 miles in its launches and *kumpits*, captured 43 craft, and arrested 113

Filipinos, all caught on the job, wading in the mangrove, or trapped at the entrance to a river or inlet. But both bark-cutters and pirates have diminished of late, and the Marine Division guardedly claims some of the credit, while keeping its launches and *kumpits* constantly on patrol.

It is not expected, however, that they could stop a pirate from attacking North Borneo. Should the deterrent value of this force be weighed, and found wanting, it would be comparatively simple for a *kumpit* or two to cross to North Borneo unapprehended. *Kumpits* come into Sandakan, Kudat and Tawau in droves from these islands, to secure a better price for their copra than that prevailing in the Philippines or in the Archipelago. A pirate *kumpit* could conceal its arms among the sacks of copra, and when intercepted by a patrol boat could give every indication of being a peaceful trader. It is the way back that he would find difficult. Loaded with bales of cloth, sewing-machines and outboard-engines, with a crew member wounded and the ship's papers unsatisfactory, even if the raided village had not passed word of the attack, the *kumpit* would be too suspicious a character altogether. And should the village be linked up by then with the radio service, and news of the raid be broadcast, the *kumpit* would stand a very slim chance indeed of escaping.

Nevertheless, it was the considered opinion of the Marine Division that further attacks would be made. The pickings are so tempting. Even tiny Tungku yielded nearly 50,000 dollars' worth of loot, and there are few kampongs now in Sulu as prosperous as that. Among the small east coast posts that would attract the pirate, and which are well aware that they may be attacked in the near future, are Mostyn, in Darvel Bay, still without radio, and reached by a chain of useful islands, and the area round Beluran, north of Sandakan, which though it possesses a transmitter has a large community of Bajaus, and is in danger of being neglected by the Government. Stephenson considers the danger as state-wide, and that there may well be attacks from the islands to the north of Kudat on Tanjong Tajan, on the Mantanani Islands, and on some of the small, peaceful, unprotected west coast kampongs: 'In fact', he said, 'wherever there is a Chinese trader living on or near the sea, as in the Lokapas case.'

The Lokapas murders, to which Stephenson was referring, could easily have paved the way for an era of sea-borne crime. The threat still hovers, but the painstaking, persistent work of the police in solving the murders, and in hanging the criminals, has created an impression, which not even the Marine Division had done, that crime still did not pay. The action taken over this case, has, more than any other single factor, re-created among the peoples of the north and east that feeling of a minimum sense of security to which they are entitled and which formerly was lacking. It was the first time since the war that pirates were apprehended and hanged by the North Borneo Government, and in the story of the Lokapas murders all the difficulties of maintaining law and order can be discerned.

Lokapas is a small kampong near the Malawali Channel, not quite midway between Kudat and Sandakan. In October 1955 Lokapas consisted of only two buildings, one a shop and the other an old store-house. The shop was run by a young Chinese named Ng Sze Lee, married to a Bajau girl named Raniah binte Ati. They had three children, aged five, three and fifteen months, and they lived there alone, trading with the surrounding kampongs and the nearby islands.

Early on the morning of October 3rd a *kumpit*, carrying ten men, tied up at the small jetty. Sze Lee, perhaps, was a little apprehensive, but he recognized several of the men with whom he had had dealings previously, and he invited them into his shop, distributed cigarettes to them, and enquired what he could do for them. He was suddenly and savagely attacked, the men drawing *parangs* and slashing at him as he stood before them. He fled from the shop, screaming in agony, fell, was slashed again and again, and, as the blood poured from a severed arm, from wounds in neck, abdomen, shoulders and back, died in an agonizing moment.

The mob turned back to the shop. Raniah, crouched over her children, was hauled off them, slashed, and allowed to run to her husband. They caught up with her by the jetty as she fell sobbing for mercy. A multitude of blows from razor-like blades sliced into her head, neck and shoulders, and she too died.

Ignoring the infants, screaming with terror, they ransacked

the small shop and took anything of value to the waiting *kumpit*. A sewing-machine, pressure lamps, rice, flour, sugar, kerosene, some gold rings, a locket . . . perhaps in value $1,500 all told. The reward for this murderous morning's work was about $50 in cash for each robber, some food and clothing, and an odd ring or two. Such was the value of two lives. With the *kumpit* loaded they placidly moved away, and vanished among the islands.

Four days later, on the afternoon of 7th October, the two dead bodies, badly decomposed and mutilated by wild pig and dog, were discovered. In the shop, lying on a mat, were the three children, barely alive. The eldest had found some sugar, and on this alone had kept herself and the babies alive. They were picked up, taken by friends to a nearby kampong, and the police at Kudat informed. The police were quickly on the scene, and embarked on a heart-breaking tour of all the islands and bays, discovering kampongs so new or so minute that they were unrecorded, and at all of them finding from the natives (Obians, or Bajaus) a complete lack of information. They were confronted with a blank wall, and as the investigating officer Basil Arrowsmith says, in his report published in the *Police Magazine*: 'Islanders remained most unco-operative throughout, and were of no assistance to the police whatever.'

One small shred of information was obtained, passed on in a frightened whisper by a Chinese shopkeeper. He had over-heard a man whom he had heard called Imam Sayang enquiring on the jetty of his kampong (which had better remain anonymous) whether the shopkeeper on Lokapas kept a large stock of stores and cloth. In his boat were some seven or eight other men, and the towkey, not liking their appearance, had not allowed them to land. They had left at dusk, the towkey said, in the general direction of Lokapas. He felt he had seen Imam Sayang before, in kampong Ungas Melantah on the island of Malawali. But no one there knew of an Imam Sayang, and his description was that of every Bajau. The hot scent grew cold; the constant circuit of islands died down; 1955 gave place to 1956, and another murder was unsolved.

Arrowsmith plodded on. He discovered, in April 1956, six months after the murder, on information again obtained from a Chinese, that there was a woman at Ungas Melantah married, it was thought, to a man calling himself Imam Sayang. Again this name, and again this kampong. She was watched as closely as possible in an obviously unco-operative area. In August Kudat heard that she had left in company with a man, and had gone to Tiga Island some forty miles away, and close to Philippine waters. The island was searched; no one was found. Another dead end, and as a last chance Arrowsmith in Kudat radioed the police launch to return to Ungas Melantah and make quite sure she had left. He reports the sequel, in which Ahmad, the police sergeant

'at first light on August 18th, 1956, using a small rowing-boat, landed at Ungas Melantah before the kampong was awake. The whole place was searched. The woman was found. She denied that Imam Sayang was with her, insisted that she had not seen him for over a year, and that he was residing in the Philippines. Nobody else could or would offer any further information. As the police were leaving the kampong, however, Detective-Sergeant Ahmad saw a *kumpit* anchored about a mile off shore, with two persons on board making a great pretence at fishing.

'Ahmad called on them to identify themselves, and the elder answered, "I am Imam Kullang—*Imam* (holy man) of Ungas Melantah." Now Ahmad just having had a conversation with an Imam Kullang was therefore somewhat suspicious to say the least. The *kumpit* was covered, Ahmad reported by radio to Kudat and was instructed to bring them to Kudat for interrogation.

'In Kudat the younger of the two men identified himself and was released. The elder man, however, at first refused to answer any questions at all, insisting that he was a "Holy Man" and should not be subjected to such indignity. Eventually, however, he agreed that his correct name was Imam Sayang, and that he had arrived recently from the Philippines on his first visit to North Borneo. He denied strongly and indignantly that he was in any manner connected with the Lokapas raid, nor had he ever heard of the place called Lokapas.

'When he had admitted that he was Imam Sayang, he was thoroughly interrogated. Discrepancies appeared in his story, and finally he admitted that he was a party to the raid, but that he was not the ringleader, but merely the follower of the headman of Ungas Melantah, and Imam Kullang at the same kampong. The police launch hovering off the island was informed, and on August 21st, 1956, the two were arrested. At last the one small lead of the whispered name from the frightened towkey had led to success. The case was broken.'

Interrogation of these three by Arrowsmith found them eager to incriminate five others. Three men were taken from Ungas Melantah, and the other two, after a frustrating search of the island-dotted sea had proved fruitless, were found sitting on the grass outside the police office in Kudat, endeavouring to overhear the interrogation of Imam Sayang. Another was caught later in Lahad Datu.

As constant cross-examination built up the story of the crime, a considerable portion of the loot was recovered from the kampong, some of it (the gold rings, the pressure cooker, a locket) identified by a Chinese shopkeeper and sister of the deceased. Their evidence subsequently was invaluable, for the kampong to the end remained blank. It transpired that the Imam and the headman of the kampong, although heavily incriminated in the raid, had not taken part, but had remained on the island. The seven others were charged with murder, and after a most difficult trial on October 31st were sentenced to death. They all appealed; one, the native arrested in Lahad Datu, was acquitted. The Governor-in-Council commuted to life imprisonment the youngest (aged twenty), and the eldest. The other four, on January 8th, 1957, were hanged at Jesselton prison.

A large number of relatives from Ungas Melantah had sailed round to Jesselton to hear the trial. They had stayed on for the hanging. On their return up the coast the small flotilla of *prahus* was struck by an unexpected storm. The boats carrying the relatives of the murderers capsized, and a number drowned. This act of God, even more than the punishment of Government, created a tremendous impression. It is still recalled in awed tones.

Lokapas is deserted today. The small jetty is in ruins, and the single shop-house and its store are crumbling down. The jungle behind is slowly advancing over the silence that once carried the laughter of happy children. The elder two are being cared for in Kudat by the chairman of the local Hokkien Association, and the youngest child is in the care of the deceased woman's sister. They are well and happy; Arrowsmith had to thwart an attempt by the brother of the murdered man, living in China, to have the young girl sent to him. He felt they should stay in Kudat until they were old

217

enough to decide for themselves, for 'I do not think', he wrote, 'that the life of a Sino-Bajau child living in China would be very pleasant. She'd more likely be treated as a slave.'

I met Arrowsmith on a rather dirty morning of drizzle, when the *Marudu* stopped her engines just before dawn, and picked up this policeman who had intercepted her. He clambered aboard from a small *prahu*, a big, jovial man dressed in jungle greens, very fit, very efficient, very well-liked; and that, in a nutshell, is the North Borneo Police. It is criticized by the unthinking, for with the medical and education departments it is the biggest spender of Government money in the country, and it provides excellent quarters for its Dusun constables that excite the envy of others. Yet should trouble flare up, should racial hatred replace the good-will among peoples in North Borneo, or the islands really begin mass-raiding, this little force will be stretched to its utmost, and those most ready to criticize now will be the first to complain at lack of protection and inadequate police. Let them be thankful for the faithful service of the P.C. 49s, and the fitness and efficiency of the few officers who lead them. Should they go, as the Lokapas murders showed too clearly, anarchy will return, and only the Suluks and Bajaus will profit from that.

12. THE SOUTH-EAST

TAWAU, the capital of the south-east coast, is the most stimulating town in North Borneo. It has one drawback, which it shares with its big brother farther north, Sandakan; it has an inferiority complex. It is constantly sneering at the west, at Jesselton in particular, in a thoroughly bad-tempered way. The rivalry between east and west coast, which has existed for over fifty years, once was pleasant; but of late the cries of the east that it is being neglected, that the Government does not help it, that no one ever visits it, and that the west coast spends all the money the east coast earns, have taken on all the querulousness of sick invalid. It is unpleasant to hear such cries from a grown man, and it denotes a maladjustment somewhere.

The cause of the illness may lie partly with Jesselton, for undoubtedly there is excessive centralization in Government, and much that the east coast could do must be referred to the west. If Tawau and Sandakan were permitted greater freedom of action this frustration might vanish, and their inferiority complex disappear. But the fault must rest partly with Tawau itself, in failing to ignore, as inconsequential, the indifference shown towards it by those outside its small isolated community, and in persisting in strident attempts to secure recognition, forgetting that the frog that croaks loudest often comes from the smallest pool.

Tawau is at its most pleasant when it forgets the outside world and becomes its unaffected self. The morning after I arrived a note came round the Rest House listing the visitors to the town by name and inviting them to play cricket. It was the friendliest game imaginable. Peter Edge, the Resident, was the wicket-keeper, the bank manager the bowler, and a most varied collection of Malays, Chinese and Europeans came and went in a most informal manner. The morning's activity was controlled by the bank manager's wife, who, from the steps of the Club gave everyone fifteen minutes' batting and some bowling. If you dropped a catch, the Red Cross benefited by a dollar; if you hit a six, which was dangerous to the children nearby, it cost you fifty cents.

The morning passed to the click of bat and ball, in an atmosphere of unforced, completely matter-of-fact goodwill between all races and grades of responsibility. The green *padang*, on which we played, was alongside a charming new

Tawau market

Club, used by all races. Sheltering in the shade of a group of *casuarina* pines, it stands by the sea, which laps its verandah at high tide. Beside it was a children's playground, sensibly fenced in, and on the other side a new concrete swimming-pool. Nearby was the Rest House, a pleasant, informal structure in which Timorese servants strove with terrible concentration to master the complicated ritual of serving a plate of food, which they watched you eat with unabashed amazement.

This was Borneo at its best, a leisurely, multi-racial community happily living together. Here I hope is the future of North Borneo and not the deserted community centre of Sandakan, for on this *padang* and in that Club I saw retained all that was good of the legacy of the past, and in the Resident, tall, lanky, unassuming Peter Edge, I met one of the finest of the few Chartered Company officers still serving his territory.

The teams gathered in the Club after the match, and each player in his own way relaxed with his friends. The Club provides a room for the mah-jong enthusiasts, and there was a group of young Chinese busily clacking the counters as we cooled off on the terrace. Another room, complete with table, was for billiards, one of the favourite pastimes of the Malay, and the bar, of course, seemed the magnet for the European.

On the terrace I met four of the leading Chinese of Tawau, and was amazed to hear that they had concluded a million-dollar copra deal with China in the Club. The four were Hakka, and had agreed to combine to meet the demand. 'But surely you discussed this in the Hakka Club, or the Chinese Chamber of Commerce?' I asked, thinking of Singapore or Sandakan. 'No, here,' said Sim Cheng Pang, the chairman of the Chinese Chamber of Commerce. 'We arranged all the details at this very table, with Malays playing billiards on one side of us, and Europeans drinking on the other.'

Hong Teck Guan, the most prominent Tawau citizen, a solidly-built man, cautious and watchful at this interview, waved a hand over his back to the water behind. Out in the calm strait between Tawau's rickety old jetty and the long-protecting bulk of Sebatik Island, a ship was anchored. 'There is the result,' he grunted. It had come to take 2,000 tons of copra to China; and to try and develop the trade still further he, Cheng Pang and William Thien, another of the *kongsi* (as a business group is called) had arranged to visit the mainland and to meet their customers.

Teck Guan is a name to conjure with in North Borneo, for his business interests range the territory. In talking to him I had the feeling of great power, in the traditional sense of a Chinese businessman. I was surprised he was a Hakka, and fascinated to hear that this Chinese, who spoke no English, who felt, I am sure, no affinity whatever towards the institutions or the ideals of the west, had yet used this all-races Club for the most holy of ceremonies, the concluding of a business deal. With his associates, Willy Thien, Cheng Pang and Richard Tai, I had a most absorbing conversation, and we met under the friendliest of circumstances; but yet I found him threatening and frightening, not by his manner, but by what he represented, for to me he represented the ruthless, overwhelming strength of China.

The east coast shares little of the political interests entertained in Jesselton, Beaufort and elsewhere. William Thien echoed half-laughingly the old saying of the Chinese: 'We do not mind who holds the cow, so long as we can milk it.' This indifference to politics extends even to the local scene. Tawau is an important port, with a highly favourable balance of trade, and with interests that conflict or compete with other centres. But it has proved extremely difficult to find a Chinese to represent the town on the Legislative Council in Jesselton, or to pause even for a moment from the amassing of wealth to participate in the affairs of the Town Board. They are all prepared to grumble in the coffee shops about the old wharf, the lack of electricity and the shortage of police, but no one is willing to devote an appreciable amount of his time to any attempt at remedying the situation. Edge fights an uphill battle for Tawau, largely on his own.

Tawau is the boom town of the territory, and is playing a role in some respects similar to that of Singapore in the 1830s. It is a well-lit and well-policed bazaar in the jungle of lawlessness that surrounds it, and it is mushrooming through the desperate attempts of the nearby islands to reach it and so secure an equitable price for their produce. Just as Singapore, by its good government and open doors flourished mightily (and still does), so Tawau, by a similar policy, stands out like a beacon amid the surrounding darkness.

In particular it is booming because of its copra trade with the Celebes. In a fatal effort to acquire funds, the Government of Indonesia, that is to say Java, has copied the restrictive practices of the régime it overthrew. The Dutch system of restraint and regulation has been taken over completely, and the economic impulses of the vast Indonesian area are

covered by a maze of controls. These stand in great contrast
to the British policy of free trade; they stand in contrast to
the Dutch as well, in that the Dutch at least could enforce
them, whereas the Javanese have found it increasingly difficult, and at times impossible, to control the export trade of
the islands now only nominally under their control.

In the areas outside Java, power now rests with the army
commanders. In the Celebes, for example, Colonel Sumual,
the commander, is in complete control, able even to restrain
Soekarno, the President, at the airport, and to send him back
to Java to the accompaniment of Makassarese abuse. It has
ever been the same in Indonesian history; the islands are not
complementary to one another, and for most of their life they
have lived independent lives. Only when there appeared a
particularly strong man, with a particularly strong navy, such
as Kertanagara in the thirteenth century, was an empire such
as Madjapahit's able to emerge. Java today has neglected its
navy, and its islands now defy it.

Colonel Sumual, in the old town of Manado, in north
Celebes, permits, even encourages, the trade with Tawau, for
by the permits he grants to the sailing vessels he secures
enough to pay his army. The levy, which is paid willingly
enough, in ports as far apart as Manado, in the furthermost
north-east tip of Celebes, Tolitoli, in the north-west, and
Butung, down in the south-east, ranges from $2,000 to $500.
Once that levy is paid the boats can sail across to Tawau, and
secure the best possible price for their copra. There are no
other regulations (except that they are denied the use of an
engine, outboard or otherwise, as Sumual would not be able
to catch them), no restriction on port of exit, no insistence
that one 'national' firm must be used, no control whatever.
The result is an ever-increasing trade, of great benefit to
both parties.

With Mr. G. R. Johnson, the Customs man, whose sun-
burnt and freckled face denoted a lifetime of outdoor activities in the New Hebrides and Solomon Islands, I spent several
hours going over the mass of sailing craft either drawn up on
the flat beach before the rows of smart new shop-houses, or
else anchored between the shore and the end of the long jetty
that stretched over the shallows to the deep water beyond.

There were over forty boats in Tawau when I was there, the largest commercial sailing fleet I have ever seen. Not one of them had an engine; they relied entirely on their large mainsail and jib, for they were all single-masted, usually of fore and aft rig. In appearance the fleet varied considerably. Perhaps the most attractive was the *lette*, with a lateen sail hanging from a huge curved boom rather like an inverted elephant's tusk. It carried no jib for'ard, and in long hauls, such as from Butung to Tawau, a journey possibly of several weeks, the danger of running before the wind would be considerable. Only extreme conservatism has retained this rig, of pre-European vintage, and kept its narrow lines, with curved upswept bows and stern. The *lambo* is a stocky, blunt-sterned schooner, with an incredibly downward-stooping bowsprit that must dip into every swell it meets. It is broad of beam, ideal for the stacking of many bags of copra. So, too, is the *jongkong*, rather similar in appearance, but gaily-painted on the side and stern, whereas the *lambo* is plain to the point of austerity. The *padangkang* has an upswept curved stern, but otherwise resembles the *lambo*. Both have a rather stumpy mast, and are gaff-rigged. Finally I crawled all over a *lipa*, a small open boat, with no cabin, no deck, a boat far more primitive altogether, not far removed from a big dug-out. Yet this has sailed from south of Tarakan, in south Borneo, and as with the others carried enough water in stone jars to make the voyage non-stop, and enough copra in piled sacks to make it profitable.

Sumual got his territory under control in late 1954. The Customs collection at Tawau the previous year was two million dollars. In 1954 it was 2·3 million. In 1955, when the *lambos* started coming across in scores, the Customs revenue rose to 3·4 million, and in 1956 it was over four million. It had doubled in four years, and it is still rising.

Teck Guan and other towkeys in Tawau feel that the trade will continue, that Java will accept it as she has accepted the Sumatra trade with Singapore, and that it will provide a much needed stimulus to the east coast. It seems to me that this hope could well be buttressed in some way by more concrete information. Tawau is a trading centre; if it is considered necessary to visit China, one of the countries buying copra

from Tawau, surely it is equally as desirable for a representative to visit the Celebes, the major centre that sells to
Tawau. Johnson knows a lot about copra, learned from the
boats, but the quiet visit of Edge, for example, might discover
a lot in Manado itself that would benefit Tawau and thereby
the territory, for whereas the *kumpit* trade with Sandakan is
from Sulu, wild and lawless, the Celebes is adequately
administrated and considerably dependent on the goods it
secures in Tawau for its standard of living. The sooner an
official relationship between the two is established the better
for both concerned.

Copra has become the third major export from the colony.
In 1956, a total of 70,000 tons, valued at over 23 million
dollars, left the territory. Over half this export had come from
the Celebes or Sulu, which had exchanged it for an astonishing range of commodities. Tawau exported $300,000 worth
of cigarettes, for example; Nescafé is another popular buy,
and material, chocolates and sugar all sell well. In and out
of sheltered Tawau has sailed over a quarter of all the small
craft listed in the colony's Customs return, some 3,300 vessels
in the course of a year.

The Government regards this trade as uncertain, and considers it too unstable a basis for any improvement plan for
the harbour. The wharf is inadequate; four ships were
anchored off shore when I was there, waiting their turn to use
it, and the thousands of tons of copra had to be stored in
various sheds throughout the town, as there was insufficient
space on or near the jetty. The Straits Steamships from Singapore are cynically convinced that the Government is waiting
for them to knock it down, so that a claim can be lodged
against them, and when meeting the *Kimanis* or any other
of the fleet that turns round here, the common procedure is
to walk back up the jetty some distance as it comes alongside,
as the few old piles bend and sway like soft butter.

If this trade is transitory (and really no one has adequate
information for a decision one way or the other), and the imports suddenly stopped coming, through piracy on the high
seas, for example, Tawau would collapse as would have Singapore in the 1830s, for nearly 70 per cent of Tawau's revenue
comes from this *entrepôt* trade. But in a few years, and it is

this, and not merely its fleet of schooners off shore that makes
Tawau so exciting, developments now beginning will snowball so that the town (its 1957 population was five thousand)
could well become within a decade the largest in the territory, and go on to match the expansion of the west coast, step
by step.

Apart from the re-export of copra, Tawau has its own
9,000 acres of coconut trees, second only to Kudat's 19,000,
in a colony-wide total of 45,000. This crop has been left
largely to smallholders in North Borneo; there are few plantations of any size, and although the coconut tree is a charming sight its crop has not been developed scientifically. There
is no increased price paid to the farmer who produces better
copra, for example, and the quality of the North Borneo
export is abysmally low. The Sulu or Celebes product is
better. Livestock flourish under the palms, but here again no
scientific investigation of maximum numbers or advisable
rotation has been undertaken. Economic use of the coir from
the husk has not been studied. Copra, for all its value to the
territory, has been ignored, and one of the steps that may well
increase the value of Tawau's export is a Colonial Development and Welfare Scheme to devise a copra grader, and an
Agricultural Department determination to investigate all
aspects of its production.

The giant of Tawau is the Colonial Development Corporation's Borneo Abaca, Ltd., which since 1950 has controlled a
number of estates on the gently-rising slopes behind the town,
including the largest rubber estate in the territory, an old
Japanese concern of nearly 13,000 acres, which in 1956 produced over five million pounds of rubber. It is one of the few
rubber estates that is not following the thirty-six in Malaya
and the half-dozen or so in North Borneo into sale and frag-
mentation; it is one of the few that is clearing new land and
is both re-planting and planting afresh with high-yielding
plants. Here is a solid and developing basis for Tawau's increasing prosperity.

The Japanese not only grew rubber here, but manila hemp
as well, and in the expansion of this crop by Borneo Abaca,
Ltd., there is another agricultural development of the utmost
significance to Tawau. Since 1950 the British Government

through its Colonial Development Corporation has spent millions of pounds in resuscitating and reviving this ex-Japanese property. Its 1957 Annual Report, for example, lists £3,400,000 as assigned to North Borneo projects, of which Borneo Abaca, Ltd., is the chief. It is money well spent and wisely administered. The estates of Borneo Abaca have become the outstanding asset of Tawau.

They are administered by 'the boy wonder', as 29-year-old Peter Wise is called. A brilliant man with an extremely competent team underneath him, he has his Company now showing a profit, and there are those who point to him as the ultimate head of the entire Empire-wide corporation. Without doubt, although the effort to restore efficiency to his vast rubber estate was painful, his major problem has been the economic production of manila hemp. This he has now achieved.

Borneo Abaca grows manila hemp on three estates near Tawau, of which Table Estate is the most important, with a total area of some 3,500 acres. It is the only manila hemp grown in the Empire or Commonwealth. Some 150 tons a month are produced, at an average cost, thanks to very efficient machinery and management, of $900 a ton. It is sold at prices that rise and fall round $1,300 a ton. Not unnaturally, the hemp acreage is being expanded, in particular at Table Estate where another 500 acres are being planted, and fresh areas are being investigated nearby.

Tawau possesses the four essentials for successful manila hemp-growing. It has an even rainfall throughout the year, ranging between 70 and 90 inches, a rich, fertile soil at altitudes not exceeding 2,000 feet, a temperature range between 70 and 90 degrees, and a strict control of a common virus disease that attacks this banana-like crop. The first three of these assets were provided by nature itself, the last is the contribution of the Agricultural Department.

The Agricultural Officer at Tawau, Mr. C. Bridge, was on a two-year loan from the Colonial Development Corporation. In this he was typical of the Agricultural Department people I met away from the headquarters office; nearly all were on some sort of loan or attachment from another country. Apart from investigating the tremendous agricultural development of the area, his primary task was to sustain the attack by the Department of Agriculture and the Colonial Development Corporation against the virus disease (called Bunchy Top). This campaign has been so successful that whereas a few years ago the Borneo Abaca project had been almost broken, today over a million pounds of hemp are exported yearly, and the disease has been largely eliminated.

Bunchy Top spreads from wild bananas, of which there are innumerable mats all round the Borneo Abaca estates. Chinese and native smallholders let them grow in profusion, and flies carry the virus into the rows of hemp. Bridge, by using half his entire vote, and three-quarters of his staff, is able to inspect once a month every single banana mat in the Tawau area. His men slog round day after day, checking and destroying, mapping and recording, until he is able now to say confidently that his monthly inspection, combined with the weekly check by the estates, has brought the disease down to one per cent of the crop. This is economic, and if it can be kept this low the development of the hemp industry is assured.

Table Estate is so called because it is grouped round the slopes of a small flat-topped mountain, which despite its un-characteristic shape is the remains of a volcano. The hemp grows well because it is planted on rich volcanic soil, a beautiful sight, and it has been the Department's second great contribution to the economy of Tawau in that Bridge has discovered a lot more of it, as yet unused.

The rest of North Borneo, the remainder of Borneo for that matter, is ancient rock, part of the Sunda Platform, formed in very early geological times, and nearly all its goodness and richness has been washed away. But in the area between Tawau and Semporna the soil is largely volcanic, extremely fertile, and waiting to be developed. A soil map of this area is being compiled. Although in its early stages, there is enough on that map to show that possibly the whole Semporna Peninsula, a long triangle of land bounded by Tawau in the south, Mostyn in the north and Semporna in the east, is fit for extensive cultivation. All that it requires— need I repeat?—are roads and people.

Bridge has established an agricultural station at Quoin

Hill, near the Apas River, and the road out to it from Tawau is first in the list of Edge's priorities. It was this road, and its suggested continuation north across to Mostyn, and east out to Semporna, that excited the Chinese I met in Tawau even more than the copra trade. They felt, indeed the whole town felt, that on this road rested to a large extent the future expansion of Tawau. From the sea the outline of innumerable baby volcanoes can be seen; there are no live volcanoes nearer than the Philippines (although Pryer at Sandakan heard the explosion of Krakatoa, a thousand miles to the south), and these long-extinct cones have had their lava long since broken up by the elements of nature. The rich soil left behind, now covered by thick uninhabited jungle, is suitable for many crops; in particular, as Bridge and his predecessors have pointed out, it is ideal for cocoa, and this, it is hoped, will be the crop of the future.

It is a crop new to North Borneo, for the rich soil necessary for its growth has only just been discovered. But in Africa and elsewhere cocoa-growing is a highly profitable occupation, and as the sixty experimental acres of Borneo Abaca, and the half-dozen of the Agricultural Department at Quoin Hill, are both flourishing, as the Semporna Peninsula satisfies the requirements of a high rainfall, a warm humid climate and a fertile soil, there seems every indication that if the Government can bring these factors to the notice of the right people, Cadbury's for example, the necessary impetus can be given. Even before the advent of any big estate, I venture to think that the younger sons of over-crowded Chinese shopkeepers will leave their packed rooms and their cramped quarters, and will move down the pioneer road, to plant rubber at least, and if given the know-how, cocoa as well.

Although the discovery of this volcanic soil is the most exciting agricultural development in North Borneo since rubber rescued it from the nineteenth century, the development of the peninsula may be retarded by the lack of labour. Only the arrival within the last few years of several thousand Timorese, and a planned migration of Cocos Islanders, rescued the existing estates from a shortage that had persisted since the war, and which was prevalent throughout the territory. There is now a small surplus of labour in Tawau, but the lack of a stable North Borneo-based labour supply is still felt, as the Timorese, appreciated though they are, show no signs of settling down in the territory.

A hundred years ago Wallace, the anthropologist, declared that Asia ended, both geographically and ethnologically, at a deep fissure that ran across the shallow Java Sea. Everything west of that line, the fauna, the flora and the people, were Asians, while to the east there was an immediate difference, and one was in another continent, an Australasia or a Polynesia. This Wallace Line has since been developed; there are now two borders, with an intervening area where both continents mix. The principle is maintained, however, and to meet the Timorese is to go out of Asia, to the islands that stretch into the Pacific.

The mixture of peoples in Tawau is disturbing to the minute police force, for here the stability of the rest of the colony is lacking. Timorese, Bugis from the Celebes, Suluks and Bajaus are all birds of passage, coming or going. Tawau is brand new, being completely rebuilt from a disastrous fire that destroyed its temporary post-war buildings several years ago, and it is extremely proud of its spick and span modern shop-houses that stretch along the sea front. It fears another conflagration, and dreads any suggestion of a riot between these different peoples that throng its streets. There are no signs of ill-will between them, however, and although Tawau leads the colony in violent crimes, thanks to the Bugis of the south Celebes, the list is not a long one. The long-bladed Bugis knife with the pistol-like grip is used occasionally, but that is all. A European's house was burgled in 1957, the first since the war; sensational in Tawau, but scarcely a crime wave.

In other ways this mixture of peoples in Tawau is part of its charm, shown most clearly perhaps whenever a concert is organized. One such, held on the spacious lawns of the Residency, illustrates this. The Residency itself was a perfect setting, close-cut grass enlivened by hibiscus and bougainvillea in all shades of red, pink, purple and orange, sweet-smelling frangipani, and flaming yellow and red cannas. Overhead, cooling the late afternoon audience, was a background of coconut trees, fan-like travellers palms, dark-green mango trees and an occasional kapok tree.

The concert itself, like the setting, could only have been provided by North Borneo. It began with a Timorese flute orchestra playing for a Timorese choir. They are all Roman Catholics, these dark curly-haired young men, and hymns are their favourite songs. Other tunes, traditional to Timor, had a thin, haunting timbre, quite unlike the Portuguese-inspired music of modern Malacca. The flutes, hand-cut in the jungle behind Tawau, had been smoothed and rubbed to a glossy texture, beautiful pieces of work. Before the war these young men sought work in the oilfields of Dutch Borneo; now they sail farther north, under the advice of their Fathers, and secure employment all over North Borneo. Wherever they go they take their flutes and their faith with them.

Following the Timorese came the Cocos Islanders, people prevailed on to migrate and settle here when their Indian Ocean home became seriously over-populated, and malnutrition was common. The war-time air-strip had destroyed thousands of coconut trees, there was no empty space on the atoll, and the British Government made a very wise move indeed in bringing them to the east coast of North Borneo, where the way of life is largely the same and there is room for all.

Their dancing showed clearly their Scottish connections through the Clunies-Ross family. What are accepted today as native traditional dances are based on the Highland reels and dances taught to the simple islanders over a hundred years ago by the Clunies-Ross and Thompson families. Eightsome reels, Strip the Willow and the Lancers, the basic form of these and other dances is still prominent, but with the easily-recognized influence of the Malay *dondang* superimposed.

The troupe that danced the reels to the music of two energetic fiddlers, consisted of sixteen men and women wearing bright sarongs and frilly blouses. The girls, their smooth black hair caught back by silver and gold combs, wore sarongs of every hue, blue, green, red and silver predominating, with long hip-length blouses and frills cascading from shoulder to hip, most unlike any other Malay or Indonesian dress I have seen. Colourful though they were, they were outshone by their men, who wore a similar costume but somehow managed to look brighter and more decorative. The more primitive the society, the brighter the male, it seems, and the Cocos Islanders, with the men looking not unlike Scotsmen in evening dress of kilt, frilled lacy shirt and *jabot*, were no exception to this rule.

The next item was again a complete contrast, a song and dance given by a party of six sea-Bajaus who had sailed down from an island near Semporna. Musical accompaniment was by drum this time, the symbolic traditional drum of—it must have been—the Hindu temple of long ago. The *orang laut* had their faces heavily covered with white powder, literally pasted on, and bright lipstick worn by men and women alike. They danced their traditional dance in a series of sinuous, measured movements of arms, legs and body, with curved-back fingers, very similar to Hindu temple-dancing, although nothing in their history connects the two together.

They were dressed alike in elaborate costumes consisting of beaded, sequin-embroidered jackets, and long loose trousers or skirts, and to add a final bizarre touch, heavy, exotic-looking gold- and jewel-encrusted head-dresses. One dance, in which the man wore a set of long, curved silver talons, seemed to mime, in slow, abrupt movements and sensuous poses, an argument which waxed hot and furious, and then died down. No one knew the story, which perhaps had passed from India to Java, and been spread during her days of Hindu greatness. This is the edge of culture here, Islamic and Christian; once perhaps it was the edge of Hinduism too.

Finally, there was a solo performance by a pagan, a Dusun from the Serudong River, south of Tawau. This runs into the wild interior almost along the Indonesian border, and the few kampongs of Dusuns there merge almost imperceptibly with the Muruts. The dance of the Serudong Dusun was to all intents and purposes the head-hunting dance of those farther inland, and as he unsheathed his *parang*, over two feet of curved steel, the hilt adorned with tufts of hair, and with shield held in front of him pursued an imaginary enemy, each step in perfect time to the fiercely-beating gongs, I wondered whether this was a dimly-remembered legacy of the past or something that is still alive. I fear it is the former, for we have abolished head-hunting, and have given them nothing but empty peace in its place.

Tawau is the southernmost town in North Borneo, close to Indonesia. The Dutch had attempted to acquire this area, in the 1880s, and the Chartered Company did not obtain undisputed possession until near the close of the century. It soon became larger than Semporna and Lahad Datu, the Chartered Company posts to the north that had preceded it, and it has now a most varied agricultural base on which to develop, all introduced into what was uninhabited jungle in the last fifty-odd years.

Between the two wars it was the centre as well of the only large-scale mining operations in the territory, with a low-grade coal being extracted from a field up the Selimpopon River, one of the six streams that flow into Cowie Harbour, on the northern slopes of which Tawau is situated. This coal mine was abandoned in the 1930s, and the rather unruly lot of Chinese there, recruited originally from labourers who went to France during the first World War, found employment elsewhere. But on the neighbouring river, the Kalabakan, a post-war enterprise of great importance to Tawau has begun.

With the relinquishing in 1952 by the British Borneo Timber Company of its monopolistic position, the way was clear for other companies to participate in the timber trade of the territory. The Bombay Burmah Trading Corporation was one of the firms attracted, and it secured a twenty-one year concession up this river, which it is now developing. It has established a log depot on Sebatik Island, where the coal company once stored their output, and this, administered as a part of Tawau Harbour and named Wallace Bay, has become a timber port of some size. The Company secured nearly three million cubic feet of timber from the giant forests fringing the Kalabakan in 1955 (the latest figures available) and over sixty ships called at Wallace Bay to take it away.

Tawau has perhaps the most diverse economy of any town in the state, and with increasing exports in timber, rubber, manila hemp, copra and cocoa it can look to a bright future. Should its northbound road be built, and stretch finally across the Semporna peninsula to the store and the log-pond that calls itself Mostyn, it may add tobacco to its list of exports, for a few miles inland from the Mostyn jetty there is a very healthy plantation run by the Segama Estate. It is small, scarcely a hundred acres, but it is successful, and its long high *attap* drying sheds are full of stacks of fine cigar-leaf wrapping, the finest tobacco in the world. Mostyn is ringed by reefs and islands, and cannot be much further developed as a port. Should the land behind it, now growing tobacco and supplying excellent timber, be opened to any extent, the products must be exported, unless deep water is discovered near Mostyn, via Tawau. That will be possible only if an all-weather road is built.

On the other side of the bay from Mostyn is Lahad Datu, a village of only a thousand people. It was once the site of one of Cowie's trading posts, when his diminutive vessel sought for rattans and birds-nests, and Bajaus who wished to buy arms and ammunition. The island-covered bay was the most lawless area in the Chartered Company's possession, and the slavers and pirates who lived there have chased traders, once even the Government clerk, to the jetty itself, and shied off only when the policeman on duty came running down it with a rifle at the ready.

It is now much more peaceful, but the young District Officer there still finds it as advisable as it is pleasant to spend much of his time in launch and *prahu*, visiting these islands, talking to the people, discovering new kampongs and by his presence keeping his unruly flock quiet. He has no outstanding chief to help (or hinder) him, for the sea-Bajau is so independent that he would never acknowledge a premier chief, and there is scarcely a leader among them able to command the loyalty of anything larger than a kampong, while those who still live in their boats, the real *orang-laut*, accept no one as their superior who is not their superior in force.

The little township of Lahad Datu squats at the foot of a rise, almost on a level with the waters of the bay, and when it floods the town suffers. Behind it, safely climbing the slope, are the few Government offices and, farther back, a new airstrip linking it to Tawau (half an hour to the south) and Sandakan (an hour to the north). Beside the bitumen road as it runs up the slope through serried ranks of coconut trees to the airstrip is the Rest House. This is simply two enormous rooms in an old wooden house. Inside the bare room there is a wire cage, and inside the cage is a bed, isolated, it is hoped, from the mosquitoes that plunge against the wire. Over the entrance to this old Rest House is a piece of a marble frieze, brought back from Greece by Dr. Dingle before the war, determined that Lahad Datu was going to have some culture. Despite his efforts, I do not think that culture is the word that one would use when describing Lahad Datu; it is more likely to be charm.

John Cresswell, the famous bank manager there ('You're going to Lahad Datu?' people all over North Borneo would say with surprise, 'Well give my regards to Cresswell'), was as optimistic as Teck Guan in Tawau over the possibilities of copra sales to China, for although Lahad Datu is much smaller than its southern neighbour, its coconut acreage, which pushes back the jungle along the coast for several miles, is only just a fraction less, and wherever you go you see the cattle grazing under the tall smooth rows of trees, and the fires under the elevated frames to dry the nut, and the smell of coconut oil is everywhere in your nostrils. To many the smell is particularly objectionable, but to me it is a quick vivid memory of a childhood spent on hot Australian beaches, when a mother smeared oil on to shoulders throughout a burning summer, until a brown body could bake and surf for hours without worry. I never smell copra now, in the lighters of Singapore or the bags at Lahad Datu and elsewhere, without being back once again looking for the wrecks of old Dutch ships out past the reefs of Rottnest Island or surfing on Cottesloe beach. How people find it nauseating I cannot imagine.

Lahad Datu is not all coconuts; the road that the Chartered Company built with much effort northwards from the town twenty miles to the Segama River now connects it to the sole survivor of the nineteenth-century tobacco boom, to the Segama tobacco estate, controlled by the great Imperial Tobacco Co. Here many of the Cocos Islanders have found work, their employment presenting new problems to a management already grappling with the difficulties of producing a most finicky crop. Constant and unremitting care and attention is needed on a tobacco estate; unlike a rubber estate, no day passes when some new problem or threat might not arise. Flooding is a constant danger, and it was this, as well as low cigar prices and the presence of innumerable pests of different varieties, that eliminated all the other estates. It may be flooding that will move the Company away from the powerful and uncontrollable Segama, an east-coast giant second only to the Kinabatangan, and force it to find new areas near Mostyn. But for the present its 300,000 pounds of tobacco, taken from 450 acres, and valued at over $3 million, is a welcome export from Lahad Datu, and an added reason for Cresswell to press for the completion of the new bank.

In addition Lahad Datu may be assisted in the future by the timber enterprise a score or so miles along the coast towards Tungku. Here the Kennedy Bay Timber Company has secured a lease of land stretching inland to the Segama, and with the thoroughness and lavishness associated with American concerns is rapidly developing its area. It may extend its operations to the thick timber land west of Lahad Datu, and in that case its production of a million cubic feet or more of logs may well be doubled.

Already it has built over eighty miles of metalled road, there being no stream convenient for floating logs, and has established an engineering section for its giant American trucks with spare parts alone valued at over $500,000. It has brought into the colony the skagit high lead logging system it has employed in the Philippines since the war, and which its parent company out of Seattle has used for nearly fifty years. This involves the use of a forest giant as the focal point for a circle of cables, attached to a powerful winch which drags down the hill the timber cut down within that radius. To hear the roar of the winch deep in the jungle, and then suddenly to see a tremendous log slithering towards you out of the greenery like an immense snake is a dramatic experience.

The most magnificent tree on the east coast, the Queen of the Jungle, which towers up in smooth unbroken symmetry a hundred feet or more, is economically worthless. Its texture is so fine, it is so brittle, that it is liable to disintegrate as it hits the ground, and it could never pass through a mill. On a drive through the Kennedy Bay area we saw many of these monsters pushing through the extremely lush vegetation of giant creepers and ferns, and in the mapping and planning section this was confirmed. Nevertheless there is enough *seriah* there, the main product of Borneo's jungle, to warrant an extension of the log pond and to justify sober optimism that if the untouched area on the other side of Lahad Datu is secured this new timber venture will be a success.

Kennedy Bay has added to the diverse population of the east coast by employing Ibans from Sarawak, reputably the best timber men in Borneo, and Filipinos from its camps on Basilan Island. I became aware of another innovation when driving out to see some timber being felled. Round the corner towards our jeep rushed a huge American truck, racing twenty tons of log to the pond. As it neared us our driver pulled to the right, not the left, and as the truck roared past, just missing us, my heart nearly stopped. He explained afterwards that as the timber road network did not link up with the territory track from Lahad Datu they continued to drive as they did in America or the Philippines, on the right of the road. I wish he had told me before.

The south-east coast of North Borneo is not merely an area of varied economic activity amid small communities of different races; it is also a place of great scenic beauty. We have nearly left the east coast, and we must soon return, via Labuan, to Singapore. Come with me then before we end our stay on a day's trip I made up the coast, and see vicariously through my eyes some of this beauty and charm, and envy, with me, the people who live there.

The trip began in Tawau in a comfortable cabin on the *Kimanis*, which loaded with copra was beginning her run back to Singapore. She left before dawn, and an early breakfast found us steaming along the edge of the Semporna Peninsula. We entered a narrow strait, or *Trusan* as it is called, passing odd-shaped hilly little islands so closely that you could watch the Bajau throw his small hand net as he stalked his fish through the calm blue water, and the housewife, at the entrance to her small hut on stilts, almost could offer you a bowl of rice. Most of the islands, and the Borneo coast itself, were covered in jungle that climbed the slopes, but some had serried rows of coconuts, a lighter green breaking the darker hues.

At 9 a.m. the white wave of our bow subsided, the anchor rattled down, and we swung into a rippling tide a few score yards off the long jetty of Semporna, strategically placed at the northern entrance to this narrow strait. Here we climbed down the side of *Kimanis*, to the envy of all doing the round trip from Singapore, and joined a small Government launch. It was a pleasant morning of blue skies and light sea breeze; as we walked down the long jetty and visited the small village half a mile away to buy some fish and sarongs the sun was warm on our backs, and I envied the small naked children diving and swimming in the cool depths and wondered how many of their parents would rob me if they had the chance.

From Semporna our host, Mr. G. Douglas, the young D.O. of Lahad Datu, took us in his launch down Darvel Bay to Mostyn, some hours away, time for him to serve four of us a three-course picnic luncheon, which we ate sitting in deck-chairs under an awning, delighting in the views of island and ocean that we passed. Douglas had two senior officers with him, and if the excellent relationship shown that day between the three as they discussed the problems and prospects of the area is typical, the administrative service of North Borneo must be a very pleasant occupation indeed. Douglas has a job that any young man would wish for; with the type of senior officer over him that there is now it is all the better.

At Mostyn, where we nosed our way in with care, past obtruding reefs and sandbanks, we found more Bajau boats, whose sails dot Darvel Bay, and a decrepit old Chinese launch. No Chinese junks are seen in these waters, very few venture far south of Sandakan, and the waters are still the preserve of the locals. The high jungle crowds close to the shore here, but inland a little there is tobacco, hemp and timber all being exploited, and the time when a D.O. will walk across to Tawau, Douglas and I agreed sadly from our deck-chairs, is not far distant.

In the late afternoon we headed out across the bay. The far hills and mountains of Borneo were deep blue in shaded haze; the shallows and reefs near the surface changed the sea to a light green, almost to a white, and overhead a perfect tropic day ended in a blaze of red that flamed the clouds. We sat on deck, the launch rocking a little, catching an occasional salty spray, sipping cool drinks and watching a timber ship swing out from Bohayan Island, where a central log pond is established; and as darkness fell we crept our way into the newly-created anchorage at Kennedy Bay.

Don Ireton, the dynamic American manager, has built himself here the loveliest home in Borneo, a long low ranch-type house with an immense lounge of highly-polished red wood, and a glorious view, over a rough stone wall only shoulder high, of Darvel Bay. His wife has decorated it taste-fully with fittings and materials from Hong Kong and Manila, and with servants from Basilan. It was a restful, luxurious setting for the end of an idyllic day; and the calm conversation of G. L. Carson, the Conservator of Forests, made me realize that not everyone in Sandakan is sour, and that life among the forests of the east coast must be good for the soul. Certainly Carson and Ireton, in their different ways, reflected a great inner tranquillity. It was shown too by Peter Edge. Does it come from service in the south-east of North Borneo? Does the beauty of it slowly enter the soul of the beholder?

13. UGLY DUCKLING

IT is very difficult not to begin and end any visit to North Borneo at Labuan. It is almost inevitable. It is possible to catch a freighter in Sandakan for Hong Kong, or for Australia (via New Guinea), and you can do the same at Jesselton, but all the regular air services, and the Straits Steamships, enter and leave North Borneo through this island. Planes from here fly to Manila, Hong Kong, Kuching, Singapore and Darwin; its airport, a flat broad strip of crushed coral, is a major transport centre in the East, and whereas before the war Labuan was the most ignored and neglected of the Straits Settlements, almost forgotten by a secretariat in Singapore, it is today, thanks to a great post-war air expansion, and to other developments, an ugly duckling that suddenly has become beautiful.

Labuan, as with the rest of West Borneo, once was part of the Sultanate of Brunei, the rump of which faces it across the broad bay off which it lies. During the nineteenth century the Sultan ceded away vast tracts of his country, rivers he was unable to control, and reluctant to raid. From the time when Rajah James Brooke acquired the Sarawak River, in the far south, in 1842, until the Chartered Company bought its last river in the north, in 1903, several thousand square miles were sold away. Of this, Labuan was the only piece ceded directly to the British Crown, which needed a base—from which to guard the sea and to attack Borneo pirates. Brooke and the Chartered Company had to pay for their rivers; the British Government had the Royal Navy, it wanted a base from which to fight pirates, and its forceful action carried the day.

The Sultan hoped that by giving Labuan to the British he would be freed from the uneasiness of further visits, and to a certain extent he was right. The island, with its protected deep-water port facing the mainland (Port Victoria as it was called), was useful enough as a naval outpost, and piracy was driven away from the coast. The British preoccupation with West Borneo in the first half of the nineteenth century was this local worry, the curse of piracy, and with that checked little further interest was taken in the conditions in Brunei. It was left to Rajah Brooke, whose relations with the Sultan were based on other things than a show of force, to bring the south into some semblance of peace, but it was not until the advent of the Chartered Company that the north was rescued from anarchy and lawlessness. In Brunei itself slavery persisted into the twentieth century, long after piracy at sea had vanished.

It was hoped that Labuan would spring to life, once the magical wand of 'Free Trade' had been waved over it, and that it would become, in the manner of Singapore and Hong Kong, a British emporium in the Far East. This never occurred. It lacked the rich hinterland the other two possessed, in Malaya and China, and the products of Borneo were minute compared with the wealth of the eastern islands that poured into Singapore. Throughout the nineteenth century Labuan remained a very small outpost indeed of the British Empire, for if it cost Britain nothing to acquire it, it cost a lot to run it, and the staff was cut to the bone in an attempt to balance the tiny budget.

Periodically it was spared the annual grants-in-aid that Singapore had to make to its poor relative by a spurt of activity in its coal mine. The flat island, with some rolling elevations of 300 or so feet, is twelve miles long and seven wide, rather in the shape of a triangle, with the point of it heading out to sea, and the base facing Brunei Bay. At the point there is coal; it is not very good coal, and there are various difficulties in working a mine where it rains possibly 150 inches a year; nevertheless this was attempted at various occasions during the nineteenth century, the Royal Navy refuelled at £1 a ton, and enough revenue secured from its export to maintain a few police and an administrator or two.

Among the Government officers who lived there was Hugh Low. He built a beautiful Residency on the gentle slope behind the village, and governed there inconspicuously for many years. Towards the end of his career he was brought back to Malaya, and thrust into newly-acquired Perak. The first Resident there, Birch, had been murdered, the Malays were up in arms, the Chinese tin miners were divided and lawless. The state was heavily in debt and on the point of collapse. With greatest sangfroid Hugh Low took it all in his stride, and by the dint of great labour he transformed Perak into a prosperous, peaceful and progressive area, and won for himself the title of one of Britain's greatest administrators in the Far East. No one has ever discovered how he learned his trade in Labuan, but it is one of its few claims to fame, that it taught Sir Hugh Low.

One of the major steps he took when in Perak, which could well be considered applicable to North Borneo today, was to live with a deficit budget. He maintained that it was impossible for a primitive state to advance if it was not developed. It was useless saving money. All the revenue, and more, should be ploughed back into the territory. Slowly the procedure would snowball. The more money spent on developing the country, the more revenue would be raised. Low constantly spent wise money in Perak, pushing out roads in particular, encouraging migration and agricultural enterprises, and within a decade Perak was transformed. It was once thought, in 1888, that he would be the first governor of a Federation of British Borneo; I wonder whether he would have transformed Borneo too?

Labuan never advanced during the nineteenth century, and the books of the time all mention its dismal collection of wood and *attap* shops lying by a swamp, its thick mangrove and its flat oppressive features, with disgust, even, at times, with horror. All the pestilences of the tropics are mentioned. Conrad paints a very gloomy picture, using all the depressing nuances of which he is master. Hugh Clifford describes the desecration of European graves, and the same general atmosphere is maintained in the more impersonal histories that chronicle the Empire. I had steeped myself in these histories, and it was with something like apprehension that I approached the island for the first time in 1953, to discover to my surprise that Labuan is lovely, charming, a little pearl of the China Sea.

There are many delightful characteristics about this island; one, which is categorically denied by every writer I have read (and I think I have read every single book on Borneo ever written), is the climate. It is merely an attitude of mind, for the climate has not changed, but the warm, delightfully, luxuriously warm, climate of Labuan was regarded with horror during the nineteenth century, and even during the first part of this. Yet there is always a sea breeze, the tang of salt air, the scent of bush and shrub and the coolness of tall timber on the island, and the humidity of the jungle has vanished. It is a dry heat on Labuan, and the evenings are cool. The greyness and dampness of most of London's months can stand no comparison with the clear sunlight on Labuan, and the stretches of beach, each one reserved for you between low red outcrops a few hundred yards from the office, seem infinitely preferable to the stale air of the pub that is the escape for London.

Another surprise to any visitor who has made the mistake of reading Maugham, or the latest text-book on Colonial Development, is the attitude of the inhabitants. I have read that they are 'Cooped up under a boiling sun, bad tempered with not enough to do'. In fact there is an air of great determination on Labuan among the keen but friendly people who are trying to make the island move. They take a delight in their pleasures, and Labuan is an easy place on which to enjoy swimming, tennis, cricket, football, shooting, fishing and golf. There is a new Recreation Club facing the blue waters of the harbour that is better sited and built than anything else in North Borneo. At the same time there is a multi-racial loyalty to the island's welfare that I did not see for example in Sandakan, or Kudat, and which augurs well for the future.

One feels here more push, more drive, than is apparent on the mainland, and therefore more irritation with Government slowness. Labuan in September 1956, after expressing much dissatisfaction with its treatment by the North Borneo Government (it had been merged with North Borneo in 1946, leaving the Straits Settlements), regained its pre-war Free Port status. A representative collection of business men of all races then took the initiative and convened a Trade Convention. Delegates from Hong Kong, Singapore, the United Kingdom, Australia and New Zealand, Sarawak, Malaya and elsewhere, represented their governments or their chambers of commerce. Although a comparatively small affair, it was the most ambitious venture of the kind held in North Borneo, and it reflects the ambitious and progressive attitude of the island generally.

It set out to sell Labuan to these visitors, and with the Convention over it formed itself into a Free Port Guild, which will maintain and develop this project. Labuan's small port, with a population of 1,500, has ample space behind it

Labuan fishermen

where large go-downs can be built, and it is the hope of the guild that the island will be used for bulk storage. Businesses can trans-ship their goods here, as in Singapore, for re-export. At present it is the port for the Brunei Bay area, including Seria, the centre of the great oil industry. Should Singapore become more unstable, or should demand rise throughout Borneo and the islands to the north, Labuan is determined to be considered as an alternative to Singapore for that bigger market.

As a free port it intends to convince Hong Kong industrialists that safety alone should induce them to put an egg or two in its basket, and it is convinced that industries begun on Labuan will prosper.

The basis for its development, whether as an industrial centre or as an *entrepôt* port, rests on its harbour. Here it has natural assets denied the rest of West Borneo. Deep water comes close inshore, and the breadth of the island spreads protective arms. The swell of the South China Sea breaks on the other coast; out past Victoria there is the calm water of Brunei Bay, 36 feet deep, where the whole U.S. 7th Fleet once lay at anchor, watching the ships of the Australian 9th Division land their men on the devastated town. The landing wrecked the town, as tanks plunged through *attap* walls, and heavy guns smacked down anything left standing, but it could not destroy these natural assets, and it is on these that the Free Port Guild concentrates.

Perhaps the dominating figure of the Free Port Guild, and of Labuan generally, is a dynamic man whom, if ever I argued with Hong Teck Guan, I would seek as an ally, R. P. G. Brodie. Red faced, white haired, muscular framed, he is known as the 'uncrowned king of Labuan', and he is the type of determined business man who must be a thorn in the flesh of every complacent Government officer. Within the last year or so the Government has built a new wharf for Labuan, replacing the Australian Army structure that gave post-war service for too long. It is 600 feet long, with a depth of 26 feet, and already a 10,000-ton freighter has been alongside. It is too small and too shallow, insists Brodie and the guild, and if Labuan is to grow there must be a bigger wharf; it is basic.

The sense of urgency that the guild is seeking to impart to Labuan's prospects is not altogether shared by a Government that has the affairs of an entire colony to consider, and it struck me as significant that although every other department in North Borneo has thrown off its pre-war hangover, has been fired with new schemes and encouraged with new equipment within the last few years, the Marine Department, with its headquarters at Labuan, is still struggling on salvaged gear and modified loot; it is the Cinderella of the territory.

This indifference to marine questions does not extend to

buildings on land, for its new headquarters, in the centre of the town, is the most outstanding public building in North Borneo; but in its inadequate slipway alongside a departmental jetty far too small, which was guaranteed by the P.W.D. to hold to a fifteen-ton strain but collapsed at seven tons, in its overcrowded shore-line and packed shed, this neglect is confirmed.

The Straits Steamships, the lifeline of the territory, despite much ingenuity, has been unable to organize a schedule which permits its ships to proceed without pause round the coast of North Borneo. At various ports they have to anchor and wait for the dawn, for there are too many unmarked shoals and reefs for a night run to be made.

The Marine Department has made what efforts it can with its Japanese buoys and old Australian and Japanese equipment to mark these navigational dangers, but the extremely expensive delay must be maintained, for the seaways are not sign-posted, and North Borneo's development suffers. These reefs and shallows, the major concern of the department, along with the majority of the government's sea transport, are away on the east coast. But the only slipway able to take ships up to 120 tons is an inadequate one in Labuan on the west, where they are hauled in by an old converted Australian army engine. Government launches from Tawau and Lahad Datu and the timber launches of the east coast must make the long haul round to Labuan for lack of adequate slips on the east coast. Yet this slipway at Labuan is not used by Brunei, twenty miles away, or by the oil launches of Seria, or by the Government launches of North Sarawak. Sea transport is essential to all three; one would think a Government would look out to sea sometimes, and include it in any comprehensive transport plan for the future.

The people of Labuan have preserved their humour, and while the prospects hoped for by the Free Port Guild excite them, they still live a typical North Borneo existence. Some of their experiences have passed into territorial lore. There is the story for example of an episode before the war, when the island was still a part of the Straits Settlements, and the district officer, slightly overburdened with his work, which involved the responsibilities of harbour master, superintendent of the gaol, executive officer for every department of government, as well as tiresome hours on the bench, managed to secure the appointment of his one and only colleague, the doctor, as a Justice of the Peace. Court work vanished from his worries, until one evening, D.O. and doctor coming back from the club by the waterfront, both slightly under the weather, forgot to turn on the lights of their bicycles, and were halted by the duty policeman. Terrified at what he had done, he then tried to withdraw, but the D.O. very solemn, insisted he do his duty. He and the doctor were duly booked.

Next morning he took the chair in court, and the charge 'that he did ride a bicycle during the hours of darkness without a light' was read out. He fined the doctor five dollars. The D.O. then vacated the chair, and took his place in the court. The new magistrate heard the charge read a second time. He eyed the accused. 'I take a serious view of this. This is the second case today, it is becoming prevalent, and I intend to stamp on it. Fined ten dollars!' I ought to say that a variant on this folk tale of Colonial administration is related in a territory thousands of miles from North Borneo.

Labuan, erased during the war, and forced to exist for many years afterwards on *attap* and wood, is now emerging as a spick-and-span little town, very attractively planned and sited. Administratively it has become a slight puzzle. The system in North Borneo is as it was in Malaya, a Resident under the governor controlling a number of district officers. Despite the pressure of the Secretariat, and of Heads of Department, who are inclined to by-pass them, the Residents remain, two on the east coast, and one on the west and in the Interior. For some reason Labuan was placed in the Interior Residency. After a few years this appeared somewhat odd, and possibly as the nearest to a political gesture that a government could make to the Labuan Chinese who wanted to be re-joined to Singapore, it was divorced from any Residency, Interior or Coastal, and made the senior district office. These arrangements I feel sure matter less in the long run than in the personality of the man who administers it; and in G. Headley, a small dark man who puffs his pipe at Brodie, the island has now a second claim to fame, for Headley has made an ugly duckling a solitary white swan.

The great days of Labuan lie ahead, and they are connected not merely to the exploitation of its free port facilities and opportunities, but to the immense development of the oil industry as well, developments which it is hoped will benefit the whole territory. The search for oil in North Borneo dates back to 1888, and throughout the twentieth century various holders of the oil rights of the territory investigated the constant reports of oil seepages. These were all fruitless (and in fact a seepage usually pre-supposes the absence of one of the essential factors in an oil field, a hard roof to contain a storage), and North Borneo had to watch with envy, as large oil deposits were developed just south of it on the east coast, at Tarakan, and on the west coast, at Miri, in Sarawak.

Miri has been a fading asset for some years, and the field is now situated even closer to North Borneo, in Brunei. It is a coastal field, a twenty-five-mile stretch between Kuala Belait and Seria, and to visit it is a fascinating experience. I expected to find rough men wearing tin hats, spurting gushers of oil, and a tough frontier-like existence. I soon discovered how wrong I was, for it is the essence of luxury and sophistication.

An attractive young woman met the private plane of the Brunei Shell Company that flew me from Labuan to Anduki, the airstrip, and a large British car drove me down a wide bitumen road, past American-style single-story homes set well back in their own lawns and gardens, and under *casuarina* pines. Only one primitive *attap* hut was visible. 'That's where the Manager lives—he is last on the list,' I was told. I was deposited at a luxurious hotel, far superior to anything in North Borneo. Nearby was the Shell Club, a large modern building that could have been transported from Santa Monica or Hawaii, with several lush bars, a beautiful swimming pool close to the sea-beach, tennis courts and badminton courts, a golf course, and only a cricket field to remind you that you were not in the States, but in a part of the Empire. There was nothing however in all this luxury and leisure to suggest that you were in Borneo, or on an oil field.

That evening however as I drove along the coast road to Kuala Belait, which lies at the other end of the field, there was all the evidence in the world. Not far back from the coast rose the jungle, silent, still, towering monsters that had lost a mile or so of their territory, momentarily, but who watched and waited for their turn to advance again, as they were doing already in half-deserted Miri, south of Kuala Belait. This was Borneo, and it was not so difficult to remember again that a few hours away from this community of 25,000 people, pagans struggled to survive, and watched their women die in labour.

Between the jungle and the sea rose numerous derricks, gaunt against the sky. Between Seria and Kuala Belait 458 wells have been sunk, and 250 of them are producing. A producing well is one of the most disappointing objects imaginable, as the drilling derrick is removed, and an inconspicuous little collection of dials and knobs on a few pipes are concreted over the hole. It is called 'a Christmas tree', and from these Christmas trees 40 million barrels, at a value of 300 million dollars, were exported in 1955, making it the seventh biggest field in the world. The Sultanate of Brunei, stripped of all its rivers except this one little stretch, struggles along on an annual revenue of 100 million dollars, managing, with great effort, to spend perhaps a quarter of it.

These wells do not draw off all the natural gas under the surface and, as an essential safety precaution, the Brunei Shell Oil Company maintains scores of outlets where this gas escapes. The flames from these outlets burn unceasingly, and as you drive along they leap and fall all round you. It is never dark in Seria, and you either become accustomed to these fires, burning sometimes from high pipes, or leaping from shallow pits, or you draw your curtains. To drive between these furious flames must be like driving through hell. Sophistication in hell; is that typical of all oil fields?

Labuan is fixing its attention not on the Seria field however but on its possible expansion seaward. The Exploration Division of Shell have covered most of North Borneo already, checking all previous data, and working with the Geological Department in mapping the territory. Prospects were so bright in one area, the Padas-Klias Peninsula, where reports of oil stretch back to the nineteenth century, that drilling operations were begun near the isolated kampong of Kuala Penyu. No oil was found, and the company has largely abandoned thoughts of any further drilling in the territory. Its eyes are focused on the China Sea, on the waters off shore.

In 1955 the Exploration Section had a thorough seismic survey made of some promising areas. In 1957 three off-shore rigs well out of sight of land were erected, one island standing in 75 feet of water, and drilling began. There are four essentials needed for a successful oil field. There must be a geological structure known as an anti-cline, a gentle curve of strata; the anti-cline must have a non-porous top and bottom; and there must be an accumulation of oil. The seismic survey has revealed anti-clines of immense size, three or four times as large as the structure on which rests Seria. The only comparison that could be made would be with one of the Middle East giants. There are over half a dozen close to the North Borneo shore; any one of them could produce a field bigger than Kuwait. Combined, they could be the largest single field in the world. But have they a hard top and bottom, and is there oil? We shall know soon enough.

While I was in Seria an 'island' had been towed from Kuala Belait and placed in position on Hankin Shoal. It is out of sight, but now part of the municipality of Jesselton. I hope it observes all the by-laws. Shell have become so excited over the possibilities however, for nowhere in the world are there structures of this size undrilled, that it is abandoning this slow off-shore Hankin Shoal rig, and is acquiring two portable rigs. The Hankin Shoal, if it is a failure, will have to be abandoned, and the costly six-month work of erecting a drill on the 'island' written off. For £1,000 a day Shell are hiring portable rigs, of the type used off Louisiana, which can sink their legs to the bottom and begin drilling immediately. If no oil is struck, up come the legs, and on she moves.

Sea drilling for oil is assuming greater importance all round the world, as the known fields on land begin to fail. Oil experts see constant improvements forthcoming in the rig and equipment for this off-shore search, and the 100-fathom line will soon be within reach. Should this off-shore drilling in North Borneo advance past the present 30-fathom to this depth, British interests will move out into the centre of the China Sea, to areas such as Spratley Island, already disputed property between four countries. Oil may bring great wealth to Labuan and North Borneo generally; in addition it might involve it in International repercussions of the utmost delicacy. For the moment however Labuan has reserved a large area on the coast, where underwater pipes can come ashore to a storage depot, and with crossed fingers watches the helicopters fly over the horizon towards the drill. Of all the exciting developments in North Borneo, this looms largest.

To travel from Seria to Brunei town, along a hard stretch of beach at 50 miles an hour, a car ferry, and then a long winding road across jungly country, is in some ways to move from modern times back to the Middle Ages, all in the course of an afternoon. Dominating the small town, towering over the miserable collection of huts which creep over the water or which cling close to its flanks, is an immense mosque, the largest in South-East Asia, signifying, as did the mediaeval cathedrals that likewise rose protectingly over a huddle of peasants' hovels, the acquisition of new wealth and the growth of an old faith.

Brunei once before had experienced a wave of religious fervour, in the fifteenth century. The Islamic faith had been carried to the shores of Borneo by Indian and Arab traders, the ruler of Brunei had been converted, and being by nature predatory added the demands of piety to his piratical instinct and embarked on a career of conquest. By the beginning of the sixteenth century the town, possessing certain natural advantages (it was on the one river in Borneo without a bar at its mouth, and it was distant from the Hindu Empire of Java and the Muslim state of Malacca), had secured the allegiance of all the lesser lords in Borneo. Every river sent tribute, and it was at the height of its power when Magellan's fleet arrived, in 1521. It had become the greatest Malay state ever to exist, and its capital has never been equalled. It is the memory of these days that excites the politicians now, while the centuries of decadence in between are forgotten.

Pigafetta, the chronicler of Magellan, has left an account of this first visit by a European to Borneo. It is reproduced in John Crawfurd's *A Descriptive Dictionary of the Indian Islands and Adjacent Countries* (1856), long out of print. I reproduce it for its great interest.

'On the 9th July the King of Brunei sent a very beautiful *prahu* to us, whose bow and stern were worked in gold. At the bow flew a white and blue banner surmounted with peacock feathers, some men were playing on musical instruments and drums. Eight chiefs entered the ship and took seats in the stern upon a carpet. They presented us with a painted wooden jar full of betel and *arica*, the fruit of which they chew continually; and jessamine and orange blossoms, a covering of yellow silk cloth, two cages full of fowls, a couple of goats, three jars of distilled rice wine and some bundles of sugar-cane. They did the same to the other ship, and embracing us took their leave. The rice wine is as clear as water, but so strong it intoxicated many of our men. It is called *arrach*.

Six days later the King sent three *prahus* with great pomp, which encircled the ships with musical instruments playing and drums and brass gongs beating. They saluted us with their peculiar cloth caps which cover only the tops of their heads. We saluted them by firing our mortars without stones. Then they gave us a present of various kinds of food made only of rice. Some were wrapped in leaves and were made in somewhat longish pieces, some resembled sugar loaves, while others were made in the manner of tarts with eggs and honey. They told us that their King was willing to let us get water and wood and to trade at our pleasure. Upon hearing that, seven of us entered their *prahu* bearing a present to their King which consisted of a green velvet robe made in the Turkish manner, a violet velvet chair, five *brazas* of red cloth, a cap, a gilded drinking-glass, a covered glass vase, three writing-books of paper and a gilded writing-case. To the Queen we took three *brazas* of yellow cloth, a pair of silvered shoes, and a silvered needle-case full of needles. We took three *brazas* of red cloth, a cap and a gilded drinking-glass to the Governor. To the herald who came in the *prahu* we gave a robe of red and green cloth made in the Turkish fashion, a cap and a writing-book of paper; and to the other seven chief men, to one a bit of cloth, and to another a cap, and to all of them a writing-book of paper. Then we immediately departed for the land.

When we reached the city, we remained two hours in the *prahu* until the arrival of two elephants with silk trappings and twelve men each of whom carried a porcelain jar covered with silk in which to carry our presents; thereupon we mounted the elephants while those twelve men preceded us afoot with the presents in the jars.

In this way we went to the house of the Governor where we were given a supper of many kinds of food. During the night we slept in cotton mattresses whose lining was of taffeta and the sheets of camboia. Next day we stayed in the house until noon. Then we went to the King's palace upon elephants with our presents in front as on the preceding day. All the streets, from the Governor's to the King's house, were full of men with swords, spears and shields, for such were the King's orders. We entered the courtyard of the palace mounted on elephants. We went up a ladder accompanied by the Governor and other chiefs and entered a large hall full of many nobles where we sat down upon a carpet with the presents in a jar near us. At the end of the hall there is another hall higher but somewhat smaller. It was all adorned with silk hangings and hung with two brocade curtains opened from it. There were three hundred foot-soldiers with naked rapiers at their thighs in that hall to guard the King. At the end of a small hall was a large window from which a brocade curtain was drawn aside so that we could see within it the King seated at a table with one of his young sons chewing betel. No one but women were behind him. Then a chief told us that we could not speak to the King and that if we wished anything we were to tell it to him, so that he could communicate it to a brother of the Governor who was stationed in the small hall, and this man would communicate it by means of a speaking-tube through a hole in the wall to one who was inside with the King. The chief taught us the manner of making three obeisances to the King with our hands clasped above our heads, raising first one foot then the other and then kissing the hand towards him, and we did so that being the method of the royal obeisance.

We told the King that we came from the King of Spagnia and that the latter desired to make peace with him and asked only for permission to trade. The King had told us that since the King of Spagnia desired to be his friend, he was very willing to be his, and said that we could take water and wood, and trade at our pleasure. Then we gave him the presents, and receiving each of which he nodded slightly. To each one of us was given some brocaded cloth and silk, which were placed upon our left shoulders, where they were left but for a moment. They presented us with cloves and cinnamon as refreshments, after which the curtains were drawn to and the windows closed. The men in the palace were all attired in cloth of gold and silk which covered their privies, and carried daggers with gold hafts adorned with pearls and precious gems, and they had many rings on their hands.

We returned upon the elephants to the Governor's house, seven men carrying the King's presents to us and always preceding us. When we reached the house they gave each one of us his present, placing them upon our left shoulder. We gave each of those men a couple of knives for his trouble. Nine men came to the Governor's house with a like number of large wooden trays from the King. Each tray contained ten or twelve porcelain dishes full of veal, capons, chickens, peacocks and other animals and fish. We supped on the ground upon a large palm leaf mat from thirty or thirty-two different kinds of meat besides the fish and other things. At each mouthful we drank a small cupful of their distilled wine from a porcelain cup the size of an egg. We ate rice and other sweet foods with gold spoons like ours. In our sleeping-quarters there during those two nights, two torches of white wax were kept constantly alight in two rather tall silver candlesticks and two large lamps full of oil with four wicks apiece and two men to snuff them continually.

We went by elephant to the shore where we found two *prahus* which took us back to the ships. That city is entirely built in salt water except the houses of the King and certain chiefs. It contains 25,000. The houses are all constructed of wood and built up from the ground on tall pillars. When the tide is high the women go in boats through the settlement selling the articles necessary to maintain life. There is a large brick wall in front of the King's house with towers like a fort, in which were mounted fifty-six bronze pieces (cannons) and six of iron.

During the two days of our stay there many pieces were discharged. That King is a Moro and his name is Raia Siripada. He was forty years old and corpulent. No one serves him except women who are the daughters of chiefs. He never goes outside of his palace, unless when he goes hunting, and no one is allowed to talk with him except through the speaker-tube. He has ten scribes called Xiritoles (present-day Malay—*juru tulis*—court clerk) who write down his deeds on very thin tree-bark.'

From the time of Pigafetta until the beginning of the twentieth century the story of Brunei is a tale of decline. Its rivers broke away or were ceded away, and the Chinese inhabitants of the town, who had covered the slopes of the river in pepper gardens, migrated elsewhere as dissolute rulers and lax administration replaced the fervour and efficiency of before. Throughout the centuries various travellers looked in on Brunei, and it was a little worse each time. When James Brooke came, in 1839, there was no Government of West Borneo, which was all that remained, even nominally, of Brunei, merely licensed plundering, and while his expansion from Kuching meant a new dawn for Sarawak, it hastened the complete collapse of Brunei.

The arrival of the Chartered Company, in 1881, introduced a new note into this movement, and produced results that may well have repercussions in the future. Charles Brooke, the successor of James, wanted to annex all of Brunei; the cession of the north-west by the Sultan had ruined that hope, but as the Chartered Company began acquiring further rivers from Brunei he moved north past the shrinking Sultanate and seized a river in Brunei Bay, the Lawas, thus interposing a barrier between North Borneo and Brunei, and encircling it by Sarawak territory.

The circumvolutions of the Brunei boundary are almost

incredible. They are understood only by this movement of Sarawak to prevent North Borneo moving south, and by its determination to secure all of Brunei for itself. After Lawas was acquired Brooke then turned to the one large stream left to the Sultan, the Limbang. The Sultan refused to cede it, for it was his life blood, but he was unable to prevent Sarawak from intriguing with its rebellious inhabitants. North Borneo too was in the argument, and the British Government, alarmed not by their quarrels so much as by the opportunity it gave to Foreign Powers to interfere, and so create a new menace to its trade route to China, imposed in 1888 a Protectorate over the whole area.

Sarawak was not to be deterred, and in 1890 it steamed up the Limbang and annexed it. The administration of Brunei benefited in no way by the Protectorate, for while warning off other powers Britain admitted she could not afford to govern it herself. Conditions became intolerable. Slavery was rife, law and order did not exist. A steady migration of people fled from the court of Brunei into the shelter of North Borneo or Sarawak. In 1902 the Colonial Secretary in London, Joseph Chamberlain, recommended that the rump of territory be partitioned and the Sultanate permitted to expire. Thus the end was reached; but not quite. For a change in policy brought a British Resident in 1905, oil at Seria was discovered in 1927 and today the state is one of the richest countries per head of population in the world.

Nevertheless there is dissatisfaction in Brunei today, and this jumble of territories, where Sarawak's Limbang divides the state in half, and its isolated Lawas separates it from North Borneo, is one of the bones of contention chewed over by such people as Azahari, the demagogue leader of Borneo's one political party, Party Ra'ayat. He criticizes too the structure of the administration, which consists almost entirely of relatives of the Sultan. The latter criticism has been accepted, and a new constitution has been introduced. The former is equally as objectionable, and a rationalization of the boundaries of British Borneo is long overdue.

Azahari and the other young men with him talk also of a 'Greater Brunei', in terms that remind one that he received his training in Java with Soekarno under the Japanese.

'Greater Brunei' is Brunei's claim to all its ancient territories, to the rivers it held when Magellan's fleet cast anchor down-stream, and when its collection of huts at the river's bend was a great capital. Such talk is listened to with horror and sus-picion by the Dusuns of North Borneo, who are neither Muslim nor Malay, and who can well remember when their grandfathers were oppressed like cattle; but what of the Brunei Malays of North Borneo, what of the rivers in Brunei Bay itself, opposite Labuan?

The outstanding man of North Borneo's Brunei Bay is the chief of the Sipitang River, O. K. K. Mohammed Yassim bin Haji Hashim, O.B.E., and to meet him I travelled from Beaufort on the decrepit old rail service that struggles through to Weston, and then by fast outboard, skimming across the glassy waters of the bay, to Sipitang. It was an exhilarating ride, and I found Mohammed Yassim a most stimulating acquaintance. He met us at the river mouth, a slim man, taller than Dato Mustapha, and far less reserved. I found him tense, dynamic, violent in conversation and passionate in his criticism of Azahari, but it was a personal criticism, not one of policy. He did not consider any absorption by Brunei as likely, rather he thought of an independent North Borneo. He visualized a British departure in ten or fifteen years. I was surprised, as he is an official member on the Legislative Council, and served for a time on the Executive Council; surely the safety of the state depended on the permanence of the British?

'Yes,' he replied, 'for the present. I can drive my Land Rover at sixty miles an hour, but my people still walk. We must be able all to move together, otherwise we will be swamped by the Chinese.' His Chinese friend beside him smiled indulgently. 'Did he think an alliance of all Muslims would prevent this?' I asked. He had thought so, he told me, but the Bajaus north of Jesselton were impossible; they would not accept even a chief *kathi* (religious head). Mohammed Yassim could see no further than 'his people', the Brunei Malays of North Borneo; and when taxed with whether he preferred British to Brunei rule he told me that his father, a silver worker in Brunei, had been one of those to flee from the kampong at the beginning of the century, and had settled in Kuala Penyu, in North Borneo. British protection had saved him, and it would serve his son too.

He had inherited his position from his father, who had joined Government service, first as a clerk, then becoming the Native Chief of Sipitang. On his death, in 1945, Mohammed Yassim who had led a band of guerrillas against the Japanese, and had assisted the Special Detachments parachuted into the bay, took over, and after a spell in business was elevated to the Executive Council of the State.

Largely because of his dominant personality Sipitang was made a Local Authority, in which responsibility for finance and administration was passed to the local members. This confirmed Yassim's belief that the British were withdrawing, and he set to work with a will to make this transfer effective.

He is not afraid of responsibility, and to raise revenue he imposed a new cess on produce leaving his area. He aims to take over all the Chinese Schools in Sipitang, and he wants a tapping course for rubber smallholders. He is anxious to have an airstrip—it takes him a day to travel the sixty miles or so to Jesselton, and there is only remote contact with the interior behind him. Above all, he wants his people educated in English, the key to the future.

It is an artificial barrier that divides this river with its little outposts at Mesapol and Sindumin from Brunei, and it is merely a caprice of nineteenth-century politics that has splintered the economic and ethnographic unity of Brunei Bay into fragments. Fortunately for the future, there are men of patience and goodwill at the helm; it is recognized that the colony of North Borneo shares many problems with Sarawak and Brunei, and that a combined effort would be more effective than three separate struggles. Talk of some sort of Federation is in the air; each year the governors meet in conference, and already there is a certain amount of inconspicuous cooperation. The Geological Department and the Judiciary are Pan-Bornean for example, and there are many other ways in which unity of goal and effort is advisable, particularly in Health and Education, but in much else as well.

Political Federation remains a topic of conversation. It is suspect to many in Brunei, as a device whereby the poor acquire access to the coffers of the rich. Many in North Borneo suspect it too, and fear it means Malay and Muslim domination. But a quiet undertow has begun, I think, which will create a more favourable balance of mind amongst all communities. The time is not far distant when the doubters in North Borneo will realize with their friends in Sarawak that by remaining isolated and independent they are remaining in the horse-and-buggy days, or the *prahu*-and-pony days, of the nineteenth century. A British Borneo looms before us.

My last evening in North Borneo was spent on Labuan. At a party begun at the fabulous Brunei Shell Company's rest villa, and continued at the Recreation Club, I discerned through the cheery haze some of the qualities that would make North Borneo an example to be admired in such a Federation, and which already makes it outstanding among the states of South-East Asia. Tolerance, multi-racial goodwill, peace and happiness; these virtues are hard to come by, yet North Borneo has them in plenty. If it can impart these blessings to its neighbours it will be a gift more valuable than all the oil in Brunei. Next morning, as my plane bore me southwards and westwards to Kuching and Singapore, and the varied views and scenes of my Borneo tour flashed through my mind, I felt that for better or worse there was something North Borneo could never share, its incomparable loveliness. And suddenly the fishing stakes of Singapore were in sight, and it had all become west coast, interior, northern islands, east coast and oil fields, two months of movement and a kaleidoscope of memories, all reduced and compressed to a single moment in time.

READING LIST

BRUCE, Charles (A.B.C. Francis). *Twenty Years in Borneo.* London, Cassell, 1924.

BELCHER, E. *Voyage of the Samarang.* (2 vols.) London, 1848.

BURBRIDGE, F. W. *The Gardens of the Sun.* London, Murray, 1880.

COOK, Oscar (R.M.O.). *Borneo, Stealer of Hearts.* London, Hurst and Blackett, 1924.

CRAWFURD, John. *A Descriptive Dictionary of the Indian Islands and Adjacent Countries.* London, 1856.

ENRIQUES, Major C. M. *Kina Balu: The Haunted Mountain of Borneo.* London, Witherby, 1927.

EVANS, I. H. N. *Among Primitive People in Borneo.* London, Seeley Service, 1922.

EVANS, I. H. N. *Studies in Religion, Folk-Lore and Customs in British North Borneo and the Malay Peninsula.* Cambridge Press, 1923.

EVANS, I. H. N. *The Religion of the Tempasuk Dusuns of North Borneo.* Cambridge University Press, 1952.

FORREST, Captain. *A Voyage to New Guinea from Balambangan.* London, 1779.

GARRY, A. N. M. *Census Report B.N.B. (Chartered) Co.,* 1931.

IRWIN, G. *Nineteenth Century Borneo.* The Hague, 1955.

KEITH, Agnes. *Three Came Home.* London, Michael Joseph, 1948.

KEITH, Agnes. *White Man Returns.* McClelland & Stewart, Ltd. 1952.

KEPPEL, Captain, the Hon. H. R. N. *The Expedition to Borneo of H.M.S. Dido.* London, Chapman & Hall, 1846. 2 vols.

MARRYAT, Frank. *Borneo and the Eastern Archipelago.* London, 1848.

MAXWELL HALL, J. *Kinabalu Guerrillas.* Kuching, 1949.

McDOUGALL, W. *British Borneo.* Oxford, 1914.

MUNDY, Captain R. *Narrative of Events in Borneo and Celebes Down to the Occupation of Labuan.* London, 1848.

PRYER, Ada. *A Decade in Borneo.* London, Hutchinson, 1894.

ROBSON, J. H. M. A. *A Bibliography of Malaya: also a short list of books Relating to North Borneo and Sarawak.* Kuala Lumpur, 1939.

ROTH, H. Ling. *The Natives of Sarawak and British North Borneo.* London, Truslove & Hanson. 1896. 2 vols.

RUTTER, Owen. *British North Borneo.* London, Constable, 1922.

RUTTER, Owen. *The Pagans of North Borneo.* London, Hutchinson, 1929.

RUTTER, Owen. *The Pirate Wind.* London, Hutchinson, 1930.

ST. JOHN, S. *Life in the Forests of the Far East.* London, Smith Elder, 1862. 2 vols.

TREGONNING, K. G. *Under Chartered Company Rule: North Borneo, 1881–1946*. Oxford, 1958.

WHITEHEAD, J. *The Exploration of Kina Balu*. London, Gurney & Jackson, 1893.

WOOLLEY, G. C. *Native Affairs Bulletins*. North Borneo Government Publications.

GLOSSARY

Arica	Fruit	*Maias*	Orang Utan
Arrach	Rice wine	*Mangosteen*	Fruit
Attap	Fibre	*Mengaris*	Tree
Bajau	Name of a people	*Murut*	Name of a people
Balignini	Pirate tribe	*Orang Kaya Kaya*	Chief, first class
Barong	Heavy Suluk knife	*Orang-Laut*	Sea people
Berongsai	3-night dance	*Orang Shantung*	Shantung Chinese
Berubat	Sea ceremony	*Orang Sungei*	River people
Billian	Hard wood	*Padang*	Playing field
Bongon	Basket	*Padangkang*	Schooner
Bugis	Name of a people	*Padi*	Rice
Chawat	Loincloth	*Pantun*	Songs
Cheongsam	Chinese type garment	*Parang*	Knife
Cutch	Bark liquor or dye	*Pengiran*	Head Man
Damar	Resin	*Pelahan*	Slowly
Dato	Title	*Pomelo*	A fruit like a grape-
Dhoti	Indian style garment		fruit
Dondang	Malay dance	*Ragus*	Harrow
Durian	Fruit	*Rajah Laut*	Admiral
Dusun	Orchard or a people	*Rambutan*	A fruit with a hairy
Guano	Bird—or bat—manure		skin
Gutta Percha	Resin	*Ranikhet*	A poultry disease
Hakka	A Chinese race	*Rattan*	A type of bamboo
Hokkien	A Chinese race	*Samazau*	Dancing
Illanun	West coast tribe	*Sampan*	Small boat
Imam	Holy man	*Sari*	Garment
Jongkong	Schooner	*Sasandangong*	Ceremonial plaid
Juru Tulis	Court clerks	*Seriah*	A type of wood
Kampong	Village	*Sherip*	Captain
Kathi	Religious head	*Serang*	Bo'sun
Kebaya	Garment	*Sisir*	Harrow
Kedazan	Tribal name	*Suluk*	Inhabitant of Sulu
Keramat	Place of miracle-	*Surra*	Cattle disease
	working	*Tabeh, Tuan*	Greetings, Sir
Kerbau	Buffalo	*Tamu*	Market
Kongsi	Chinese business	*Tanjong*	Point on Cape
	group	*Tapai*	Rice alcohol
Kulintangan	Gong-playing	*Tid' apa*	What matter? (Don't
Kumpit	Vessel		worry)
Kwan-chai	'Rest for a long time'	*Tongkang*	Vessel
Lambo	Schooner	*Trusan*	Straits
Lallang	Wild grass	*Ubi kayu*	Tapioca root
Lette	Lateen sailed vessel	*Xiritoles*	Court clerks
Lipa	Small open boat	*Zebu*	Breed of cattle

INDEX

Printed in England under the authority of Her Majesty's Stationery Office by William Clowes and Sons, Limited, London and Beccles. Wt. P77870. K28.

S.O. Code No. 88-388*